Dreamscaping

New and Creative Ways to
Work with Your Dreams

Dreamscaping is the first anthology in Roxbury Park's
New Visions series, bringing to readers cutting-edge writings
in psychology, spirituality, science, literature, and the arts.
New titles for this series include:
Dancing on the Edge of the World:
Jewish Stories of Love, Faith and Inspiration
Edited by Miriyam Glazer
New Visions series editor: Mark Robert Waldman

also by Stanley Krippner:

Dreamworking

Dream Telepathy

The Mystic Path

Dreamtime and Dreamwork

Broken Images, Broken Selves

also by Mark Robert Waldman:

The Art of Staying Together

Love Games

Dreamscaping

New and Creative Ways to Work with Your Dreams

Edited by Stanley Krippner, Ph.D., and Mark Robert Waldman

ROXBURY PARK

LOWELL HOUSE
LOS ANGELES
NTC/Contemporary Publishing Group

Published by Lowell House
A division of NTC/Contemporary Publishing Group, Inc.
4255 West Touhy Avenue, Lincolnwood (Chicago), Illinois 60646-1975 U.S.A.

Lowell House books can be purchased at special discounts when ordered in bulk for
premiums and special sales. Contact Department CS at the following address:
NTC/Contemporary Publishing Group
4255 West Touhy Avenue
Lincolnwood, IL 60646-1975
1-800-323-4900

ISBN: 0-7373-0268-2
Library of Congress Catalog Card Number: 99-74528

Roxbury Park is a division of NTC/Contemporary Publishing Group, Inc.

Managing Director and Publisher: Jack Artenstein
Editor in Chief, Roxbury Park Books: Michael Artenstein
Director of Publishing Services: Rena Copperman
Series Editor: Mark Robert Waldman
Editorial Assistant: Nicole Monastirsky
Interior Design: Susan H. Hartman

Printed and bound in the United States of America
99 00 01 02 DHD 10 9 8 7 6 5 4 3 2 1

I dream of grass, astonishing as that seems.

Of an apeman.

No, that's a lousy term. *Hominid* is more appropriate. The creature walks under a bright tropical sky, minding its own narrow business. A male, I realize, I'm sitting in the future, watching it from ground level and feeling waves of excitement. Here is an ancestor of the human species, naked and lovely, and it doesn't even notice me strolling past and out of sight. I have seen through time, changing nothing. Aren't I a clever ape? I ask myself.

Not clever enough, a voice warns me.

A quiet, almost whispered voice.

> Robert Reed,
> "Killing the Morrow"

In memory of

Shari Lewis
Fran Waldman
Bruno Bettelheim

*May their dreams live on through those
who have been touched by their gifts*

CONTENTS

PART 2
Working with Your Dreams

PART 3

Understanding Dreams

ACKNOWLEDGMENTS

SPECIAL THANKS to Michael Artenstein, Nicole Monastirsky, and the staff at Roxbury Park for bringing this dream book to life. To Steve Hart, Susan Van Vonderen, and the many individuals who dedicated their research and time to the development of this book— may your dreamscapes enlighten the night.

A NOTE CONCERNING REFERENCES

For the purposes of making this book more user-friendly, notes and references have been kept to a minimum. References appear at the end of each original essay. References for chapters 19 and 24 are listed in *Dreamtime and Dreamwork*, edited by Stanley Krippner. For all other chapters, please refer to the original text listed in the permissions section at the back of this book.

Dreamscaping: Exploring the Landscapes of the Soul

The dream's here still: even when I wake, it is
Without me, as within me; not imagined, felt.

William Shakespeare, *Cymbeline*

MY INITIAL journeys into the dreaming world were fraught with disappointment and angst, for no matter how hard I tried, I just couldn't remember my dreams. Everyone else did—my friends, my family, my teachers—but even the insistent prodding from a well-intentioned therapist could not cull a fragment from my soul. The best I could do on the analyst's couch was to reflect on a childhood nightmare or two.

The earliest dream I could recall—I was five or six years old when it occurred—featured an enormous eyeball, a menacing image that was triggered by a movie I had watched that evening. In the film, young children were swallowed up by glassy-eyed alien monsters living underground. The nightmare that followed was typical, but when I awoke, I found myself staring at the light fixture on the ceiling above my bed. Suddenly, the frosted-glass cover became the cracked eyeball of my dream. I didn't scream, but for weeks thereafter I crawled into my bed without glancing up, lest that scary eyeball spring to life again.

Perhaps now, as an adult, I was refusing to remember my dreams for fear of encountering more nightmares. "And perhaps," my therapist countered, "it symbolized your fear of being seen."

The process of interpreting a childhood dream seemed highly speculative to me, and so I quietly mumbled, "Perhaps." Deep inside, however, I felt that that eyeball dream was mostly a reminder to avoid watching horror films, particularly before going to bed.

I had more luck with my second childhood nightmare, again just a fragment of a dream. I was all alone in the house when suddenly, a little man jumped up onto the window ledge. I awoke, opened my eyes, sat up in bed, and there, on the ledge, was the little man in the dream. He seemed so real that I screamed, and my father came running in. I told him what I saw, but instead of telling me that it was just a scary dream (as so many parents unhelpfully do), he put on his robe, picked up a baseball bat, and went outside the house. I knew he would kill the sinister creature of my dream. When he returned, he assured me that the little man was gone and then gave me the bat to keep by my side. I felt so proud and safe.

Twenty years have passed since I first interpreted that dream, and my impression remains the same: how I wished my father could be there for me whenever I felt scared and alone. But no one, it seemed, could help me remember more of my dreams. I kept pen and paper by my side, woke myself with alarm clocks, pleaded, prayed, and cursed, but all to no avail. And so I took another tack: I simply presumed that my dreams were helping to resolve my inner conflicts and concerns. When I awoke each morning, I seemed to feel refreshed, happier, and clear-headed. This was the first glimmer I had that people could use dreams in unusual, alternative ways.

Then, suddenly, I began to recall my dreams. Not only did I remember them, but I began to analyze them *in my sleep*. When I awoke, the imagery would quickly fade, but the interpretations remained, allowing me to apply them to various conflicts in my life. Once again, my appreciation for the creative potential of dreams increased.

One day, as I was struggling with an insidious writer's block, I decided to test the power of my dreaming world by seeking a resolution as I napped. I found myself going back and forth between imaginary fantasy and actual dream, and when I awoke some twenty minutes later, I had discovered an intriguing story line. The process worked so well that I often use it to gain new insights about my relationships and my work.

As I began to formally research the field (more than 1,500 books on dreams are currently in print), I discovered that people often would have the kinds of dreams their therapists expected them to have. Freudian patients, for example, might dream about sexual repression and parental conflicts, whereas Jungian patients may visualize archetypal images of shadowy demons and gods! Dreams, I concluded, could be easily influenced and shaped.

I also discovered that no two people (no matter how expert they may be) interpret the same dream in exactly the same way, and so I became suspect of the "objective" truth of one's dream. Thus, the dream itself is rarely a fact; rather, it is a tool, a stimulus, an event to contemplate, make sense of, and apply to one's life. Indeed, as research has shown, the essential meaning of a dream lies within the dreamer, not in a therapist or friend or book.

Dreams are the personal property of the dreamer, to be played with in whatever manner the dreamer sees fit. We can use our dreams to analyze the past or speculate about the future, expose unconscious thoughts, gain insight into problems, or divine creative solutions to obstacles big and small. We can even use dreams to deepen relational bonds by sharing them with family, colleagues, and friends, for they are intimate portraits of the soul. Ultimately, a dream is a dialogue, whether it is with another person or between two aspects of one's inner personality—an uncensored glimpse into the nature of self, society, and the world.

Today, dreamwork continues to intrigue professionals and non-professionals alike, spawning dream appreciation groups, artist's dream galleries, Internet journaling, experiments with lucid dreaming, and explorations into the dreaming practices of indigenous cultures and groups. *Dreamscaping: New and Creative Ways to Work with Your Dreams* brings together this vast menagerie of research and practice, highlighting essays by the leading authorities in the field.

Part 1 focuses on the individual journeys that teachers and therapists have taken as they introduce new techniques for working with dreams: overcoming personal resistance, educating children, healing prison inmates, transforming wounded souls, and changing society bit by bit. The reader even steps into one dreamer's world as he struggles with his religious fears and concerns.

In Part 2, we describe how to explore dreams using traditional and nontraditional techniques, such as working with sensual dreams, family dreams, repetitive dreams, archetypal dreams, "dead-end" dreams, and dreams reflecting anger and abuse. Experiment with these techniques: read one chapter each night before going to bed and observe how it influences your sleep. Create a dream journal and record your feelings and thoughts; within a month or two you may be astonished as a whole new world of dreamscapes appears.

Part 3 is a representative selection of cutting-edge research and theory: reviewing the spiritual and psychological history of dreams; examining the relationship between metaphor, myth, and dreams; and reflecting on the power of a dream to predict neurological disorders and death. From inner space to cyberspace, *Dreamscaping* reflects a changing landscape that has evolved from its Freudian roots and is beginning to reshape social consciousness throughout the world.

We are such stuff as dreams are made of—as Shakespeare poetically quipped—and so, dear reader, I bid thee well as you browse the chapters of this book: to read and reflect, to sleep, perchance to dream.

MARK ROBERT WALDMAN
Woodland Hills, California

INTRODUCTION

Dreamscapes:
Yours and Mine

STANLEY KRIPPNER

WHEN I WAS in high school, I began to recall my own dreamscapes and started to record my dreams. Then, in the early 1950s, my interest was dampened when one of my psychology professors at the University of Wisconsin informed the class that dreaming in color was a symptom of schizophrenia. My friends and I had all recalled colorful dreams, and we now decided to be cautious about sharing those experiences. Apparently, our professor was unaware that investigators at the University of Chicago had already discovered that dreams are naturally occurring phenomena that take place periodically during the night, usually during stages of rapid eye movement sleep. Soon afterward, it was observed that most dreams contain color, although these hues and tints are easily forgotten and often omitted from dream reports.[1]

A dozen years later, I was invited by Montague Ullman to become director of a dream laboratory at Maimonides Medical Center in Brooklyn, New York. Our research team conducted the first study of dream diaries kept by preoperative male transsexuals, as well as one of the first investigations of pregnant women's dreams. Our laboratory, however, was best known for studies that investigated unusual forms of communication, such as telepathy, during dreams.[2] Our basic procedure was to fasten electrodes to the head of a research participant, place him or her in a soundproof room, and randomly select a sealed, opaque envelope containing an art print. A psychologist would then take the envelope to a distant room, open it, and study the print while the laboratory participant (in bed and asleep) attempted to incorporate material from the art print into his or her dreams without ever seeing it. Upon completion of a series of experiments, a team of judges compared the typed dream reports with the total collection of art prints, attempting to identify the print used on the night of each experiment. About two out of three times, we obtained statistically significant results, with odds against chance so great that coincidence was unlikely. One participant, for example, dreamed about going to Madison Square Garden to buy tickets to a boxing match. On that same night, the psychologist in the other room was focusing on a painting of a boxing match.

Several prominent dream researchers attempted to replicate our results. The success rate from other laboratories was mixed, so we did not claim to have demonstrated conclusively that communication in dreams can transcend space and time; however, our research did open a promising line of investigation. Several years later, my colleague Michael Persinger and I reviewed the entire body of research data from the Maimonides studies, selecting the first night that each research participant had visited our laboratory.[3] We then matched the results with data collected at weather stations and discovered that the participants' "successes" were higher during calm nights with little sunspot activity than during nights marked by electrical storms and high sunspot activity. We repeated this analysis with one research participant, a psychoanalyst, who had spent more nights in the Maimonides laboratory than anyone else.[4] The results were similar. If these results stand up, they indicate a potentially predictable pattern in such events, and an association with the environment that may lead to a natural rather than a supernatural explanation of unusual forms of communication.

After a decade of laboratory work, I joined the faculty of Saybrook Graduate School and Research Center in San Francisco, where many of our students use dreams as the topic of their doctoral dissertations. I have served as president of the Association for the Study of Dreams and continue to write extensively in various journals and books about the cross-cultural investigation of dreams.[5]

For the purposes of this book, Mark Waldman and I use the term *dreamscape* to encompass the world of dreams, the process of dreaming, and the ways in which dreams can be studied, interpreted, appreciated, and applied to one's daily life. The essays in this anthology were chosen to help you realize the potentials of your dreamscapes and to cherish the gifts they have to offer.

Throughout history, several individuals have claimed that their scientific, technological, athletic, or artistic breakthroughs resulted from dreams that were serendipitously recalled. Jack Nicklaus, for example, discovered in his dream a golf swing that brought him out of a slump. On a societal level, Harriet Tubman claimed that her dreams helped locate the routes for the Underground Railroad, which rescued hundreds of slaves in the years before the Civil War. Many other creative people—writers, musicians, dancers, and so forth—make deliberate use of dreamscapes in their work.

Dreams have an intrinsic connection to issues of morality and freedom, states Montague Ullman, a professor of psychiatry at Albert Einstein College of Medicine.[6] As a result, the dream's ability to challenge the dreamer's current values and behavior patterns often reveals his or her unused potential to make positive life changes. There is an underlying polarity between the goals of dreaming and wakefulness: dreaming seeks to help the dreamer navigate more effectively through the turbulent waters of an often unpredictable inner world, whereas wakefulness helps the individual to make decisions about day-to-day functioning in the outer world.

Dreams can serve us both individually and collectively. Ullman has been one of the few psychotherapists who has drawn attention not only to the significance of the dream for the dreamer, but also to the significance of the dream for the social context in which the dream occurs.

Dreams, Conflicts, and Personal Myths

Dreams also reflect the "personal myths" that may unconsciously govern an individual's life (a theme that Joseph Dillard and I take up in chapter 26). From a psychological perspective, myths are statements or stories that address important human concerns and have direct consequences for people's behavior. There are cultural myths, ethnic myths, institutional myths, family myths, and personal myths—all of which may emerge in dreams. These can be used to highlight a person's development and growth or point him or her toward a specific direction or goal in life. They even illuminate a dysfunctional or potentially destructive behavior, attitude, or wish.[7]

Personal myths can help coalesce dream images into a coherent story, and the dreams you record can help you to identify personal myths that may adversely influence your life. I once worked with a woman who had frequent dreams about warfare. In her personal life, she felt ambivalent about her work: she wanted to be more socially involved, but something seemed to hold her back. Through her dreams, she was able to identify and resolve an ongoing inner conflict between her family's traditional concepts of female passivity and her friends' insistence that she become more active in her community. She resolved this mythological conflict by playing a dynamic role in starting up a child-care center and a family counseling clinic.

In another example, I worked with a man whose dreams reflected a common mythological theme: an "approach-avoidance" pattern in his relationships with women. When a relationship started to become too intimate, he would pull away, making inappropriate comments and engaging in senseless behavior. In his dreams, he was in the basement of his childhood home. He heard a muffled voice crying for help and found a person who was virtually smothered in plastic—a child who resembled himself as a boy. As he worked with this image, he recalled how frightened he felt whenever his alcoholic mother flew into a rage. One time, as he began to cry, she covered his head with a plastic bag, almost smothering him. He decided never to expose his feelings to her again, and this resolution carried over into his adult life. As a result, he sabotaged promising relationships because they reminded him of this earlier life-and-death struggle. Once the mythological conflict was brought to the surface, he was able to interrupt his dysfunctional behavior and express, instead, his tenderness and love in his subsequent contact with women.

The personal myths in dreams often reflect opposing themes. Some, for example, center on achievement, whereas others focus on failure. Some contain stories of nurturance, whereas others are obsessed with deprivation. Other polarities include creation and destruction, completion and fragmentation, affirmation and cynicism, acceptance and rejection, empowerment and debilitation, reconciliation and alienation, wisdom and ignorance, safety and danger, independence and dependence, trust and suspicion, celebration and betrayal, intimacy and separation, questing and passivity, death and rebirth.

Montague Ullman proposes that sharing such dreams in a group can expose and explode dysfunctional personal myths. He writes about Paula, a young woman whose personal myth cast her as Superwoman: a person who needed to excel and star in all her undertakings while maintaining autonomy and independence. One day, Paula dreamed about a piano contest in which she felt she was too old to compete. Her dream group helped her to realize that she could lay to rest the Superwoman myth without compromising her autonomy. By understanding that dependence was equally a part of her personality, Paula was able to modify her drive to become supercompetent in everything she did.

Dream Groups: A Postmodern "Dreamscape"

In the United States and throughout the world, groups of dreamers are gathering together to work on their dreams. Such groups offer an opportunity to explore personal, social, and cultural dimensions of dreaming in both structured and informal settings. This grassroots dream movement, as it is sometimes called, also is marked by the appearance of dream appreciation groups, which are often leaderless or facilitated by people without advanced academic degrees. There are artists' dream groups, women's dream groups, and dream groups for recovering alcoholics. Some focus on the creative aspects of the dream, others search for spiritual dimensions, and still others emphasize personal growth and development. Many community-based groups cut across race, age, gender, and socioeconomic boundaries.

A colleague and I guide monthly dream groups in Berkeley, California, following a user-friendly model developed by Ullman. Our two basic principles are that the dreamer must remain in control of the process while his or her dream is being discussed, and that the group serves as a catalyst, helping and supporting the dreamer's efforts to understand the images. Theoretical material is minimized, except for a few basic concepts, such as day residue, the linkage of dream images to the recent and remote past, the dream's use of a visual modality to engage in metaphorical expression, and the tripartite structure of the dream—setting, development, and resolution.

I have called this a postmodern approach because it maintains that dreamers can appreciate the significance of their own dream reports without always having to rely on the interpretive guidance of psychotherapists. This questioning of the power of experts has a distinctly postmodern tenor, yet it implicitly supports Freud's often disregarded view that the task of interpretation ultimately falls on dreamers themselves.

Ullman's model begins with a dreamer presenting the manifest content of his or her dream, what postmodernists would refer to as the text. Realizing that they will project their own experiences into the dream, members of the group reflect back any feelings experienced while listening to the dream and by imagining that they themselves had just had the dream. The group then turns its attention to each dream image, "deconstructing" it and responding to it in a metaphorical way. The dreamer "reconstructs" the text in response to the group's projections, which usually is helpful in increasing his or her appreciation of the dream. Next, the dreamer describes the events of the day previous to the dream, defining the context that helped to shape it. The dreamer and the group then engage in what postmodernists term a *discourse*, working collaboratively to make connections among the dream images, the dreamer's current life situation, and the dreamer's past experiences. The dreamer responds with as much self-disclosure as he or she feels comfortable providing, and the process continues until the dreamer feels a sense of closure.

One member, Myrna, told our dream-sharing group about a dream in which she survived an atomic bomb explosion. Seeking refuge, she headed toward a church, but as she neared it, she heard evil voices coming from within. She bypassed the church and continued on her lonely way.

Glen, another member, commented, "If this were my dream, I would relate it to the way that I survived the explosions in my family. The traditional institutions of my childhood stood for values that I considered destructive, and so I set out to find my own way in life."

Johanna, another participant, added, "When I experienced this dream, I felt it related to my seemingly solitary concern about the fate of the planet and the way that most 'good' people ignore the threat and make the problem worse."

After each group member treated the dream as his or her own, they discussed each image separately: the explosion, the church, the evil voices. At the end of the process, Myrna shared what she had learned about her dream, engaged in additional dialogue with the group members, and thanked them for helping her understand the meaning that the dream had for her.

In using this technique or any of the other methods described in this book, it is important to remember that the content, text, or story line is not the dream itself—it is only the material that the dreamer has recalled and reported. Dreams do have the potential, however, of serving as the core of people's capacities to assimilate major changes in their lives. Your dreamscapes can enable you to revise your pictures and stories of the present and to rehearse your future responses. Dreamscapes can provide guidance and direction in troubled and uncertain times, as well as nourish your creativity, spirituality, and self-understanding.

NOTES

1. Kahn, E., Dement, W., Fisher, C., & Barmack, J. E. (1962). Incidence of color in immediately recalled dreams. *Science, 137*, 1054–1055.

2. Ullman, M., & Krippner, S., with Vaughan, A. (1989). *Dream telepathy: Experiments in nocturnal ESP* (2nd edition). Jefferson, NC: McFarland.

3. Persinger, M. A., & Krippner, S. (1989). Dream ESP experiments and geomagnetic activity. *Journal of the American Society for Psychical Research, 83*, 101–116.

4. Krippner, S., & Persinger, M. (1996). Evidence for enhanced congruence between dreams and distant target material during periods of decreased geomagnetic activity. *Journal of Scientific Exploration, 10*, 487–493.

5. Krippner, S., & Thompson, A. (1996). A 10-facet model of dreaming applied to dream practices of sixteen Native American cultural groups. *Dreaming, 6*, 71–96.

6. Ullman, M. (1999). Dreaming consciousness: More than a bit player in the search for answers to the mind/body problem. *Journal of Scientific Exploration, 13*, 91–112.

7. Feinstein, D., & Krippner, S. (1997). *The mythic path*. New York: Tarcher/Putnam.

Personal Journeys
into the
Landscape of Dreams

To be, or not to be: that is the question:
Whether 'tis nobler in the mind to suffer
The slings and arrows of outrageous fortune,
Or to take arms against a sea of troubles,
And by opposing end them? To die: to sleep;
No more; and by a sleep to say we end
The heart-ache and the thousand natural shocks
That flesh is heir to, 'tis a consummation
Devoutly to be wish'd. To die, to sleep;
To sleep: perchance to dream: ay, there's the rub;
For in that sleep of death what dreams may come
When we have shuffled off this mortal coil,
Must give us pause. . . .

William Shakespeare,
Hamlet

1

The Hesitant Dreamer

JEREMY TAYLOR

YEARS AGO, when I had been teaching my course in "The Mean-ings in Dreams and Dreaming" for about five years, a young man came to me at the Starr King School for the Ministry in Berkeley and asked if there was any point in his taking my class if he never had any dreams to share.

"You don't have to give your speech about how 'everybody dreams.' I've read the literature," he said, "and I know that I actu-ally do dream every night and just don't ever remember it. From what I've read, I have the idea that my dreams might be very interesting and useful to me, if I could only remember them. My question to you is, is there any point in my taking your class if I never have any dreams to share?"

I blithely answered that he should go ahead and sign up for the class because simply having a place where he was regularly expected to have a dream to share would increase his recall. I said this to him because my experience up to that point had convinced me that the

main reason why most adults do not recall their dreams with any frequency, even though they are dreaming regularly (the laboratory
researchers tell us we all regularly dream five or six or even more
times every night), is that they have no socially and emotionally supportive contexts in their lives in which to share and think about their
dreams. As soon as such a context is created—for example, by sign-
ing up for a class where remembering and sharing a dream once a
week with other class members is part of the "homework"—it almost
invariably has the effect of increasing even the most stubbornly dim
recall of dreams.

However, I turned out to be wrong. The young man—I will call
him Mike—did take the class. His attendance was exemplary. He was
there every week, bright-eyed and interested, and quite articulate
about his ideas regarding the possible meanings in other people's
dreams, but he never had a dream of his own to share.

Eventually, I began to have some qualms about his participation
in and experience of the class. Though his suggestions often provoked
substantial aha's of insight for other dreamers, he was still relatively
aloof from the process in important emotional ways. By never allowing himself to be at the emotional center of everyone else's caring
attention by working on a dream of his own, he was missing out on
an important social and emotional dimension of the work.

The point of the formal, academic classes in dream work that
I teach at various institutions of higher learning in the San Francisco
Bay area and elsewhere is not simply to develop an intellectual facility at the analysis of symbolic forms and structures. That kind of skill
is important, but is far from the main point of the work. Equally if
not even more important is the experience of authentic emotional
contact and the building of reliable communities of creative intimacy
and psychospiritual support. The fundamental element in the building of this kind of authentic community is the willingness to be emotionally vulnerable—to experience the risk and acceptance that goes
with sharing one's own dreams.

For this reason, I almost always share and work with my own
dreams in those groups that I facilitate. In my view, Mike was missing
this basic aspect of the work because of his inability to remember

and share his dreams. So, I started to hassle Mike about his lack of dream recall much more aggressively than I ordinarily do. I started to question him closely at the beginning of every class about his lack of recall—what had the awakening been like? Had any fleeting impressions of the mental activity just prior to waking up been left at all? Finally, when the answers to these questions turned up no new information, I suggested to him that he simply *make up* a dream.

"What would your dream have been like this morning if you had been able to remember it?"

I went on to point out that this was not as bizarre a suggestion as it might at first appear. All forms of interior imagery and experience come from essentially the same unconscious place that the dreams come from, and for this reason, they inevitably carry essentially the same freight of symbolic meaning and import as the "real" dreams remembered from sleep. Had Mike been willing and relaxed enough to take me up on my playful but serious suggestion, it is quite likely he would have produced a conscious fantasy narrative that would have lent itself quite well to the same group process of exploration that we were using with the regular nighttime dreams shared by the other members of the class. This, however, was not to be.

Mike sidestepped the suggestion by saying that, yes, he understood the theory, and that it was probably even correct, but that he didn't want to do it "because it felt too much like cheating."

As I was sitting there, wondering what to do next, Mike suddenly said that it was odd, but while we were talking, he had a curious thought:

"Maybe there were some pastel colors in my dreams last night."

I thought to myself, "maybe pastel colors"! I've heard some *skinny* dream fragments in my time, but this one is definitely the skinniest! We probably won't get anywhere trying to work on something this insubstantial, but it is the *only* opening he has offered all semester to be the center of everyone's attention, so on grounds of group process alone, I'm going to go for it.

At that time in my life, I was under the mistaken impression that there were two kinds of dreams—the kind that appeared to have a beginning, a middle, and an end, which were worth working with, and the kind that were only "random" fragments, which were not worth working with. I fully expected the work with Mike's dream would stir genuine emotions in Mike and the rest of us, but I anticipated that it would not be particularly productive from the point of view of actually "unpacking" any substantial meanings from the tiny fragment that he offered.

When we started to work on the fragment, I tried hard to think of questions to ask and things to suggest, and so did everyone else in the class, all to little avail. Finally one of the class members spoke up and asked, "Is there any association in your mind between the word *pastel* and the word *pastoral?*" (The technical name for such a not-quite-rhyming word similarity is a *klang association.*)

Mike made a funny face—the sort of face that I have come to recognize over the years as an expression of an aha—and said, "Well, yes. Now that you mention it, there is."

Everyone wanted to know what the association was, but Mike said it was "embarrassing" and that he wasn't sure he wanted to share it.

At that point, without any prompting from me, the class began to push him good-humoredly, assuring him it couldn't be any worse than any of the other things that had come up in the group.

Mike laughed and said, "Okay! Okay! I'll tell you! When you asked me that question, I had this aha that everybody's been talking about all semester, and my aha is that my commitment to the 'pastoral life' is distinctly 'pastel.' . . . I'm here in theological school not because I really want to be a Unitarian Universalist minister, the way I always thought I wanted to, but because I am fulfilling the expectations of my parents!"

I was stunned by the depth, strength, and significance of this revelation, coming as it did out of a tiny little dream "fragment"— a fragment that I had been just as willing as everyone else to disparage and toss aside as "meaningless"—but now that we had spent the time and energy to work with it a little, it had yielded this amazingly elegant and succinct metaphor of what I perceived to be his greatest problem at that moment. In fact, I was not really surprised by the content of the revelation. I had already concluded on the basis of our several interactions that it was likely that Mike didn't really have his heart in being a minister the way he seemed to think he did. What surprised me was the way in which this seemingly innocuous little dream fragment brought him to understand consciously that this was the case.

From that point onward, I became very interested in working with such seemingly meaningless dream fragments. I told my classes that I didn't want to hear any more of their fragments, because I wanted to see if the experience with Mike's dream was an anomaly, or whether *all* dream fragments had this amazingly concise quality of "Zen telegraphy."

The people in my classes were obliging. We quickly discovered that the experience we had with Mike's dream fragment was *not* an anomaly—most fragments had the same condensed quality, as if they had been edited down into the same sort of charged and dramatically revealing metaphors that Mike's "fugitive pastel colors" had turned out to be.

The work with Mike's dream fragment also reveals one of the short-term "problems" when working with dreams. Having admitted to himself, wide awake, in front of attentive witnesses, what he truly felt in his heart about not wanting to go on with his ministerial training, he found it impossible to go back to the old denial system that had provided structure and meaning to his life for so long. His behavior, and even his appearance and personality, suddenly deteriorated. He was no longer "Mr. Nice Guy." He ceased arriving on time for classes and appointments. He stopped turning in his written assignments and even stopped being particularly civil when spoken to in the hall or on the street.

He struggled more and more with the conflicted feelings that the work with the tiny dream fragment had revealed and released, until finally at the end of the semester, he couldn't stand it any longer. He called his parents and told them that despite their lifelong shared enthusiasm about his becoming a minister, he now realized that he didn't like it and was not going to carry through with it.

Having broken the news to them, he left school and moved across the Bay to San Francisco and got a job in a bank.

Subsequent reports of his life suggest that he is much happier and more productive in the world of banking and finance than it appears he would ever have been in the ministry.

To this point, the story is all verified by Mike's own aha's of insight and can thus be presented as a "true story" about the meaning of his dream. From here, the story becomes an exercise in theory. Dreams come with multiple levels of meaning and subtlety to expand and develop our individual and collective consciousness and serve our evolving health and wholeness. Knowing this, I found myself thinking that there was more to Mike's dream than just the struggle with being a minister.

That night, when we first unpacked the "pastel colors" at the level relating to Mike's vocational "call," a thought ran through my mind. If it were my dream, one of the "pastel colors" I'm not remembering might be lavender, and another of the things I might be doing, just to satisfy my parents' lifelong expectations and not because my heart was really in it, would be being straight. If this were my dream, it might also be about being gay.

However, that evening, it seemed to me to be too much to push the work with the fragment any further, so I kept my fleeting thought to myself, and subsequently, there was never any easy opportunity to share it with Mike. In retrospect, it seems to me that the issue could probably have been raised in a gentle, supportive, and productive way, but at the time, I was still so stunned at the result of the work with the fugitive fragment that I didn't gather my wits to do so.

However, a few years after Mike left school and moved away, word came back that he had "come out of the closet" and become a fairly well-known political figure in the gay community. So, it seems to me that my original thought may have had some validity, though, of course, the only way to be certain would be to have Mike's own aha of verification.

In any case, even if this is not an accurate speculation about Mike's dream, it is a clear example of the larger truth that *all* dreams and dream fragments can support projections of multiple meanings. It is not a question of their size or apparent complexity—the "over-determined" quality of the dream is inherent in the structure and nature of the dreaming experience itself, no matter how small or "fragmentary" the memory of that experience may appear.

Let me expand the point even further. We know from Mike's own aha that the tiny dream dealt with a fairly profound self-deception about his desire to become a minister. There is also strong inferential reason to believe that it carried a level of meaning about his sexual orientation. By inference, I believe that at least two more distinct layers of significance were woven into his tiny dream fragment as well.

Whenever anyone erects a "fake identity" in the world and begins to believe and behave as though it is his/her "true self," this self-deception (like all sustained efforts of thought and feeling, be they conscious or unconscious) requires increasing amounts of psychological and emotional *energy* to maintain. The greater the disparity between the false idea we are harboring and putting forth about ourselves, and the true nature of our circumstances and interior life, the greater the energy required to maintain the denial. This energy drain may be unconscious, or at least preconscious to a great extent, because to admit this energy drain consciously would result in a conscious recognition of the falsehood, thus defeating its original "purpose." Maintaining a system of denial *always* drains more energy from consciousness than is appreciated.

For this reason, one of the most ubiquitous "symptoms" of denial and self-deception is an all-pervasive feeling of "tiredness," a feeling of always being just on the brink of some physical illness, and a sense of depression and irritation that despite all efforts to streamline things and make them more efficient, there are simply not enough hours in the day to get even the most necessary and pressing things accomplished, let alone to have any time for leisure and spontaneity.

Because this is always the case, Mike's self-deception about the validity of his vocational choice (let alone his denial of his authentic sexual/relational orientation) would inevitably make him feel "tired" all the time. Therefore, there is also substantial theoretical reason to suppose that the pallid, forgotten "pastel colors" of his dream also make direct metaphorical reference to his physical health, as well as his vocation and his sexual orientation. At this level, the dream reveals a "washed-out," "pastel" picture of his general lack of physical vitality, caused by the continuous drain of his preconscious denial and self-deception.

By the same token, I believe the dream gives us a poignant picture of Mike's spiritual life as well. The original family drama that cast Mike in the role of "the spiritual one" and the "would-be minister" was shaped not only by his father's and mother's projections of their own unlived creative potentials out on their "hero son," but also by Mike's own genuine sensitivity and attraction to spiritual life and experience. However, when he actually arrived at seminary, he discovered to his dismay that being a seminary student tended to alienate him from the very spiritual life that had attracted him there in the first place. The somewhat repressed, fragile, competitive, and hypocritical lifestyle of many of his brother and sister seminary students, combined with the intense but bloodlessly theoretical and abstract academic studies—experiences that he had imagined would bring him closer to satisfying the spiritual longings of his childhood and young adulthood—tended to alienate him from any felt-sense of the presence of the Divine, rather than to support and enhance it.

In this sense, I believe the "pastel colors" represented Mike's increasingly pallid sense of spiritual connection and religious commitment in response to the disappointing realities of seminary life.

Mike's work with his fragment points out clearly once again that the magic mirror does not lie. Even the tiniest splinters of the shattered mirror reflect deeply true images. The dreams do not support the fantasies and self-deceptions of the ego, even when that ego is shaped by massive energies of denial and repression. The dream does not come to flatter and support the dreamer's conscious worldview or self-image (unless, of course, that is what is required to truly serve the dreamer's evolving health and wholeness).

2

The Twilight Zone of Dreams: Telepathy and Transformation

ROBERT L. VAN DE CASTLE

IF OUR SPIRIT journeys to the "other side," does it ever return? Does it accompany us through other lifetimes? Perhaps if dreams serve as a portal through which recently deceased spiritual entities can "enter," they may allow us to "exit"—to journey "outward" on this same mysterious plane to catch glimpses of our own past lives in earlier times. Shirley MacLaine has focused popular attention on the possibility of reincarnation and Dr. Ian Stevenson, a psychiatrist in our department at the University of Virginia, has presented the results of his careful scientific investigations on this topic in several scholarly books.

I have had a few dreams that had a reincarnation feel to them. In one, I was with a group of several dozen spear-bearing Aztec warriors going through a sort of close order drill. In another, I was in a hut with several other people, including a shaman or priest. The shaman engaged in various magical activities by a small fire and I found myself frustrated because I could only communicate through various grunts and guttural sounds. In another dream, I was an Indian brave in battle, with a beaded quiver on my back. I was busily shooting arrows at a group of enemy warriors. At one point a spear that had been thrown at me deflected off my belt and broke, but later in the dream I experienced some pain as two arrows struck me in the back.

As a sentient being, I was pleased that my dreams intimated other planes of reality or existence, but as a scientist, I felt they left something to be desired. There was no trace, no tangible remnant of their appearance: you could receive a precious gem in a dream and awake empty-handed. For me, psychic or paranormal dreaming represents the experience of awaking with a gem in your hand, because you have a report or record of your private internal dreaming scenario that can be compared objectively with some external "real world" scenario. If an impressive correspondence between a dream and some highly unlikely incident exists, it offers evidence that your dreaming mind didn't just *imagine* but actually perceived the incident, even though that information lay outside the apparent sensory boundaries within which we operate during our waking hours.

I had read a little about parapsychology as an undergraduate student and found the subject intriguing. My serious interest in parapsychology began after Dr. J. B. Rhine invited me to discuss some of my informal ESP work with him at the Duke Parapsychology Laboratory in 1951. Rhine encouraged me to continue my developing interest in ESP, and I wrote my M.A. thesis on a parapsychological topic. I later spent a year as a research associate at the Duke Parapsychology Lab and became familiar with the experimental studies of individuals with apparent psychic abilities. Although I achieved some low level success at guessing ESP cards, I would not have considered myself as possessing any unusual ESP talents. Certain experiences at the Institute of Dream Research, however, began to convince me that it took the state of dreaming to facilitate whatever ESP ability I might have.

Calvin Hall and I had had several discussions regarding the credibility of paranormal dreams. Although he claimed to have a fairly open mind on the subject, his attitude seemed to me a rather skeptical one. On March 12, 1964, I was spending a night in our lab as a dreamer, and Calvin got a very strange look on his face after he heard me report a dream. Here are a few excerpts from that dream:

> There was a boxing match going on. There were two young lightweight boxers who were fighting and one of them was doing much better than the other. It seems his opponent became vanquished and then another lightweight contender got into the ring with him. This new contender now started to give a pretty savage beating to the other boxer. . . . I remember standing up and throwing a few punches in the air myself because I was so involved with the action in the ring.

After I recounted my dream, Calvin told me that while he was monitoring the EEG machine in the next room, he had been concentrating on the Sonny Liston-Cassius Clay (Muhammad Ali) fight during the REM period from which he had just awakened me. He had decided to find out firsthand whether it was possible to influence a dream telepathically, but had not informed me about his intention. Calvin had wanted to add a little live action to his imagined activities, so he had thrown a few punches into the air himself as he was thinking about the boxing imagery.

Five nights later, when I was again sleeping in the lab, one of my REM reports involved specific and detailed skiing imagery. The imagery that Calvin had been concentrating on during that REM period was a skiing scene! Could coincidence explain these striking correspondences between my dream imagery and Calvin's waking imagery when he was trying to influence my dreams? Maybe boxing and skiing were themes that I often dreamed about. A frequency count of these elements in my home dreams ruled out that explanation. I had recorded a total of ninety-seven dreams at home, and punching activity in any form appeared in only four of those dreams. The only time I reported a boxing match was during the REM period when Calvin had concentrated upon boxing imagery. Similarly, there were no occurrences of skiing imagery in any of my home dreams; the only time I had dreamed about skiing was when Calvin concentrated on skiing imagery during that REM period. Calvin's skepticism soon eroded and he was so impressed by his successes with me and five other male subjects that he published a paper describing his results.

I later participated as a telepathic dream subject for Montague Ullman, a psychoanalyst, and Stanley Krippner, a psychologist, at their Maimonides Laboratory in Brooklyn. I participated a total of eight nights during a forty-four-week period and was successful enough with three different agents or senders to be dubbed "Prince of the Percipients" (telepathic receivers). A chapter bearing that title and recounting my results appears in their book *Dream Telepathy*. My experiences as a telepathic dreamer in four different laboratory settings have firmly convinced me that telepathic dreams, by which I mean dreams in which messages are received from another person, are possible and that they occur with much greater frequency than is generally recognized. There are more ways of communicating with each other than those acknowledged by current science.

. . . I participated in some monthlong dream workshops sponsored by the Association for Research and Enlightenment (A.R.E.), where personal and spiritual growth were emphasized. The A.R.E. is an educational organization located in Virginia Beach that disseminates information about the trance-based "readings" of Edgar Cayce, the psychic known as the "sleeping prophet." Through my activities with A.R.E., I met Dr. Henry Reed, a former psychology faculty member at Princeton University, and we became involved in some A.R.E. research projects. One of the guiding principles of A.R.E. was that everyone participating in a research project should have an opportunity to experience personal growth as a result of his or her participation. This was a new twist for me. I had been accustomed to carrying out studies similar to those at Denver or Chapel Hill, where I collected data from subjects about something that I was interested in, but the subjects, who were obliged to participate, received only class credit. I wasn't used to thinking about how to enhance the personal growth of a research subject.

Henry had been aware of my participation in the Maimonides studies and approached me to ask how some happy fusion might be found between the experimental protocol developed at Maimonides and the humanistic service-oriented protocol that was typical for A.R.E. projects. I wasn't sure that such a rapprochement could ever be accomplished, but as Henry and I traded thoughts on the topic, we eventually developed a protocol that we called the "dream helper ceremony."

We decided to utilize telepathic dreaming in a group context as a way to be of service to others. Rather than focusing upon a target picture, the "dream helpers" focus telepathically upon a target person. This target person acknowledges that he or she has some troubling emotional problem but does not discuss it or give even the slightest hint what it is. The dream helpers dedicate all of their dreaming activity for that night to helping the target person better understand the problem and place it in a new perspective. . . . The goal in the dream helper ceremony is to dream collectively about a target person's problem and to help that person find a solution to the problem.

The telepathic dreamers are called dream helpers. Before retiring for the night, these dream helpers gather around the designated target person and engage in some activity to create a feeling of bonding. They might meditate, pray, sing together, or sit silently holding hands. It's useful if the target person can loan some personal object—jewelry, a photograph, or an article of clothing—to each dream helper. Wearing that object or having it by the bedside will enable each dream helper to feel a special connection with the target person when they go to sleep that evening. The target person does not disclose, or even hint at, the nature of the problem for which he or she is seeking guidance.

The dream helpers renounce the right to experience any personal dreams that night and dedicate all their dreaming activity to being of service to the target person. They ask to be used as a psychic vehicle to achieve understanding and healing for the target person. At home they might not make the special effort to record every one of their dreams for themselves, but since they have dedicated all of their dreams to the target person, they work diligently to maximize their dream recall during the night. They don't want to cheat the target person out of the dreams to which they are entitled. The next morning, the dream helpers gather again with the target person, and each one describes in detail the dreams remembered from the preceding night. A fascinating pattern emerges as the warp of one dreamer's images is laid against the woof of another's and dream strand after dream strand is woven into the rich collective tapestry.

In one of our ceremonies, the dream helpers reported a black car driving into the town of White Hall, someone being hesitant to accept an Oreo cookie, someone ordering an ice cream cone with one scoop of chocolate and one of vanilla, someone noticing the black and white keys on a piano keyboard, and Martin Luther King, Jr., preaching in front of the White House. With each successive report, the theme of black and white became more predominant. Several dreams also dealt with family dissension and parental lectures about obedience.

The target person, a white woman, was very surprised by these dreams. Most of the dream helpers were strangers to her and none were aware that she was dating a black man struggling with the question of how to deal with the negative reaction she anticipated from her family. One of the helpers dreamed that his watch was slow, and another about seeing a movie in slow motion. As the dream helpers discussed these dreams about slow motion, they suggested to the dreamer that she might move slowly in bringing up this relationship to her parents until she was sure she wanted to continue it.

The group was astonished and delighted at what they had accomplished. They felt they had been so successful because they were not attempting to gain anything for themselves; they were engaged in a healing service nourished solely from a sense of love. Everyone benefited and felt energized by their participation. The target person was deeply touched by the obvious sense of caring that the group communicated to her. Although she had not verbalized the problem she sought help with, the dream helpers had been able to comprehend her problem, empathize with her feelings, and reflect on how she might lessen the anguish her conflicts generated.

Seldom does any single dream helper grasp the full significance of the target person's problem. Like the proverbial blind men and the elephant, one describes the tail, one the leg, one the trunk, one the tusks, one the ears; but only when these discrete bits of information are assembled it is possible to grasp the nature of the elephant.

The dream helper ceremony can be a very powerful technique for uncovering ordinarily hidden issues. It should not be attempted unless everyone is fully committed to dealing with whatever emotional issues are uncovered. The target person's problem should not be something trivial (What sort of car should I buy?). It should be some emotional concern that one might discuss with a very trusted friend or counselor in the hope of reaching a better understanding of the overall problem.

For one dream helper ceremony, the target woman's question, which she revealed after all the helpers' dreams had been reported, dealt with whether to enter some new, as yet undetermined, vocation. Almost every dream helper reported dreams of extreme violence: wild animals were involved, someone was hit on the head with a hammer, and other acts of aggression were mentioned. There were also several mother-daughter dreams with disturbing content; one had a mother duck and several drowned baby ducks. When I asked the target person why she thought there was so much violence in these dreams and why the troubled mother-daughter relationships were portrayed, she broke down and confessed that her mother, who had been a psychiatric patient, had been quite violent and cruel to her when she was younger. Her mother had once tried to drown her in a tub of boiling water, which helped explain the image of the drowned baby ducks. The subsequent group discussion suggested that maybe the target person needed to resolve this old issue with a therapist before moving on to a new vocation.

During one dream helper weekend, we had so many participants that we divided up into two groups, with Henry leading one and me leading the other. We discerned that although each of the target persons was a female of about the same age, education, and socioeconomic status, the dreams of the two helper groups diverged widely. The dreams for target person A were right "on target," but did not apply to target person B at all, and the dreams for target person B were amazingly specific to her problem but had no pertinence for target person A. It seemed as if each target person were a psychic magnet attracting only dream filings of a very specific metal.

I think the dream helper ceremony is a convenient way for an open and interested person to observe psi in action and to experience the inner personal and collective power that results from shared awareness.

If the time ever comes when we all agree to use the formidable power of our dreaming mind as dream helpers for each other, we will witness a positive change in planetary consciousness greater than the negative change in planetary consciousness following the dropping of the first atomic bomb.

3

Dreams and Social Responsibility: Teaching a Dream Course in the Inner-City

JANE WHITE-LEWIS

I FEEL VERY lucky. I have always loved my work as a psychotherapist and Jungian analyst. The intimacy of the analytic hour and the analytic relation is a very precious experience. It is a rare privilege to enter into the imaginal life—the dreams, fantasies, and concerns—of another. In my work I am, it seems to me, a midwife—assisting, enabling new life to come into being. And as I bear witness to another's transformation, I am changed.

Quite content with my chosen profession, I was startled a few years ago when I was at a college reunion and the partner of a classmate challenged me on my work—the exclusiveness, the elitism of my work. We had been discussing therapy, short-term therapy and group therapy versus long-term individual psychotherapy or analysis. A cognitive therapist, my challenger believed wholeheartedly in the efficacy and value of short-term therapy. He asked me, "How can you do what you do—spend so much time with so few people, a privileged few—when there is so much to be done, so many people in need of therapy?" It was true. Given that I usually see my patients two or three times a week for years, I have worked, compared to this short-term therapist, with very few people. My response to his question was this: "Yes, I work on a small canvas, but my practice is composed mostly of therapists and educators, also a lawyer, an executive in a construction firm—and mothers and fathers, and potential mothers and fathers—that is, people who are in a position to impact others, to affect the lives of others. If I can work deeply and increase the consciousness of these people who are in contact with many others, then there will be that much less toxicity in the world, and, through the ripple effect, my practice does not seem so small." That was my answer.

But this question—"How can you do what you do?"—stayed with me, troubled me, and began to take on a broader significance as I witnessed the appalling deterioration of life around me. Repeatedly, I would see the homeless struggling to survive as they huddled in cardboard boxes on the streets of New York or in the less public corridors of Grand Central Station. Repeatedly, I would read in *The New Haven Register* of drug-related crimes and the tragic deaths of young men of color in New Haven, the "City of Elms." Repeatedly, I would hear accounts from friends and patients of muggings, robberies, and street crimes. I ached with pain for the children, women, and men victimized by the social and economic conditions of their lives, and I raged at the previous president and administration who persisted in defending their privileged position, with no vision, no heart, no sense of social responsibility. But was I fooling myself? Perhaps I was no better, reassuring myself of the social impact of my practice as I worked as an analyst with mostly upper-middle-class, white patients in my comfortable office in the beautiful, serene New England town of Guilford, Connecticut. Wasn't this a luxury? But what could I do? The problems were too immense. What could I do that would make a difference?

About the time I was wrestling with these questions, I decided to start graduate work at the Union Institute, which is a nontraditional, alternative, interdisciplinary graduate program. On applying to the program, my plans were clear. I had written on the psychology of nightmares and nightmares in literature. At Union I wanted to focus on the interface between psychology and literature and planned to study literary theory, theories of the imagination, and feminist criticism. One requirement of the program has to do with social responsibility. As stated in the catalogue, "The Union Institute does not support research in a vacuum, and it defines doctoral study as a force for social change." Each student must consider the social relevance of her/his work.

This aspect of the Union program—social responsibility—was given special emphasis in the particular opening colloquium I attended. To prepare for the colloquium our group was asked to read Jonathan Kozol's book *Savage Inequalities* (1991). In this powerful book, Kozol describes the appalling conditions he found in some of city schools and compares these schools with public schools in affluent suburbs and towns. Kozol argues that in many ways our schools are now more segregated and less equal than before the Brown v. Board of Education decision in 1954; elite public schools have arisen within our public school system. By describing the conditions of inner-city schools and by relating his conversations with the school children, Kozol effectively conveys the real tragedy, alarming injustice and "savage inequalities" within our educational system. In my opinion, *Savage Inequalities* should be required reading on everyone's list. It is the kind of book that changes one's thinking, you learn something and can't unknow it, life just isn't the same after you read the book—at least that is how it was for me.

When I went to the colloquium I had been considering teaching a course on dreams in the local high school, in Guilford, to fulfill the internship requirement of the program. But after I read *Savage Inequalities* and after I heard one of my colleagues, a successful Afro-American executive, describe his plans to work with young men of color in the inner city to help them gain some sense of self-empowerment—it all fell into place for me. What is more empowering than knowing oneself, one's inner life, one's dreams, one's potential? I decided that I would not teach a course on dreams in Guilford, but rather in the inner city, in New Haven.

My next step was to visit the High School in the Community (HSC), an alternative public high school in New Haven. Founded in 1970 by a group of innovative, dedicated teachers in response to turmoil in the schools and in the city in the late sixties, HSC has attracted, over the years, students who are interested in more creative approaches to education and who are interested in interdisciplinary studies. The school is small (about 240), informal (everyone is on a first-name basis), and there is a lot of individual attention. Students apply to this magnet high school from all over the city. Because of too many applications, the students are chosen by lottery in each school district, and, as a result, the student body is diverse in both academic ability and ethnic/racial backgrounds. There are children of Yale faculty; there are students from the poorest, most stressed, most beleaguered neighborhoods in the city. From what I had heard about HSC, I thought that this school *might* be receptive to my proposal.

With some trepidation I called to set up an appointment with the principal. I was told that there is no principal at HSC; the school is run by the teachers. ("A good sign!," I thought to myself.) The helpful voice on the phone suggested that I come to a teachers' meeting the following day to talk to the teachers about my idea.

Early the next morning I drove into New Haven and, without too much trouble, found the school—an old red sandstone building sitting on a tiny lot and looking like a child's tall and square drawing of a school. As I sat in my car for a few moments, I started to feel queasy and to hear voices saying, "A course on dreams? You must be crazy!" Taking some deep breaths and finding a wee bit of inner courage, I managed to get out of the car and locate an open door (the front door was locked). On entering, I found myself in a vast, dark hall. In a state of semi-paralysis I was contemplating my next step when a cheerful soul moved toward me and asked if she could be of help. I started to explain that I wanted to teach a course on dreams, but after only a few sentences, she stopped me. "What a great idea! But wait!," she said, "I want the others to hear too," and she called to a group of teachers to come and hear what I had to say. As the teachers listened with obvious interest, I told them why I wanted to teach a course on dreams and what I hoped to accomplish by teaching such a course.

I said that it seemed really strange that one hears almost nothing about dreams in school. We spend almost a third of our lives sleeping; dreaming is, as we all know, a wondrous aspect of being human. We are blessed with a dialogic imagination. Psyche loves stories—we love to listen to stories, we tell stories to others, we tell stories to ourselves in our dreams. But we don't talk about dreams in school. What a waste! There is so much we can learn from our dreams.

Studying dreams, I argued, had educational, creative, psychological, and social value:

1. By considering the images of their dreams as metaphors and imaginal expressions of their feelings and concerns, the students could move from concrete to more abstract, symbolic ways of thinking, thereby increasing their capacity to think symbolically.

2. By studying and reflecting on their dreams and by tapping into their imaginal worlds, the students could get a sense of their own cast of characters and inner literature, both as a source for their own creative expression and as a bridge to literature, to the imaginal worlds of others.

3. By considering dream figures as aspects of themselves and the dream as an expression of their inner conflicts, the students would begin to know themselves better. In dreams we find missing parts of ourselves that point the way to our psychological development; we also find the rejected parts, the inner enemies, the seeds of prejudice.

4. Increased self-awareness fosters self-empowerment, self-esteem, a fuller sense of agency and more responsible life choices—all of which have social implications.

To the extent that one is more psychologically conscious of inner conflicts, the less likely one is to project these conflicts, this toxicity onto the world and the less likely one is to act out in destructive ways.

The faculty response to my proposal was enthusiastic; they loved the idea. "Wonderful! It would help the kids with abstract thinking," said a math teacher (who teaches a course on math and art). "Connecting dreams with writing and literature—terrific!," said an English teacher. "I wish we could take the course," said several of the teachers. Within twenty minutes, I was signed up to teach an elective course entitled "Dreams and the Imaginal World" during the second quarter, November through January.

Before starting the course on dreams, I had had minimal teaching experience. Through an odd set of circumstances my first job had been teaching. Although my field in college had been economics (international finance), I found myself—after graduating from college in 1957—teaching seventh-, eight-, and ninth-grade English at Hillsdale's School for Girls in Cincinnati, Ohio—not exactly preparation for teaching in a New Haven public high school in the 1990s.

Although I had certainly been thinking about the course for months, I had not done much actual preparation—no course design, no lesson plans. As this was new territory (to my knowledge, no one had ever taught a course like this), I felt that I had to get a sense of the territory before I could determine which direction I wanted to go. A few days before starting to teach, I did, however, begin to panic at my lack of preparation. Trying to comfort me, an experienced teacher friend reassured me by saying that I had been preparing all my life for teaching this course—which was true, I guess—but undoubtedly more teaching experience would have helped.

And so at the beginning of November I started teaching. About a fourth of the school had wanted to take the class; eighteen juniors and seniors were picked to be in the class. We met for an hour four days a week, Monday through Thursday for nine weeks. Then in January, I decided to teach a variation of the course the next quarter to a group of ninth- and tenth-graders. The comments that follow generally refer to both sessions.

On the first day of teaching I entered my assigned classroom and found a huge room, one of the four rooms on the first floor. Two walls were cut with enormous windows; large blackboards covered the reachable areas of the other walls. Radiators (which could not be turned off) clanked away; several windows were open in an effort to deal with the overheating and peculiarities of an antique heating system. I noticed odd iron doors on one wall, the remains of an even older heating system. Later I was told that this school was built in 1880 and is the oldest school in New Haven.

Several students were in the room eating lunch. The High School in the Community has no lunchroom—in fact, no gym, no library, no varsity sports, no lockers, too few computers, and no auditorium (PTA meetings and plays are held in the halls). But when the students, my students, entered the room, none of the dated, inadequate facilities mattered. Immediately the room became filled with energy and very contemporary as the students tumbled into the room with their bright colors and voices, laughter, flashy earrings, baseball caps, book bags—and curiosity. And so, with the aroma of lunchtime fried chicken still in the air and some sticky soda spillage on the floor, we began to get to know each other and to talk about dreams.

In one of the first classes, as an introduction to talking about images, the students made collages—picking out images that appealed to them from a pile of magazines. We talked about some of the images. For example, cars turned up in a lot of the collages. So we talked about cars—what is a car? How is it different from other modes of transportation? What might a car mean in a dream?

Because the students were most interested in understanding their own dreams, we spent a lot of time talking about dreams. At the beginning I tried a rather disciplined approach to group dreamwork with the students asking the dreamer for clarification of the images in the dream and for associations. What started as dream*work* usually shifted quickly into dream*play*," a free-for-all as everyone started associating to the dream, talking at once and addressing comments to a neighbor, if not the dreamer. At some point during this process, something would click for the dreamer, the "aha" phenomenon that dreamworkers speak of. I tried to get a word in now and then, generally making some effort to push for a more symbolic understanding of the images. It was primarily my task, I felt, to make sure that the experience was emotionally safe for the dreamer. As it turned out, there seemed to be something protective and self-protective operative in the room which kept the expression of feeling and dreamwork at a safe level. At the end of class, I would speak privately with the dreamer to make sure s/he was all right, to comment on the dream, and to suggest something to think or write about.

Other class activities included creating dream theater by enacting a dream, and drawing a response to her/his dream or to a dream told to the group. Sometimes the class would write about their dreams—dream the dream on (continue the story) or engage in an "active imagination," a dialogue with one of the dream figures. The students also wrote about their earliest memories, family stories, their own personal histories—that is, the imaginal context of their lives and their dreams. To understand projection and our tendency to color what we see, a couple of classes were devoted to projective tests—the Rorschach and the TAT. We talked about the literary use of dreams in novels and short stories and dreams in movies. A published poet friend of mine came, read some of her work and spoke of her own process of transforming her dreams into poetry.

The major project for each course was to keep a dream journal, to make daily entries. If the student could not remember a dream, there were many other possibilities—for instance, childhood dreams, in fact any dreams from the past, dreams of friends or family members, any dreams encountered in novels, short stories, poems and on television. The journals were mostly kept at home; I would, however, review them and comment on them several times throughout the quarter.

Although I had had an intuitive sense that a dream course could be valuable, it was only in the classroom that I fully recognized the powerful potential and endless possibilities inherent in teaching a course on dreams at the high school level. Let me give you a few examples of what can happen.

There was Rick's dream, for instance. As I listened to Rick telling his dream, I was startled by the remarkable similarity to the beginning of Dante's *Divine Comedy*. The next day I brought in a translation of the *Divine Comedy*. No one in the class had heard of Dante (although one girl said she had a friend named Dante, who, in fact, turned up in the second course). It was a marvelous moment (especially for Rick) when I read his dream and then the beginning of Dante's poem, and the class recognized the connection between the two, the connection between our dreams and great literature. They *got* it—the fact that creative possibilities that lie within each of us, in our dreams.

And then there were those students who claimed that they could not write well or hated to write, but who discovered a "voice" when they wrote out of their personal experiences and feelings. Often associations to remembered dreams led to painful events and current concerns—the death of a father from AIDS, the sudden death of a beloved teacher, a devastating house fire, the break-up of a family because of divorce, the terror of living in New Haven and the fear of being shot. When these students wrote about their dreams and the associations to their dreams, they began to discover not only their potential for writing powerful and eloquent prose, but also the relief that comes from giving expression to the pain and tension within.

There is, I discovered, a real societal value in talking with high school students about their dreams. Dreams proved to offer an amazing opportunity to talk about issues in a nonjudgmental way. For instance, many of the students reported dreams of police. A fairly typical dream involved the student being engaged in some drug-related activity and hiding from, arguing with, or running from the police. I asked the class, "If the dream is a reflection on an inner state or conflict, who is the cop?" Their own inner authority figure, their conscience? If the student can consider the cop as an inner figure and the image of the dream reflecting an inner conflict, then there is the possibility of taking some responsibility for the choices

being made and not unconsciously acting out, projecting the disap-
proval onto the outer cop/parent/authority figure.

Another example: Many of the young women dreamed of having a baby, and usually jumped immediately to a concrete interpretation—the baby in the dream represented the baby they wanted to
have with their boyfriend. Teenage pregnancy is a real problem for
many of these girls. One of my sixteen-year-old students was a
teenage mother. What if the baby in the dream is understood as
some young part of the dreamer, some potential that needs to be
mothered? A literal pregnancy is not the solution for a young woman
who wants to fill her inner emptiness with a baby, to feel more
important by becoming a mother. The last thing in the world these
young women, these children, need is to be trapped into a lifestyle
that will interfere with any attempt to get an education. If the child
in the dream can be considered as an inner child, inner potential,
that needs to be mothered, cared for, educated—there is a possibility of choices and a chance of escaping the hopelessness and despair
of being poor and uneducated with few options.

As you can imagine, the teaching was not always easy. Some
days were difficult and discouraging. And I made mistakes as I struggled to learn what worked and what did not. Whenever I got into
my lecturing mode—talking about Freud versus Jung, or archetypes
or whatever—I could see their eyes glazing over (the fact that the
class was right after lunch and the last period of the day didn't help).
When I let go of having to *teach* them and stayed with their imaginal material, anything I wanted to teach emerged; that is, the theory would naturally come out of the practice. For example, one of
the students, Tina, dreamed of a girl she hated, an excellent example of what Jung calls the "shadow." Her image was engaging and
memorable and offered an opportunity to talk about this useful Jungian concept without my launching into a boring presentation.

In the first group I made a major mistake trying to teach
Wuthering Heights which I had adored when I had read it at about
age twelve. Brontë's literary use of a dream in this novel is brilliant.
In the third chapter, a nightmare appears which shapes and resonates

throughout the novel. But most of the class hated the book; the language was so difficult that it was like reading a foreign text. They refused to read it. I even tried showing a film version of the novel; most of the class dozed off during the viewing. In the second group, instead of watching *Wuthering Heights*, we watched an episode of the popular soap opera "All My Children" and ended up having a lively discussion of themes and archetypes.

All in all, teaching the dream course at the High School in the Community has become an important part of my life. This experience has had an enormous impact on me; I suspect the same is true for many of my students. And, of course, the effect of introducing dream studies into the curriculum had been felt beyond my particular classes. Often my students introduce me to their "dream characters," their friends who appear in their dreams, who then proceed to tell me one of their dreams. Teachers in the school are curious about the course, frequently ask me about their dreams, and bemoan not being able to take the class. On occasion I am invited to a literature class to speak about a dream in a text (e.g., *MacBeth*). In addition, students who are not in my class stop me in the hall and ask, "You're the Dream Lady, aren't you? Well, I had this dream last night and . . ." or "What does it mean when you dream that. . . .?"

I realize that I have been especially fortunate to have found such fertile ground; perhaps not all schools would be so supportive and receptive to including dream studies in the school curriculum. And yet, perhaps my experience is not so unusual after all. Dreaming is, after all, a universal phenomenon. Let us not underestimate the innately human fascination with dreams and the desire to find some meaning in a dream. Maybe it would *not* be so difficult to introduce dream studies into school curricula.

It seems to me that there is a danger in the field of dream studies of a certain smugness and self-satisfaction. We know how important dreams are to us and we talk to each other about them. I do not, in any way, want to diminish the importance of this exchange, which can be enormously valuable both personally and professionally. But can't we do more in terms of the world around us? Are we doing the best that we can do? When are we going to put social responsibility as a priority? We have enormous unrealized potential and each one of us has the capacity to "make the difference."

My choice has been to work in an inner-city school. Listening to the dreams of inner-city kids and taking the students and their imaginal lives seriously, has made me acutely aware of the power of dreams in an educational context. Schools are an obvious place to start, as there are many opportunities at all levels no matter what one's interest. Each one of you—writers, psychologists, psychiatrists, anthropologists, teachers, artists, dancers, dreamers all—could find a way to contribute in a school setting. But there are, of course, many other forums in the community besides the schools where we can contribute. Isn't it time that we *do* contribute and share, more consciously and conscientiously, our riches with others?

4

Healing Crimes: Working with Dreams in the Criminal Justice System

BETTE EHLERT

ARMED WITH my years of client interview experience and a few basic dreamwork techniques, I started a private weekly dream group of friends and acquaintances, and began teaching "Practical Dreaming" through the University of New Mexico Community College.

Once I had got my feet wet in dream groups, one dream-related friend suggested, almost facetiously, that I should next contact Gordon Bernell, the education coordinator at our city/county jail. Envisioning nothing more noble than a lot of available dreamers to practice on, I called to volunteer. Gordon, who is also a lawyer, set aside his skepticism and allowed me to give it a try. He said, "We are

---

Bette Ehlert is a New Mexico attorney who, becoming disillusioned with the American criminal justice system, decided to take her dreamworking experience into the local jails, working directly with prisoners to help them identify and overcome destructive attitudes and behaviors. Her story exemplifies how creative dreamwork can lead to both personal and social transformation. —Ed.

open to new things here since, God knows, what we do doesn't work." He scheduled me a regular time and space to come offer dreamwork to women inmates.

I was not prepared for what I found. What I found was that jails are psychically filthy places—full of bloody dreams and gory feelings that are never mopped up. Pieces of them lie around in the corners and stick to your shoes. The odor of them clings to clothes and hair, and the feel of the place stays with you for hours after you leave. Dreamworking in a jail is like nursing in an E.R. People arrive in critical condition, present you their most horrific wounds for emergency treatment, and then leave again before you get to see anything heal.

What you do get to see is that people in jail live close to the bone. They have no cars, houses, jobs, families, clothes, jewelry, activities, or other props to announce who they are, or to hide behind. Their feelings of humiliation, frustration, indignation, and anger shine on the surface of their skin, a little like sweat. Just below the skin, and only slightly less visible, are the other feelings of guilt, pain, fear, self-doubt and loneliness.

You also get to see that people in jail live in a state of emotional starvation. They live with a near total deprivation of all the kinds of emotional nourishment that make it possible for the rest of us to survive from day to day. They are desperately hungry for the interest, attention, concern and affection of anyone with any emotional surplus to share.

My first dream groups (usually with four to eight women) met in a small conference cubicle designed to accommodate one lawyer and one client. The groups were interrupted by the incessant slamming of the glass and steel sliding doors that separate the women's "pods" from the hallway to the elevators. Groups were interrupted by the arrival of medications, methadone, commissary, caseworkers, lawyers, lunch, and recreation, as well as by the comings and goings of dreamers who got bored or "OD'd." We would start our meetings at about 10:00 am, when everyone was up and showered. Lunch could be served at any time from 10:30 am to 12:30 pm. Outdoor recreation (a walk on the roof) was at 1:00 pm. On most days, the corrections officers would allow me to stay for lunch, so that if some women decided to pass up recreation, the dream groups could last until 2:30 pm—which was lock down and head count.

To help us "clean up" after these groups, I was (after intercession from Gordon) allowed to carry in Tupperware containers of water and sand. We would all run our hands in the sand as we worked the dreams, and then at the end of the group, we would wash our hands, letting the water run off into the sand. After leaving the jail, I would drive down to one of the bridges over the Rio Grande, and dump the dirt into the river. In this way, I let the Great Mother dispose of the stuff that I couldn't carry.

Despite my lack of experience and the unbelievably lousy working conditions, the dream group, which met continuously for about nine months, was well received by the women inmates, and well worth the efforts. Three extraordinary gifts came to me as a result of it.

The first of these gifts was the support of Gordon Bernell, the education coordinator at the jail. Bernell was sufficiently impressed with the inmates' feedback to introduce me to other correctional educators and administrators. These introductions eventually led to the creation of other dream groups and the establishment of other invaluable contacts within the correctional system. The groups that grew out of the original Bernalillo County Detention Center women's group included the following: (1) a group for adult male offenders, offered as part of the "Comienzos" program, on the Men's Education Floor at the Bernalillo County Detention Center; (2) a group for male and female juvenile offenders offered to volunteers from the general population at the Bernalillo County Juvenile Detention Center; (3) a group for adult female offenders, offered as part of the "Pre-Release" program at the Corrections Corporation of America's New Mexico Women's Correctional Facility; and (4) a group in "Community Corrections" for adult male offenders with multiple DWI (driving while intoxicated) convictions.

The second extraordinary gift to come out of the original women's dream group was a personal discovery. In addition to Gayle Delaney's "interview" technique and Jeremy Taylor's "imaginative" or "If it were my dream, I would . . ." technique, I used the group to explore an adaptation of Anne Sayre Wiseman's "Mapping the

Dream Problem on the Paper Stage" technique (described in her book entitled *Nightmare Help for Children from Children.*) This technique seemed especially good for the days when I needed the dreamers to do more work than me. With this technique, the dreamer is invited to consider how the shapes, colors, and arrangements are working and whether all elements are completely satisfactory, or if any aspect of the map "wants" something. If something is "wanted," the dreamer is encouraged to consider the options for change, the price of any change, and then whether and how to implement the change.

While the women were at work on their maps, I mapped my own dream from the preceding night. The dream was:

> *Two hyenas are released into the wild, but in something like a game preserve. They are observed by two men seated before a radar screen. The radar tracks the animals through their body heat. They leave a "thermal signature" on the screen. The radar operators watch as two diagonal orange lines, representing the animals, intersect downward across the middle of the screen. One operator comments nervously to the other that the animals are moving more powerfully than had been expected.*
>
> "Hyena in the Wild," circa November 1992

I mapped this dream by putting a small, round, explosive looking hyena on the left side of the page, and then a large square radar screen with an "X," and two male radar operators on the right side of the page.

The next day, I introduced the mapping technique to my private group. I recalled no dreams from the night before, so while these women were working, I used the time to map my earliest remembered childhood dream. The dream was this:

> *I am in the basement of the turn-of-the-century school building where I attended kindergarten. The room is small and rectangular, with a low ceiling of exposed*

*pipes. It is filled with simple wooden benches. At the
front of the room is one windowless wooden door which
opens inward. The door, the walls, the pipes, and the
benches are covered with many coats of pale 1950s green
paint. I am there with my father. We are attending a
parent-teacher's meeting. I am the only child. During
the course of the meeting, a terrible and ferocious
monster enters the back of the room. All the adults leap
up and run out the front door, knocking over all the
benches as they go. I run for the door, too, but because I
am small, I have a hard time getting over the benches. I
am the last to reach it and when I get there it is closed
tight. Everyone else is outside, leaving me alone in the
room with the monster. I am terrified. I pull on the knob
with all my might. I manage to open it just far enough
to look out. I see that many people are on the other side,
pulling to keep the door closed. I see that my father is
also right there. I cannot tell whether he is pushing
against the crowd to let me out, or whether he is one of
the people pulling the door closed to keep me in.*
                    "Monster in the Basement," circa 1954

I mapped this dream by putting an orange and black explosion
on the left side of the paper, a bunch of criss-crossed lines to represent benches in the center of the paper, and a door with men's
heads peeking in around it to the right of the paper.

As I put my "Monster" image away, I saw it side by side with
my "Hyena" image. I realized that I was looking at two versions of
the same dream, separated by forty years of experience.

The vague and terrifying monster from childhood had become
a specific threat—one (or two) hyenas. The benches that had been
the child's obstacles, had become the hyenas' paths. The closed door
had become a "transparent" remote viewing device. The parent/
teacher adults who had exerted themselves to keep the monster and
the child shut in, were now focusing their whole attention on monitoring the hyenas' progress on the outside—in the wild—with the

implication that not only were the creatures dangerous, but they were also precious and endangered.

Like all children, I needed to be safe from the monster. Ultimately, I, myself, became so good at containing the monster that I almost completely choked it off and could no longer hear its voice. Due to this harsh treatment, the monster developed asthma. Asthma for me was always a problem of the exhale—the expression. In cutting off the monster's voice, I had cut off the voice of my own inner wisdom that should have inspired and directed all of my positive, outgoing activities and expressions.

My personal struggle to find a way to contain but not crush the monster/mad woman within me has developed into a career activity. Inwardly, that activity has been to get to know both my wild and emotional inside and my containing and intellectual outside, and to attend to the doorway between the two, so that it works well and easily. For me, the dream is the doorway through which we can hear the underground voices most clearly, and through which all the monsters, children, hyenas, mad women, teachers, radar operators, captains, and base commanders must pass freely in order to conduct their essential business with one other.

Outwardly, that activity has been to seek out America's most powerfully symbolic doorways—the doorways to prisons and jails—and to get them to open and close for me as I go back and forth between the waking-life monsters, children, hyenas, and mad women on the one hand, and the teachers, radar operators, captains, and base commanders on the other. As more of us go back and forth through these doorways, the less opaque they will be, and the more like transparent remote viewing devices through which we can gather necessary intelligence about something natural, precious, and endangered that lives close to the source of wisdom and energy that powers and guides all outer world activity.

In the course of conducting our war on crime and monsters, America has made herself into an armed camp. We are now staggering under the weight (and cost) of our own fortifications, and growing more and more hopelessly estranged from a growing number of "institutionalized" or chronically criminal citizens. While we need protection on the one hand, we also need these people on the other.

In corrections, there is—at least metaphorically—a peculiar equivalent to the remote viewing device that reads a thermal signature. It is the electronic bracelet. Because of the overcrowding of jails and prisons, and the horrendous expense of keeping people incarcerated, more and more jurisdictions are experimenting with "community corrections." In some instances "community corrections" means the offender is required to wear a bracelet and to check into a central computer from his home telephone at prearranged times throughout the day. It is a form of house arrest that accommodates a work schedule and does not uproot lives and families. If the offender does not answer the call for check-in so that the computer can "read" the bracelet, the computer will call every ten minutes for a certain number of hours, until finally an arrest warrant will issue. The average cost of a day's stay in jail is $50.00—and borne by the state. The average cost of a bracelet and phone is pennies a day—and is borne by the offender. We must focus on the offender and the doorway, not on the fortifications.

The electronic bracelet is an example of a "doorway" that provides security for the public, while it allows the monster its preserve, and permits the public and the monster to continue observing and learning from one another. It is a promising solution from some right-brained innovator somewhere who no doubt dreamed it up.

The last and greatest gift to come to me out of the original women's dream group was my first opportunity to consciously stand in the doorway of the dream and hear the voice of the monster/child/hyena/mad woman. After hearing that voice (I have now heard it several times), I am prepared to make several outlandish assertions about crimes and criminals.

1. There is no such thing as random violence or crime. Victims become perpetrators, and perpetrators commit highly specific crimes. They commit crimes that are perfectly, metaphorically, linked to their prior experiences of victimization or abuse.

2. At the moment of the crime, the perpetrator experiences the precise form of mastery that was missing to him/her at the

moment of victimization. Crimes are reparative attempts by victims.

3. Perpetrators are people who have poor boundaries. As victims, no perimeter stopped the world from impinging too far in. Now, as perpetrators, no perimeter prevents them from spilling too far out.

4. Perpetrators are not deterred from crime by the prospect of punishment, or "rehabilitated" after crime by the experience of incarceration. Their crimes hold the promise of a ritual and symbolic benefit, the importance of which overshadows the concern for other consequences. For most offenders, this benefit is the healing of the childhood wound. The wound established the child as victim. Through crime, the child establishes himself as perpetrator. The wound and the crime are the two parameters within which adult self-boundaries will be established.

5. Dreamwork is the solution to much of what is wrong. Through dreaming, perpetrators confront the image of the wound and the image of the crime and recover the feelings attached to both. Through dreamwork, perpetrators "negotiate" the boundary between the two. As the skill of dream negotiation is perfected, it can be applied to future wounds, so that future crimes need only be committed in imagination, and future boundaries can be negotiated in accordance with preestablished rules of procedure.

The first dream in which I could hear the voice of the monster/child/hyena/madwoman was shared by a dreamer in one of the earliest women's groups at the Bernalillo County Detention Center. This person was a white female first offender in her early twenties. She had honey-blond hair, a kind and pretty face, and a soft Southern voice and was in every way the picture of the girl next door. I met her, and she had this dream, about one week after her arrest. She had never been arrested before.

Juliette and the Beast
I am in a room, sitting with my boyfriend, Richard. Maybe we're talking. The room is dark. The only thing I

*can see clearly is Richard. I feel sad and scared.
Something is wrong. The room has doors. Richard
leaves. I don't see what door he goes out. He just
disappears. I walk around and can't find him. I feel
abandoned and sad. Then the doors fly open. Except
one door. It's a rubber door. Something is pushing it. I
run to it and hold it closed. I can see fingers pushing
through the rubber. The fingers have nails like a beast.
There is no light. Nothing but darkness. I don't see
anything. I'm screaming to Richard: "Come back! I want
to go with you! I need help!" I don't want to let the door
go and go after him. I need to hold the door. I am scared
to even move.*

Juliette cried bitterly throughout the retelling of the dream, and
throughout the dreamwork, but the dream had kept her awake for
many nights and she wanted to understand it. She gave powerful def-
initions of almost all of its elements, but I will relate only those most
pertinent to this discussion:

Juliette described her boyfriend, Richard, as a wonderful man
for whom she would do anything. He was totally accepting of her,
and was "like her family." He was also a true multiple personality,
who "had little voices," and did, in fact, slip out through different
doors in his head. He was part intelligent, manipulative con-man,
and part ruthless, violent thug. She attributed his violence to the fact
that he had been sexually abused as a child. Like her own father,
Richard was also notable for the fact that he had abandoned her into
a life-threatening situation.

Juliette described the dark room where she felt sad and scared
as being like the closet in her grandmother's house where, as a child,
she used to hide from her uncle and grandmother. Juliette had
repeatedly been abandoned by her teenaged mother into the care of
her grandmother. During the periods she spent in her grandmother's
home, she was sexually abused by her mother's younger brother. Her
grandmother was aware of the abuse, did nothing to stop it, and
sometimes punished Juliette for provoking it. Juliette also described

the dark room with the many doors that opened and closed as being like the jail. Interestingly, she further defined "jail" as something like a father: "It keeps you safe, gives you food and shelter, and makes you do what you're supposed to do."

Juliette described the hands with pointy, long nails coming through the door as belonging to a beast or a creature, or to something that she did not want to see. She identified the hands with her mother who had also had long clawlike fingernails, and who had used them to scratch and threaten her. Juliette said that her mother would drink and beat her and then lock her in her room.

Juliette described her crime as follows: She was hitchhiking with Richard. A man gave them a ride. Richard assaulted the man. As the victim was struggling, Richard told Juliette to go through the man's pockets and possessions to find his wallet and valuables. At the end of the terrible drama, Juliette was in a car, groping for a wallet through the clothes of a beaten and terrified man, just the way that her uncle had so often been in the closet, groping through the clothes for her. After the crime, Richard vanished. Juliette was apprehended and charged with "strong-armed robbery."

Juliette went from being the good, innocent, defenseless little victim in the closet, to being the evil, premeditated, and powerful perpetrator in the car. She went from being strong-armed herself, to strong-arming another.

At the end of the dream interview, Juliette could see herself as both the victim/child, and the perpetrator/beast. The victim/child and the perpetrator/beast, however, could not see each other. We encouraged Juliette to find a way to make the dream come out better. We suggested that she find out what the beast wanted and then try to negotiate. We offered her the following "If it were my dream, I would . . ." suggestions for revision: Get the beast to chill out, and then go around and close the doors until you feel more comfortable. Or, get the beast to chill out and then, since there are a lot of doors open to you, go out and look around for your boyfriend. Or, since Richard and the beast are both outside, ask the beast to go look for Richard. Or, just ask the beast what it knows about Richard.

Juliette listened to our suggestions and came back a week later with one final dream before transferring out of the institution. In this second dream, she was running through the woods, pursued by a gang of men. As she jumped over a stream, a huge alligator rose up, grabbed her pants and began pulling her down.

This second dream was less frightening than the first. The perpetrator was no longer a mythical beast, but only an alligator. Juliette was no longer trapped in a closet, but on the move in the woods. While Juliette's self-as-victim and self-as-aggressor images were by no means reconciled and integrated, they could at least see each other. Juliette and the beast were almost touching.

This second dream also seemed to have richer possibilities for negotiation and revision. We made several suggestions. Maybe the alligator only wanted the pants. Maybe Juliette could trade the pants to the alligator in exchange for protection from the gang in pursuit. Maybe Juliette could tame the alligator by rubbing its stomach. Maybe the gang in pursuit was not really after Juliette, but only wanted the alligator. Maybe she could trade the alligator to the alligator hunters in exchange for getting out of the woods. Maybe with help from the gang, Juliette could transform the alligator into a purse—something with a prized but tough exterior that could hold her I.D.

Juliette's first dream was typical of many first dreams that offenders bring to dreamwork. It presented, in one tableau, an overview of all the interlocking conflicts at many levels of Juliette's life. It presented, on its face, a dream victim and a dream perpetrator, in conflict, at opposite ends of a spectrum, and connected by a metaphor. That is, it presented the good and defenseless child who was strong-armed, fighting the evil and powerful beast who had the strong arm. At another level, the dream implied a present day, waking-life perpetrator (Juliette the strong-armed robber), and a present day, waking-life victim (either the man in the car, or Juliette in jail). At yet another level, the dream implied the historical, waking-life perpetrator (the uncle), and the historical, waking-life victim (Juliette as a little girl).

Juliette's second dream was also typical of many subsequent dreams that offenders bring to dreamwork. It showed the confrontation continuing, but improving. It also showed possibilities for further negotiation and improvement emerging more clearly. As the image of Juliette in the dream is reconciled with the dream image of the beast, I believe that healing is happening at all the levels, and that a good *and* well-defended young woman is beginning to emerge.

The following dream came to a man named Daniel whom I worked with on the Men's Education Floor at the Bernalillo County Detention Center. Daniel was a very handsome, very fair-skinned African-American in his late twenties. He had a quietly commanding presence. He was big, soft-spoken, intelligent, and aware of everything going on around him. He should have been well on his way up the corporate ladder. He was, in actuality, a successful crack dealer who lived in a house full of beautiful women junkies who brought him money. He had this dream a few days after being sentenced to an unusually long jail term, given his record. At the time of the dream, he had already served almost two years jailed awaiting disposition on the same charges. Daniel's dream was also a recurring dream, although earlier versions had had different details.

Daniel and the Dark Entity

> *I don't remember how this started. I am asleep. All of a sudden, this entity is in my bed, holding me down. He is dark. I can't tell if it's his clothes or his skin that is dark. He exudes darkness. He has a thick mane of bushy hair. He is holding me down hard, as if to say, you can't get up—I won't let you. He's on my back, but somehow I can see him. I feel highly frustrated. I can't believe I can't get up. This thing tricked me. He deceived me. He had to get my permission to get this close. I didn't have to allow this to happen. I am really going. I finally get up and run away. He either let me go, or I broke away. While it is happening, it isn't too scary—but it is more scary afterwards.*

In fact, Daniel had been so disturbed by this dream that he had persuaded the corrections officer to let him out of his cell, so that he could spend an hour or so in the day room until he found the courage to go back to sleep.

Daniel mapped this dream, depicting himself in a bed, pressed beneath a large, dark entity. To help the small dream ego in the bed—to get it some "perspective"—he eventually moved it to a floating position in the upper right corner of the paper. There, it was safely disassociated from the frightening activity below.

During the dream interview, Daniel gave a wordless acknowledgment that he had been abused sexually as a child. He associated the large dark entity to his childhood assailant, to the judge in black robes who had sentenced him, and interestingly, to a "dope fiend" customer of his whom he often befriended with free "product," and who wore a similarly strange hairdo.

During the dream interview, Daniel conceded that he himself had been a "large dark entity" on a lot of people's backs and that about eighty users had needed desperately to "get out from under" him. His crime was "pushing."

Like Juliette's dream, Daniel's dream showed interlocking conflicts at many levels. On its face, Daniel's dream gave the child-victim and the Dark Entity–perpetrator, in conflict, at opposite ends of a spectrum, and connected by a metaphor. The connecting metaphor was that the good and defenseless little kid who "got fucked," grew up to be a real "Evil Fucker." The little kid who got pushed down on the bed grew up to be the pusher. (The metaphor continued to explain the "trick" in the dream. The trick was that when you deal with the "Dark Entity"—in this case, the devil, the drug business, or the child molester—you get "fucked in the end." Sensing this, he had developed "eyes in the back of his head.") At another level, Daniel's dream implied the first historical victim (the innocent little boy), and the first historical perpetrator (the original evil fucker). At still another level, it implied the present-day victims (all the people with someone "on their backs"—meaning both Daniel himself and his customers), and the present-day perpetrators. In this case there seemed to be two: the judge who gave the stiff sentence, and the junkie. I believe that the junkie appeared because he was the one who "ratted Daniel out," although I didn't discuss this part with Daniel.

The Dark Entity's unusual hair proved to be a clue for how the little boy who "gets fucked" and the "Evil Fucker" might eventually be integrated. When Daniel mapped the entity, he depicted its hair as being bound into two large bunches. When asked what this hair might look like it were untied, he replied that it might look like a lion's mane.

From here, Daniel connected to the expression "King of Beasts." Daniel himself had roughly the skin color of a lion. As a wealthy drug dealer, he had, in fact, been a sort of King of Beasts. He had also allowed his females to hunt for him and bring him food. However, in the image of the lion, the potential for "beastliness" co-exists with the potential for kingly, magnanimous, and noble behavior—which I think is the direction in which Daniel is headed. We also talked about the story of Androcles and the Lion, in which the slave first frees the beast, and then the beast frees the slave.

We encouraged Daniel to think about ways to make this dream come out better. Within about a week, he reported that he had had the dream again, but that this time, instead of getting so scared, he had been able to simply stand up and walk away. My feeling was that Androcles' lion had come into his own.

The following dream gives an example of victim-perpetrator negotiations which conclude successfully in rapprochement. This dream came to an eighteen-year-old Hispanic man named Arthur, whom I worked with at the Juvenile Detention Center. He was there on his second or third offense and would remain in custody until his twenty-first birthday. Like Juliette and Daniel, Arthur was an unusually attractive, intelligent person who was also an extremely gifted artist. It would have seemed more natural to be meeting him in some studio in the art department of the university than to be seeing him in jail. His dream was this:

Arthur and the Knife
I am watching a knife falling. It's falling and slowly turning end over end. It lands and sticks in this square piece of wood. Dark blood begins to ooze out of the

wood. It spreads until it gets my feet wet. I wake up real
scared.

The message of this dream was so powerful that when Arthur
did awake, he found himself standing in his stocking feet, in his drive-
way, in the rain. He had sleepwalked out of his house and down to
his car.

Arthur gave an action/feeling summary of his dream as follows:
(1) "I am curious about a falling knife." (2) "I watch the knife stick and
the board begin to bleed. I am still curious, but feeling like I should
get out of there." (3) "When my feet get wet, I am real scared, like I
should get out of there." He connected this action/feeling summary of
the dream with the events leading up to his arrest. Even after he had
got his feet wet, he failed to get the message that it was time to get out.

Arthur described the knife in his dream as follows: The blade
of the knife was the blade of a hunting knife. It was black steel with
big, serrated teeth. He had seen his stepfather use a hunting knife
to "field dress" game. He defined "field dressing" as the process
whereby the hunter cuts the guts (the stomach and intestines) out
of the deer, so he can haul home only those parts of the carcass that
are valuable to him.

The handle of the knife was the handle of a kitchen knife. It
was pearlized white plastic. Arthur had seen his mother use such a
kitchen knife to chop meat and vegetables for dinner.

We asked Arthur if there were some way in his life that he was
involved in stripping, chopping, or "field dressing" big game. He said,
yes, that he was a car thief, and that all his many convictions were
related to auto theft. Car thieves, he said, may strip, chop or gut the
vehicle, so that they can dispose of the desirable parts in the most
effective way.

We asked Arthur if there was also some way that he, himself,
was being "field dressed." He eventually said yes, and explained that
there was a lot of "bad blood" in his family because his mother and
stepfather were afraid he had become a "chip off the old block."
Arthur's biological father was an offender and was incarcerated at

the time of the dream. Arthur conceded that, in a way, his mother and stepfather were "ripping his guts out," as they did not want to take with them any of his deep feelings, or any other parts of himself that might be connected to his father.

Like Juliette's and Daniel's dreams, Arthur's dream implied a present day, waking-life victim (the auto owners who got "stuck" and Arthur who went to jail). It also implied an historical, waking-life victim (Arthur as a young child). But, Arthur's dream is also very different from either Juliette's or Daniel's. While it *implied* both a deer and a hunter, it *featured* a knife.

There was surely a time in Arthur's life when he was a deer. There was also clearly a time in his life when he was a hunter. The deer was innocent, natural, and without adequate defenses. It got killed and field-dressed. With respect to the hunter, it was only prey. The hunter was deliberate, premeditated, well-armed, and destructive. With respect to the deer, he was only a predator. The knife, however, knew both the deer and the hunter, and yet, a full understanding of "knife" could not be reached just through understanding "deer" and "hunter." The knife was an unusual composite with enormous possibilities of its own.

As the dreamwork progressed, some of the knife's possibilities proved to be that it was "sharp," was "hard but subtle," "had a point," could "cut through the bullshit," could "cut to the heart of the matter," and could "chop things down to size."

Arthur's knife was an image of authentic self. It was also the basis of a new self-image. It united Arthur's self-as-victim with his self-as-perpetrator. It joined the innocent naturalness of the deer to the protective power of the hunter. The image of "knife" seemed to spring from a level of self that is beneath the level of wounds and crimes, and it seemed to contain the energy needed to sustain the behaviors that it suggested. Upon Arthur's transfer from jail to prison, the knife self-image was already doing its work. He seemed to leave with a serenely optimistic state of mind—something for which he had not been noted during his other incarcerations.

Juliette, Daniel, and Arthur all found in crime an experience of mastery that precisely, metaphorically, offset an earlier experience of abuse and victimization. However, in the time we had available, only Arthur was able to get beyond the wound and the crime to secure an *image* of integrated authentic self. In mythological terms, all these heroes got the "call to adventure." All these heroes entered the "Heart of Darkness" and confronted the dragon. But after the confrontation, only one hero actually "seized the treasure."

This third step—achieving the integrated image of self, or "seizing the treasure"—is indispensable. It is also the step that all repeat offenders fail to take. Seizing the treasure is, after all, the real point of the whole journey. Heroes who leave the underworld without integrating the decency of the victim with the power of the perpetrator—without seizing the treasure—those who leave without the handbag or the lion or the knife, are obliged to return again for them later.

The three steps: (1) the wound, (2) the crime, and (3) the integrated image of authentic self; or (1) the call to adventure, (2) the confrontation in the heart of darkness, and (3) the seizing of the treasure, are the three acts of one play, variously titled "integration," "individuation," or "initiation."

The drama begins at birth, when we inherit a life situation. For some, the inherited situation includes a list of high-risk factors like poverty, unloving caregivers, addiction, neglect, and various kinds of physical or emotional abuse. Some one of these adverse inherited circumstances becomes the central childhood "wound."

As we mature emotionally, we learn ways to tend the wound. These include: exploring it, nursing it, protecting it, hiding it, denying it, and overcompensating for it. The sum of the treatments we learn to give ourselves becomes our repertoire of coping skills.

Nature however seeks healing and wholeness. It wants to be free of both the wound and all the treatments. It favors a direct approach that either kills or cures—definitively. When a person reaches the end of childhood, nature craves a test. It craves something so difficult as to exceed the power of all the puny skills acquired through tending the childhood wound. Those who don't die of the test, succeed in drawing out of the depths of themselves some heretofore unknown quality. This new quality is unique with each individual. Seen in dreams, it is the image of the authentic, adult self. With the emergence of this quality/image, the individual becomes more than just the sum of the problems—and solutions—given in childhood. He or she becomes healed of them and "initiated" into adulthood and the authentic self.

Traditional societies supplied ritual challenges through which young people could test their way into their authentic adulthood. Contemporary society supplies similar challenges. The acceptable ones include military service, college, graduate school, professional training school, trade school, marriage, and responsible parenthood.

Unfortunately, too many of us arrive at the end of childhood too battered and too uneducated to undertake these acceptable challenges. Where no acceptable challenge is available, nature reverts to the default. The default initiation is, like the straight line, the shortest distance between two points. It makes use of the ancient eye-for-an-eye, tooth-for-a-tooth principle. The default initiation is simply stepping through the childhood wound, and turning it inside out. In this way, the initiate becomes his/her own worst nightmare. The child in the closet becomes the beast at the door. . . . The deer becomes the hunter.

The default initiation can entrain terrible complications. These complications often obscure the benefits to be derived. For example, where the original childhood wound is horrific, the offsetting reparative act is horrific. It takes place under dangerous, volatile (and probably illegal) circumstances, and it involves a high risk of police intervention and consequent criminal penalties. Under such circumstances, there is little likelihood that the restaged reparative drama can be made to come out better than the disastrous original. There is every likelihood that it will result in new wounds to the offender, the other participants, and maybe the bystanders, too. Then, even the benefit of the sought after symbolic triumph is lost in the confusion.

The last and best gift of my original women's dreamwork group at the Bernalillo County Detention Center was my understanding that dreams will get us to the solution for what is wrong with our criminal justice system. When we approach the fortifications that are our prisons and jails, we can look through the doorway of the dream to see the answer to the question, "Why do people commit crimes?"

The answer is that crimes are nature's default initiation into healing and adulthood. They are designed to provide the victim with precisely the form of mastery that was missing to him or her at the moment of the victimization. After the crime, the offender is poised between the two parameters within which his or her adult self-boundaries will be drawn. The offender is poised between the decent self-as-victim, and the powerful self-as-perpetrator. After the crime, the offender is finally in a position to grow up—to fabricate the hand-bag, become the real King of Beasts, or seize the knife. Knowing how to do dreamwork, and knowing why people commit crimes, we should be able to see to it that no one ever commits more than one.

By looking through the doorway of dreams, we should also eventually be able to fix it so that crimes won't be necessary at all for healing. We should be able to reorganize our fortifications so that, in the future, they will protect the public, but without imprisoning the children, the monsters, the hyenas, or the mad women. We need to learn how to turn our fortifications into a preserve and an obstacle course for the benefit of our wild and belligerent minority whose emotions are likely to explode out into crime. We need to offer them something besides the conventional initiations (school, military service, apprenticeship, marriage, etc.) for which they do not qualify, so that we can prevent them from seeking the default initiations (crime and incarcerations) which unnecessarily endanger, impoverish and disrupt the rest of us.

Finally, by looking through the doorway of dreams, we can help the children and monsters already trapped in the fortifications. Through dreams and dreamwork, offenders can begin to develop many of the cognitive skills in which they are so notoriously deficient. These include problem-solving skills like "critical reasoning" (issue-spotting, fact-finding, identifying casual connections, estimating and anticipating developments) and "social perspective taking" (developing empathy, awareness, and sensitivity, leading to better interpersonal problem-solving).

When a unified image of authentic self emerges from two opposing images of self-as-victim and self-as-aggressor, I imagine that what has gone on behind the scenes is a sort of process of negotiation. All negotiation is founded on the premise that each party has something of value to the other. In a negotiation, the details of both parties' needs and resources are explored for ways that things can be combined or exchanged to everyone's advantage. The objective of negotiation is to arrive at a win-win result. Unless the win-win result can be reached, it effectively becomes a lose-lose situation.

Dreaming and dreamwork are about possibilities for negotiation. They bring things to consciousness. They bring disparate characters to the table together. They permit the dreamer to familiarize him/herself with everyone's fears and desires, strengths and weaknesses, motives and goals. They help the dreamer to understand who seeks what changes, and what the costs and benefits of each change might be. They also permit the dreamer to explore the implementation of change. Then, as the dreamer explores, understands, and appreciates the position of each dream character, he/she somehow also incorporates, integrates, and absorbs them.

It is interesting to me that in the default initiation, the offender generally does not attempt to bring about the better outcome by *revising* the traumatic scene. Instead, he/she tends to seek the better outcome by simply *recasting* him/herself in the aggressor's more powerful and more desirable role. The offender thereby changes an I-lose-you-win situation into an I-win-you-lose situation. This is like switching places with the opposition in a negotiation. It does not efficiently advance the parties toward a win-win outcome. It suggests, among other things, a lack of skill at negotiating.

Good dreamwork demands the same cognitive skills as good negotiation. Dreamwork, like negotiation, trains the dreamer to explore the opponent's position. This exploration leads to the discovery of increased possibilities for action and outcome. Dreams are nothing if not expositions of possibilities. As a reliable method for exploring the possibilities is learned, the inevitable connection between trauma and crime as the default healing response, is broken.

At present, despite all the lip-service that we give to "criminal justice" and "corrections," we want not just "deterrence and inca-pacitation," but also punishment and revenge. We send people off to prison the way we might send them off to the woodshed to deal with a stern father. Like stern fathers, prisons have to do with struc-ture, containment, organization, rules, and discipline. The guidance they offer usually takes the form of reprimand. We expect prison bar-riers to *instill* boundaries in people. We expect offenders to *imbibe* good boundaries from the experience of being in prison. It is almost as if we expect people to "set up" in prison the way Jell-O sets up in a mold. We cannot make Jell-O without a mold, and we cannot make Jell-O if we do not allow enough time, but all the molds and all the time in the world won't help us get the dessert if we fail to add the magic powder. Given the right mold, the right time, and enough Jell-O, the dessert takes shape. Offenders are the same. With enough dreams, everyone takes shape. Up until now, we have been forget-ting the real magic powder.

5

Enjoy the Ride:
An Inner Dialogue
with a Dream

JENNY DAVIDOW

HAVING AN "Inner Dialogue" with your dream can show you how you may be stopping yourself from fully enjoying or entering into a relationship with someone. By exploring your relationship with yourself first, you can discover ways in which you can improve your relationships with others.

One of my clients, Louise, had a scary dream that seemed, at first, totally unrelated to her real-life relationships:

> I get into the elevator of an office building, and I push the button for the seventh floor. The elevator goes up, but instead of stopping at my floor, it gathers speed at an alarming rate. Now I'm frightened. I try to stop the elevator, but the buttons don't respond. The elevator goes faster and faster, then shoots out of the top of the building and goes into outer space! By now I am

> *hysterical. I don't believe there is a way for me to return*
> *to Earth. I am trapped in this runaway elevator.*

To Louise, this was a horrible dream, and the elevator was a very upsetting symbol. She could see no redeeming value in this dream. She could not even make a guess as to why she would have such a dream.

I guided Louise through the Inner Dialogue steps so that she could arrive at her own understanding of the message her subconscious was sending her. I began by asking her to imagine her dream again, and then shift her awareness so she could imagine being the elevator. Then I asked, "As the Elevator, please describe yourself. What do you look like?"

"I am the Elevator," said Louise. "I am a large metal box. I have doors and a control panel inside."

Next, I asked, "Now, as the Elevator, just tell me what elevators *normally* do."

"I take people up and down. Up and down in the building."

To fill in as much detail as possible, I asked, "Elevator, please tell me about yourself. What is unique about you, and how you are different from other elevators?"

Louise continued to respond as if she were the Elevator: "My unique qualities are . . . my walls are a golden color, inside me, where people ride. I'm a gold-plated elevator! I have unusual powers. I can shoot through the top of the building and go into outer space. I'm different from other elevators because I have a much wider range of where I can go. Also, I'm gold-plated. That makes me more valuable and special."

Now we could begin to find out what Louise's subconscious was trying to tell her. I asked, "What is happening from your point of view, as the Elevator?"

"I am going up in the building, and I just keep going up. I shoot out of the top of the building and start traveling into outer space. Louise is inside of me. She's going nuts, she's so scared—*but I'm having a wonderful time!* She thinks something is wrong, but this is what I do naturally!"

Louise looked surprised at how different the Elevator's personality was from her conscious personality. I asked the Elevator, "How do you *feel* as this is happening?"

"I feel great," Louise replied. "I like not having any limits on where I can go."

I asked the Elevator if it had something more to say to Louise. Louise, as the Elevator, responded: "I want you to give me the benefit of the doubt. Loosen up and have some fun with me! Trust me and enjoy the ride! Let's go have an adventure, and then I'll bring you back."

While speaking as the Elevator, there was a dramatic change in Louise. Her voice and body language became bolder and more zestful than they were before. These changes also were a marked contrast to the fear and powerlessness that Louise previously felt as the dreamer. The Elevator's different point of view represented a valuable subconscious part of Louise. Speaking as the Elevator had shed light on the subconscious, unused abilities that the Elevator represented: a zest for life that encourages adventure and a desire to push beyond the normal limits that Louise assumed her life must have.

As Louise and I explored these subconscious metaphors, I gave her room to discover her own meanings and apply them to specific areas of her life. Louise realized that her subconscious was pointing out that she needed to reclaim the very capable, confident adventurer in her. Up until now, she had been afraid to use the valuable "gold-plated elevator" part of her—the part that wanted to take risks and meet challenges. Because of her Inner Dialogue, Louise was willing to begin to change the safe and habitual limits she had set for herself, so she really could use—and enjoy—her abilities.

Next, I asked Louise, "To what areas of your life might you want to apply this subconscious message to take more risks and use more of your abilities?"

Louise said she was in a good relationship, but she was confused about it. She liked her boyfriend's self-confidence, but she didn't like feeling pressured to keep up with him in areas where she wasn't as confident as he was. For instance, when they went skiing, he liked to go fast and take chances; she didn't. She said she preferred to ski safely, which meant going more slowly and staying on easier slopes.

I asked Louise if the Elevator also might represent the adventurous energy in her boyfriend that was pulling her toward taking more risks. As she thought about her responses to the Elevator, and then to her boyfriend, Louise's eyes widened. After we talked about it, she said she was convinced that her relationship was a waking dream. Her subconscious was sending her the same message, both in her dream and in her relationship: take more chances and enjoy the ride. In fact, she told me, it was her boyfriend's ability to enjoy himself that had attracted her to him in the first place. Now it was time for her to learn how to more fully enjoy herself, too.

Over the next few months, a transformation took place. Now Louise enjoyed the challenge of new situations that were outside her old, safe routine. The resolution of conflicts in her subconscious had set her on a different path, moving toward a more fulfilling outcome.

Later that year, Louise told me that she had experienced a breakthrough in her skiing, and now she had fun going faster on steeper slopes. Her new confidence gradually rippled out into other areas of her life—including her relationship. Significantly, a year later, she made the decision to get married. She was ready to enjoy the ride.

6

Exploring a Terrifying Dream

AARON B. ROCHLEN AND CLARA E. HILL

CLIENTS WHO have gone through dream interpretation sessions have reported being very satisfied with their experience and have indicated that they have gained higher levels of self-understanding and insight than have clients in regular therapy sessions (see Hill & Rochlen, 1999, and Hill, 1996, for a more thorough review of this research). These results suggest that working with dreams helps clients discover new things about themselves and resolve problems in their lives. Unfortunately, however, many clients or potential clients are not familiar with how a dream might be used in therapy or what to expect from a dream interpretation session and may therefore be reluctant to take a dream into therapy. Hence, we provide an example in this chapter of what a client could expect from working with a dream in therapy using the Hill (1996) model of dream interpretation.

The Hill (1996) cognitive-experiential model evolved from a number of different theoretical orientations (e.g., Freudian, Jungian, cognitive/behavioral, and humanistic/experiential) and involves three stages: Exploration, Insight, and Action. In the Exploration Stage, the individual parts or elements of the dream are examined and the client is encouraged to experience the dream as if it were actually happening in the present. This process helps the client to access the feelings, thoughts, and previous experiences that are represented in the actual content and emotions of the dream. In the Insight Stage, the therapist and client collaborate to construct a *new* understanding of the dream. The word *new* is emphasized here, because some clients come into sessions with preconceived notions of the meaning of their dreams. In this model, we try to extend on this prior understanding of the dream and help clients in learning something new about themselves. In the Action Stage, the therapist and client jointly figure out what changes the client might want to make based on what he or she learned in the dream.

Critical to this model is the assumption that all three stages are needed for a complete dream interpretation. In addition, it is equally important to emphasize the collaborative nature of the model. Rather than the therapist having the answers about what the dream means, the therapist serves as a facilitator and collaborator in aiding the client in figuring out the meaning of his or her dream.

In the remainder of this article, we demonstrate how a client and a therapist can work together collaboratively to construct a meaning of a dream and decide what to do about it. We do this by sharing an abridged version of a session with "Ranjit" (pseudonym), an eighteen-year-old Indian-American client (note that this case was first presented in the chapter by Hill & Rochlen, 1999).

The Dream

I'm driving in a car around a winding road leading up to the top of a mountain. It is a very peaceful, enjoyable ride. Signs appear frequently on the road, but I can't seem to read them, and I'm not particularly interested in trying any harder. I look up at the top of the mountain, but I can't see very well. It appears that the peaks of the mountains are turning into skyscrapers, which is very odd and somewhat troubling. Now I'm driving faster and faster. I suddenly crash into a barrier right at the edge of the cliff. I am terrified. The car is rocking back and forth, coming close to falling off the cliff. I try to scream out for help, but I can't make any sounds. I wake up terrified.

THE EXPLORATION STAGE

The aim of the Exploration Stage is to put the client back into the dream experience and to explore the major images of the dream. This goal is achieved by having the client describe (i.e., paint a verbal picture of) the dream images fully and then associate (i.e., say what comes to mind) to the images. In the next part of the Exploration Stage, therapists work with clients to identify "triggers" in waking life that stimulated dream images. Frequently, clients spontaneously think of triggers as they describe and associate to images. Other times, however, therapists probe clients to help them identify triggers.

Therapist: OK, let's try to take a close look at some of the details of the dream. Could you tell me a little more about the car? What did it look like?

    Client: Well, it was one of those old classic luxury cars, a Cadillac I think. It had a leather interior and a very strong motor. Actually, now that I think about it, I remember it being a convertible because my hair was blowing in the wind.

Therapist: Good. Now could you describe what the scene was like at the top of the mountain and what you were feeling as you were looking up toward the top?

    Client: It was a very strange and disturbing scene. The mountains were changing into huge skyscrapers. One of the mountains looked like the Empire State Building. Sometimes the tops of the mountains looked like they had windows in them—like big buildings you would see in New York City.

Therapist: OK, now we are going to try to get some of your associations to these images. You described the car as being a Cadillac with a leather interior. What does a Cadillac make you think of?

Client: Well, I kind of think of the "all-American car," something of status that you feel really comfortable driving around in.

Therapist: And what does the "all-American car" mean to you?

Client: When I moved here from India, I was amazed at how big and fast the cars were. I always wanted my own American car. I guess I associate a sense of control and independence with owning a car.

Therapist: And what is a vehicle?

Client: What do you mean?

Therapist: Well, if I had no idea what a vehicle is, how would you describe it?

Client: A vehicle is something that moves you from one place to another. Sometimes people also refer to their own bodies as "vehicles."

Therapist: Good. Now earlier, you described the road as being a very tight, winding road surrounded by mountains. Do you have any memories of such a road?

Client: When I was a kid, there were a lot of roads like that in India.

Therapist: And were you driving the car as a kid?

Client: No, my parents were driving. I remember sitting in the back seat and feeling afraid, like maybe we were going to fall off the road. It was a much more comfortable feeling being on my own in the dream, driving around the tight turns.

Therapist: Now what about the barrier the car crashed into? Any past experiences with this?

Client: No, not really, none that I can think of.

Therapist: OK. Now if I had no idea what a barrier actually is, how would you describe it?

Client: Well, it's something that can keep you or your car from falling down a cliff, something that can cause a lot of damage, but it can save you from more potential damage.

Therapist: So a barrier keeps you from falling into danger—something that can cause a little damage but keeps you away from a lot more. I'm wondering what your own personal "barriers" are?

Client: Yes, well, in thinking about it that way I have several barriers in my life. One of them is my best friend. We went to high school together and are here studying in college. He encourages me to go out and have a good time, but he always looks out for my best interests. If he knows that I have work to do, he won't let me go out and get in trouble.

THE INSIGHT STAGE

The purpose of the Insight Stage is for clients to come to new understandings of the meaning of dreams. Again, therapists and clients work together to construct the meanings, building from what they learned in the Exploration Stage. Dreams can be understood at one or more levels: (1) the experience of the dream, (2) waking life, (3) past experiences, or (4) inner dynamics or conflicts (how different images/characters in the dream represent parts of the client's personality). Therapists typically encourage clients to work first at the "level" that is most comfortable or makes the most immediate sense. For example, if a client presents a dream that is very vivid and frightening and seems like an important experience in and of itself, the client and therapist would likely work to understand that experience without resorting to interpreting the dream "as if it stands" for something else. Alternatively, if the client presents a dream that is very concrete and related directly to waking life and the client has no interest in looking at images symbolically, the therapist and client work to understand the dream in relation to waking life. Finally, if the client seems to be acting in present life on the basis of past experiences more than present experiences, the therapist can work with past experiences (e.g., childhood, trauma).

Therapist: What do you think this dream means?

    Client: I see this dream as representing myself, kind of maneuvering my way through obstacles that come with being on my own in college as I try to reach my own goals.

Therapist: Can you say more about how you came to this conclusion?

    Client: Well, in the dream I'm enjoying being in my own "vehicle" and making my way toward the top of the mountain. I'm by myself and am "enjoying the ride," but there are signs telling me to be careful as I progress forward. Sometimes in college, I've decided to ignore the warning signs and just do the fun things that come along with college life. I think one thing this dream is telling me is to be careful, as there is the potential for harm to myself and disappointment to my family.

Therapist: Your interpretation makes sense, but let's work with it further. There seems to be much more in this dream that remains unanswered. What about the curiosity and anxiety you were experiencing as you looked up at the mountains and described how they transformed into skyscrapers? Your associations were to New York City, where you noted you would like to work sometime.

    Client: Actually, I think that this may represent some uncertainty regarding my goals and what my true peak performance is.

Therapist: I'm not sure I understand. How does that relate to your dream?

Client: In high school and at the start of college, I thought I wanted to be a financial analyst in New York City. My parents were very enthusiastic and supportive about this career choice. In college, though, I haven't enjoyed or done very well in the business courses, and I prefer classes like psychology and journalism. Another thing I'm thinking about now is whether I really want to live in New York City. The truth is that I really love the countryside and the relaxed, calming atmosphere of the mountains.

Therapist: OK, good, but how do you see this latter part about where you might want to eventually live being represented in the dream?

Client: Well, I see the transformation between skyscrapers and mountains as a representation of the uncertainty I am experiencing about both the type of job I want to have and where I might want to live.

Therapist: Nice connection, Ranjit! Now let's move into another area. As you were giving some of your associations, I became curious as to how your background with your family and experiences in India fit in with your dream. You said the mountains remind you of how you didn't feel comfortable or safe when your parents were driving in India. You also mentioned that at times your parents don't listen to you or respect your independence.

Client: Well, I do think that this dream is getting at some of my feelings about my parents. Growing up I never felt I had much control over my life. I also felt like my parents would hint at what they thought I should be doing to prepare myself for life. I would also feel angry at never having the guts to speak up to them about my desire to do what I want with my life. I am very close with my parents, but they are very strict and seem to forget that I am an adult and need to make my own decisions.

Therapist: And how do you see this represented in the dream?

Client: Well, in the dream I am on my own, moving forward and enjoying having the freedom of driving in my own car.

Therapist: Which is a Cadillac, an American car. What do you think is the significance of this?

Client: Well, I don't talk about this very often, but there is definitely a cultural tug-of-war between my parents and me. I think the Cadillac might represent my identification with the American culture. I see myself as very much American, whereas my family still practices all of the Indian customs and traditions. Sometimes they give me a hard time.

Therapist: OK, I can see how this dream represents the cultural struggle, as well as your preference for being more independent, but what about the crashing into the barrier and the inability to call out for help? That sounds frightening! What do you think that barrier represents for you?

Client: I have always had a hard time asking for help. I think I struggle in this area not only with my parents but in school.

Therapist: Say more about this.

Client: Well, as I mentioned earlier, I am often intimidated by my parents and can't seem to speak up to them. I wish I could let them know that I love them but that I want to be my own person. I would also like to be able to tell them about the tough times at college without worrying about disappointing them.

Therapist: You mentioned trouble speaking up in school?

Client: Well, I think that it is a very practical matter. I should talk more in classes but I feel nervous. There are also many tutoring resources on campus that I have not used but probably should.

THE ACTION STAGE

Once the client has an idea of what the dream means, the next step is to talk about what the client can take away from the dream to use in waking life based on his or her new awareness. Hence, the Action Stage aims to integrate information gained from the Exploration and Insight Stages to facilitate or discuss possible changes in the dreamer's life. Making changes is important both because it is the ultimate goal of therapy and because making changes helps to consolidate the insights gained earlier in the Insight Stage.

Three different types of action are possible: (1) changing the dream in fantasy or during sleep, (2) making changes in waking life, and (3) continuing to work on the dream. Often these areas of possible change are related to one another. For example, the client and therapist could discuss changing the dream and then discuss how these changes relate to those the client could make in waking life. As in the other two stages, the therapist works collaboratively with the client exploring what he or she wants to do. Thus, the therapist does not instruct the client to do anything, but instead works with the client, to determine potential areas of change and how these changes could be accomplished.

Therapist: So, if you could change this dream in any way, how would you change it?

Client: Well, I think I would make the signs in the road a little bigger, so I could see the dangers up ahead. I would also like to have another person in the car with me to enjoy the ride.

Therapist: And what else would you change if you had the opportunity?

Client: Well, I think if crashing into the barrier was unavoidable, I would at least call out for help and have people come to my rescue.

Therapist: Anything else?

Client: I guess I would have the top of the mountains either be mountains or skyscrapers. It was very annoying that I couldn't see exactly what it was up there and that it kept changing.

Therapist: OK, great. Now you mentioned that you wanted to be certain whether a peaceful country scene or New York skyscrapers are at the top of the mountains. What change in your waking life does this represent for you?

Client: Well, I think I would like to know exactly what is in store for my future! It makes me very anxious to be so indecisive about my professional career goals. I would like to be more certain about the direction that I'm going in life.

Therapist: OK, I'd like for you to listen to these changes you suggested in the dream. I'm going to read back some of the changes you had wanted to make in the dream, and I want you to just think about how they sound and what implications they might have for your waking life. You would like to be able to better recognize signs of upcoming danger, have company by your side, and be able to call out for help in times of trouble. Are any of these realistic changes for you in your waking life?

Client: Thinking about it that way, I think many of those are things I would like to work on.

Therapist: How so? Let's start with warning signs.

Client: I think I would like to be more conscious of the potential downfalls that come with partying too hard in college and ignoring my responsibilities.

Therapist: And what about the company in the car?

Client: Well, this part isn't too difficult to interpret. For some time I've been searching for a girlfriend.

Therapist: And the calls for help?

Client: As I mentioned earlier, I think I need to be more comfortable asking for help when needed. I think this applies not only to my schoolwork, but also with my parents.

Therapist: How so?

Client: Well, I would like to have much more of an honest relationship with my parents. Instead of being scared of disappointing them, I would like to be able to tell them about everything that has been happening for me in college.

Therapist: Ranjit, what could you do right now that would make it easier for you to see the "warning signs" as well as "calling out for help"?

Client: I think it would be very helpful if I could be more self-disciplined in deciding when it is time to study and when it is time to have fun.

Therapist: So maybe you could make a schedule with specific times allotted for studying?

Client: Yeah, I think I could do that. In fact, that's a good idea. I think it could work if I set up a specific time and maybe even a specific place to study each night, especially if I didn't force myself to do it for too long.

Therapist: And how about calling out for help?

Client: Well, I think going over this dream has definitely made me more willing to make an appointment with an English tutor to work on my writing skills. Also, I think I should probably talk to try to figure out some of my career-related goals.

Therapist: These all sound like very good, practical ideas. Now, if you wanted to remember this dream or create a physical reminder of its messages, what could you do?

Client: I'm not sure what you mean. Sounds like a dumb idea.

Therapist: It might be a dumb idea, but let's try it anyway. It just seems like there were some really important messages in this dream. If you wanted to remember them, how might you do so symbolically?

Client: Well, I think that I could use "signs" to tell me what I need to look out for and how I can take better care of myself.

Therapist: So could you make some sort of sign to represent the dream? What would the sign have on it?

Client: I think it would be a Yield sign with a picture of a winding, high-rising road on it.

Therapist: Sounds great. Maybe you could get a small Yield sign and hang it over your desk where you could see it and use it to remind yourself of what you learned through this dream interpretation.

Client: That's a good idea. I think I'll do that. I can picture right now where I would put it.

Therapist: OK. Now, if you were to give this dream a title, what would it be?

Client: The Crash of the Cultures.

Therapist: Great! That really captures it and can give you a way to keep thinking about this dream.

CONCLUSIONS

As we have tried to illustrate, working with dreams in therapy is an excellent way for clients to gain insight and make changes in their lives. Although working on dreams alone can be useful, research has suggested that clients tend to get more out of working with a trained therapist (Heaton, Hill, Petersen, Rochlen, & Zack, 1998). When working alone, it is easy to get blocked and give up on working with the dream. Working with an objective person, who is invested and trained in the dream interpretation process, can be helpful. In addition, working with dreams can be a way to get to a "deeper level" than might arise naturally in therapy. Because clients do not know what the dream images and characters represent or symbolize in dreams, they are often less defensive or guarded in sessions than they might be when discussing waking-life events. Finally, as we have seen in the work of Ranjit, working with dreams in a therapeutic context can be a good way to help identify some concrete goals and personal objectives that can be used to help structure and guide the remainder of the therapy. In closing, we hope that this example of the Hill (1996) model dream interpretation has given you a better idea of what clients might experience in a dream interpretation with a trained therapist. If you are a present or potential client of counseling services, we encourage you to stay open to the idea of therapeutic dreamwork and to seek out trained therapists who will help you make sense of your dreams.

References

Heaton, K. J., Hill, C. E., Petersen, D. A., Rochlen, A. B., & Zack, J. S. (1998). A comparison of therapist-facilitated and self-guided dream interpretation sessions. *Journal of Counseling Psychology*, 45, 115–121.

Hill, C. E. (1996). *Working with dreams in psychotherapy*. New York: Guilford.

Hill, C. E., & Rochlen, A. B. (1999). A cognitive-experiential model for working with dreams in psychotherapy. In L. Vandecreek and T. L. Jackson (Eds.), *Innovations in clinical practice: A source book* (pp. 467–480). Sarasota, FL: Professional Resource Press.

7

A Shamanic Dream Journey

GRAYWOLF SWINNEY

IT WAS OUR first "journey." Jane was a client with whom I had been working for some time with limited success. Her reasons for coming to me were complaints of marital problems and self-discomfort. "I know there's something drastically wrong in me," she reported, "but I can't really put my finger on it. It makes me drive everyone away from me." She saw herself [or rather, I saw her] as frigid, hard, and cold.

In therapy, we discovered that Jane's four older brothers had sexually molested her repeatedly from the time she was five through age sixteen. Her parents took the brothers' side; they wouldn't believe her when she tried to tell them about it. She felt unwanted and barely tolerated in this family. There was pressure for her to be "one of the boys." The effect was that she became frigid and unavailable both emotionally and physically in her dealings with the world. We made breakthroughs in understanding the origins of her condition, yet neither of us was satisfied. The problems lessened slightly but deep resolution was elusive.

One day, she brought in a very disturbing dream. In it, she was strapped to a cart on rails that was being slowly drawn into a spinning hub on which were mounted thousands of razor-sharp knives and blades. She had awakened in terror just before contact, deeply disturbed by the dream. I was in a particularly exploratory mood that day, and so I took a direction with her that was somewhat unusual for me. I suggested that she use her imagination and let herself be pulled into the whirling blades. I had in mind a shamanic technique, in which the dreamer directly faces the most frightening parts of the dream and blends them with the gestalt approach of working within the personal experience of the dream. I, too, allowed myself to be drawn into the dream and to share my experience with Jane. I had no idea what to expect or where this shaman-gestalt journey might lead.

Jane reported being slashed and cut into tiny bits, with blood and flesh splattering in all directions, but strangely, all she experienced was the sensation of the razor-sharp coldness of the blades. I asked her to give in to that sense-image of the icy coldness, and as she did she experienced herself becoming a thick layer of ice: frigid, very hard, and cold.

This report intrigued me, for it was a sensory expression of the issue that had brought her into therapy. "Stay with it," I urged. "Go even deeper into this sense of cold, become it." As she did this, she reported the sensation of falling into a bone-piercing cold where nothing moved or even existed, where all was frozen solid and dense.

Not knowing what else to do but trust that her imagination was taking her where she needed to go, I encouraged her to follow the experience farther. When she did so, her body became more rigid and hard, reflecting the frozen image within. I, too, traveled into the icy coldness of her dream. We remained there for a while, and then I noticed that her body started to change and relax. The muscles in her face softened and showed a visage I had never seen on her before. Then I noticed that her body began to soften, as if she were melting into the pad on which she lay.

I asked her what she was experiencing.

"I am the water that was beneath the ice and feeling warmer," she reported. "I am soft and flowing here, I feel flexible and wave-like. I have no boundaries, and it feels like I extend forever. I'm safe, no one can hurt me as water." Her once rigid body relaxed even further, and she remained quiet for a very long time. Then she opened her eyes and told me that she had had a new experience of her self. This new sense of self was very deep and continued to evolve over the following days and weeks.

The work we did together was similar to guided imagery, but was also different. The changes were dramatic and proved to be durable. For example, a few weeks following the journey, she asked permission to speak with a group of family sex offenders that I was facilitating. She had previously chided me for working with them, opining that they did not deserve anything better than castration and jail. I carried her request to the group and received permission for her to visit.

The night Jane met with them was poignant. She spoke of her pain and theirs, and how their pain had driven them to the deep, dark coldness where one could commit such an act. She pleaded that they continue to get help and change. There wasn't a dry eye in the group that evening, but more important, she provided them with a motivation to honestly deal with their pathology—a motivation that in many of these offenders had been lacking.

Some years later, I encountered Jane by accident in a store. We were both surprised and delighted, and her first words were about the Journey, the impact it had on her then, and how it had changed her innermost sense of being. Although twelve years had passed, she had found that the experience continued to positively affect her life, giving her an ongoing sense of well-being. Her marriage had blossomed and their children were doing well. She was still very soft and flowing.

In hindsight, I recognized that an important event had taken place: a deep healing that was seldom, if ever, reached through the traditional psychological methods. "Could this be the mechanism by which the placebo effect works?" I asked myself. I felt justified with such an explanation, since this healing satisfied the criteria that I use to define placebos: the healing had come from within her and had been accomplished using her own imaginative flow. I had merely accompanied her in a state of co-consciousness, invited her to follow her own sensory imagery no matter how frightening, and remained with her in that flow throughout the experience. Nothing external had been administered except support.

My experience with Jane was an encounter that changed both of our lives in remarkable ways, bringing transformation not only to her inner life and family, but also to the way I work with myself and others within the therapeutic process. By fully entering the dream experience with a client and encouraging him or her to go beyond the traditional forms of dream interpretation—integrating imagination, creativity, and intuition—a deeper consciousness can be reached in which restrictive patterns of behavior and personality can be changed.

8

Catholic Dreams

RICHARD A. RUSSO

I

*I have a golden crucifix with a hole in its center.
Bright globules of light move through my body like
living creatures of mercury. I hold the cross up to my
brow, where my sixth chakra would be, and center it over
one of the globules. A brilliant beam of light shines out
through the crucifix, illuminating all that I see. . . .*

II

I WAS RAISED a Catholic, and dutifully attended church each
Sunday until I was about ten, when I developed a disturbing psychosomatic reaction. Whenever I entered a church for any reason
(even a family wedding), I would begin to suffocate. After five minutes, I'd have to bolt for the door or else would pass out or vomit.
After a few such episodes, my parents stopped making me go to
church.

73

By college, I considered myself an agnostic, and thought my Catholic upbringing was behind me. I began to study Western mysticism and practice meditation. Then, in my mid-twenties, I had the following dream:

> *I'm in my old church, waiting to enter a large*
> *classroom, when a stern-looking priest says he will hear*
> *my confession. I'm nervous because it's been years since*
> *I went to church and I no longer remember the ritual.*
> *I decide to say, "Father, it's been a long time since*
> *my last confession. I want to tell you my doubts about*
> *God"—but then my friend H. appears* [in the dream,
> he resembles my father], *and we begin talking*
> *about sex.*
>
> *Now I'm about eight years old. "Has the boy done*
> *something wrong?" the priest asks. "Not exactly," H.*
> *replies. "Let's say it's sort of a family matter." Some*
> *pretty girls from the Catholic school are watching. I act*
> *tough. "I didn't come to talk about sex," I yell at the*
> *priest. "There's nothing wrong with sex!"*
>
> *Now I'm an adult again, standing at the podium in*
> *the classroom continuing my lecture on sex. The*
> *audience of churchgoers is shocked. I wink at one of the*
> *girls sitting nearby and whisper, "Wait till I hit them*
> *with my arguments against the existence of God. . . ."*

Thus began a vivid sequence of dreams in which my Christian upbringing again became a live issue for me. During the following months, I continued to dream of arguing with the Church authorities and disrupting services. In one fanciful dream from this period, I was a starpoint of light dancing on the lawn of the Vatican, taunting the people inside. Then, two years after the initial dream of rebellion, the issue shifted to a new level:

> *I'm kneeling in a huge cathedral, asking God to heal*
> *me but feeling uncertain what I believe. I want a sign. I*
> *look down at the floor and see two star patterns burned*

*into the stone, the aftereffects of an intense light. One is
yellowish, the other blue. I realize that Jesus and Mary
have been here, and left these marks in the stone.*

This dream had a profound impact on me. My memory of it
was so vivid that it came to seem part of my waking experience. I'd
been given the sign I wanted, but was not satisfied; the marks were
just afterimages, not the real thing. Yet they were beautiful. I drew
a picture of the two stars and kept it on my desk. I was no longer
sure what I believed.

A year later, I had a very long dream in which I was part of a
plot to assassinate the Pope. In the dream, I lived through most of
a day, complete with detailed meetings and preparations. Finally I
climbed a long flight of stairs to the top of a cathedral tower, carrying a package of poison. I was supposed to wait there for a signal
from one of the other conspirators, but accidentally dropped the
package. It fell to the cathedral floor just as a procession of Bishops
and Cardinals was entering. The High Mass was about to begin. I
rushed downstairs to retrieve the poison and ended up in the front
row as the Pope began the ceremony.

> *I'm kneeling at the railing before the altar. I look up
> at the altar and see a large crucifix there. I realize it's
> life-sized, then, to my astonishment, that a living person
> is hanging there. It's Christ Himself! The Pope is saying
> that we are all "in the service of Christ," whereupon
> Jesus blesses the congregation, then turns to me, smiles
> and says, "Even you, Russo." Suddenly, I know in my
> heart that it's true, and that I could never carry out my
> part in the assassination plot. . . .*

A few months later, I had a lovely dream in which I stepped outside to receive a "blessing." It was raining, and I realized that that was
the blessing, for I was being splashed with "little drops of holy water."
Then, almost exactly five years after it began, the long sequence of
Catholic dreams came to an end. I was in a church very much like
the one in my first dream. My son and his friends were there, but the

priest was late. I was going to have to fill in for him. At first I was nervous, then I began to sing a hymn, and the congregation joined me, and I realized it wasn't going to be so hard after all.

III

For several years I had no more overt Christian dreams. Then, on February 13, 1978, I had two profound dreams during the same night.

In the first dream, I was in the bedroom of my childhood home. I asked my mother who the three priests in our living room were, and she replied, "That's Father Bramman . . . they're all Brammans." When I walked into the living room, no one was there. Father Bramman was waiting for me in the kitchen. I had to go through the Purification alone.

> *I'm kneeling, holding a candle whose flame has gone out. As I concentrate on it, two lighted candles appear, hovering in the air to form a triangle with mine. The three small candles merge to form one. Then I have a vision of an even greater and brighter candle, burning in mid-air before me.*
>
> [In one version of the dream, the flame jumps from the smaller candles to mine; in another, the three candles merge; in yet another, the greater, incorporeal flame lights my candle, then the three become one. It was all of these, and none; I cannot explain it].
>
> *My candle is lighted. As it burns gently in my hand, I hear music coming from the next room: a gospel song about "The Greater Love."* [The music slowly grows louder, matching my swelling emotions, until it permeates the dream]. *My little candle begins to connect to the incorporeal one beyond. I start sobbing. The music swells, I can't stop crying. A voice says, "Isn't it time you stopped resisting? You were here once before, and didn't go on—isn't it because you were afraid of failing?" I'm crying uncontrollably as my little candle*

merges with the Greater One. Father Bramman peers out
from the kitchen. Tears and mucous are streaming down
my face, but I can't stop crying. Energy is being released
all over my body. It feels so good. . . .

I awoke from this dream around three in the morning, still
trembling from my sobbing. My body was limp. I wrote down my
experience, then went back to sleep.

Three black-robed, hooded monks enter the field next
to our house. I am frightened and step out into the front
yard to investigate, but one of them holds up his hand to
indicate that I should come no closer. What is about to
happen is not for me.
The three figures kneel in the field. The tall one in
the middle pulls back his hood. It's Max Von Sydow!
[who played the Knight in Bergman's film, "The
Seventh Seal"]. *He gazes upward. Dark clouds are*
gathering in the sky. A storm is brewing. Suddenly the
clouds part and a beam of celestial light shines down on
his face. A voice is saying, "It was Laughter, it was Holy
God." He floats off the ground, still kneeling, and slowly
ascends the beam of light, leaving the others behind in
the field. As he passes through the opening into the
heavens, the clouds close behind him and he disappears
from view. . . .

I awoke feeling shaken and humbled by what I had lived
through that night, and could not go back to sleep. The three monks
entering our field had frightened me because I sensed that their
presence meant Death—yet almost immediately I'd been given a signal that the dream was not about me in any literal way, that I
shouldn't be afraid I was going to die. The arrival of three priests
(a central "Father" figure flanked by two assistants) and the theme
of merging with a "Greater Light" clearly linked the two dreams,
and in the days that followed, I thought of them as a unit. My body
felt shaken and empty from the deep sobbing. I felt that I'd reached

a turning point in my life, heralded by the first dream. The second dream seemed to be a gloss on the first, primarily to insure that I didn't mistake the transformation I was going through for a physical process (my death).

As the days passed, I gradually came down from the intense energy of the dream, and felt a little sad that life was returning to normal. Then, about three weeks later, my sister called long distance to tell me that my father was in the hospital and had been diagnosed as having cancer. I was stunned. I hung up and started crying. I *knew* he was going to die. Later, when I had calmed a little, I realized how I knew: I'd been shown what was going to happen in my dream. The hooded monk who'd gestured to me had been right; my role was to serve as witness.

IV

My father died four months later. His illness brought me closer to my family and intensified the feelings and confusion which had been raised by my dreams. It would take more than a year to live through and resolve those issues and feelings in my waking life, yet everything, from my father's death and my grief to the need to reexamine my life, had been given to me in that one night of dreaming.

During the four months of his illness, crucifixes began appearing in my dreams. In one, I drove Satan away by holding up a cross; in another, I held a crucifix over my brow chakra and golden beams of light shone forth. (I loved that image with its double meaning: I *saw* through the crucifix, which illuminated everything before me, and I "saw through" it, the way one would see through a ruse.)

My earliest relationship to the Numinous had been through Catholicism. Now, in a time of personal crisis, my dreams had seized that channel to forge the connection anew. The important thing was the connection, the reawakening of the spiritual dimension of my life. I no longer needed to *believe* or *deny*. I could simply accept with grace whatever experience was given to me.

V

I continued to dream of my father for many months after he died. In some dreams he was telling me things. In many of them he was leaving or getting ready to leave—to slip away from his hospital room, to move out of our old house, to journey aboard a UFO.

Then, one last dream. It reminded me of another dream I once had in which Time had stopped, and I had to go to the basement of a great library to write the name of each book in golden letters on its spine. As I did my work, the books came alive, until finally Time started moving forward again.

This dream seemed to be the reverse of that earlier one. I felt detached from it, like it was someone else's dream, even though I experienced it as my own. When I woke from it, I immediately thought of my father.

Perhaps it was his dream.

> *Someone gives me a book as a gift. It's a hardcover copy of* Ragtime. *I put some glue on it to bind it, but instead the binding starts to dissolve. The glue had sulphuric acid in it! As I watch, the binding continues to soften, then the words begin to fade away, until finally the whole book is blank. . . .*
>
> *. . . Now the world is dissolving. I'm afraid that death will mean the end of me. Details keep fading away until finally there's nothing left. I'm in a reddish void. But I am. The point of consciousness that is me endures. . . .*

PART 2

·············

Working with Your Dreams

Romeo:	I dream'd a dream to-night.
Mercutio:	And so did I.
Romeo:	Well, what was yours?
Mercutio:	That dreamers often lie. . . .

Mercutio: *That dreamers often lie. . . .*
Through lovers' brains, and then they dream of love;
O'er courtiers' knees, that dream on court'sies straight,
O'er lawyers' fingers, who straight dream on fees,
O'er ladies' lips, who straight on kisses dream,
Which oft the angry Mab with blisters plagues,
Because their breaths with sweetmeats tainted are:
Sometime she gallops o'er a courtier's nose,
And then dreams he of smelling out a suit;
And sometime comes she with a tithe-pig's tail
Tickling a parson's nose as a' lies asleep,
Then dreams, he of another benefice:
Sometime she driveth o'er a soldier's neck,
And then dreams he of cutting foreign throats,
Of breaches, ambuscadoes, Spanish blades,
Of healths five-fathom deep; and then anon
Drums in his ear, at which he starts and wakes,
And being thus frighted swears a prayer or two
And sleeps again. . . .

William Shakespeare
from *Romeo and Juliet*

9

Six Steps for Incubating Dreams

GAYLE DELANEY

WHILE THE spontaneous dreams you have every night will help you to better understand and solve your intellectual, creative, and artistic problems, you also can learn how to elicit dreams on a given night that will help you out with specific problems. Suppose you need a new idea for a creative project, such as a paper you are writing or a picture you are painting. By using a form of "dream incubation" you can target your dreams to help you. If, instead, you want your dreaming mind to work on a problem you are having, such as getting along with a business partner, your spouse, or your child, or if you want to explore a particular problem you have with anger or fear, you can incubate a dream on that. Dream incubation is easily learned. If you carefully follow these instructions, you should be able to dream about the issue you target the first time you incubate a dream.

SIX STEPS FOR INCUBATING DREAMS

Choose the Right Night. Choose a night when you are neither intoxicated nor overtired, and one that will allow you to get a full night's sleep followed by enough time in the morning to record a dream or two. As you gain experience in incubating dreams, you will be able to abbreviate the method; but in the beginning, and whenever incubating dreams on very sensitive issues, you will have the best chance of success if you follow every step. The process will take about ten minutes before sleep and enough time to record your dream upon awakening.

Record Your Day Notes. Before going to sleep, write down the highlights of your day in the dream journal, which should be kept beside your bed. Ask yourself what you did during the day and what you felt. If you felt exhausted after a frustrating day at work, write that down. Note anything that stirred your feelings, even if the day's most moving event was a phone call from your brother. By learning to note the emotional news of the day, you will become more aware of thoughts and emotional reactions that trigger your spontaneous dreams and that may inspire you to incubate a dream. These notes are much more useful in helping you to understand a dream than are those written upon awakening. If you keep your day notes brief, you will be much more likely to keep them faithfully.

Incubation Discussion. Next, write a few lines about the issue you would like to dream about. Describe the problem, your readiness to take a fresh look at it and to alter your position, and what benefits you might have to give up if you resolved it. Stir up your feelings. Don't write much more than a page, or you may turn the process into a chore. Keep your notes brief.

Incubation Phrase. Now write a one-line phrase that clearly states what you would like to understand about your problem, or on what matter you need a new idea. This is the most important step in the process. Be sure to write out your incubation question or request on a separate line in your journal. Choosing your question may be easy, or it might be very difficult. This step will help you to focus your thinking and to clarify your problem and your relation to it, and it will force you to decide upon the next step you are willing to take in its exploration.

A good deal of insight can be gained by struggling to formulate a clear, succinct question, a troublesome issue, and actually writing the question in your journal will insure that you focus thoughtfully and carefully enough. It will also give you the necessary discipline to choose only one issue and to settle on one among many ways of phrasing the question.

Repeat the Phrase as You Fall Asleep. Place your journal beside your bed, turn out the light, and close your eyes. Repeat over and over your incubation phrase as if it were a lullaby or a mantra. Each time your mind wanders, bring it back to your phrase. You will fall asleep quickly, because you are not allowing yourself to ruminate or worry about your problem. As you repeat the phrase, feel the desire to learn something new tonight, to make a shift in your perspective. This is a very comfortable way to fall asleep and is far more productive than counting sheep.

Record Whatever Is on Your Mind When You Awaken. When you awaken, whether in the middle of the night or in the morning, write down whatever is in your mind. Learn to ask yourself, "What was I just thinking?" Frequently, a dream memory will feel like an ordinary thought that you might dismiss if you asked yourself, "What was I just dreaming?" And to the surprise of many, answers to incubation questions sometimes come in the form of ready-made ideas and formulations, or in the form of songs playing through one's mind in the morning.

Most often, however, the answers are embedded in the metaphors of the dream and are easily overlooked by the dreamer until he or she takes the time to explore those metaphors and interpret the dream. If your dream seems to have nothing to do with your question, write it down anyway. Wait a few hours, and then work on understanding the dream without trying to make it answer your question. Remember that whatever your dream is about constitutes an important issue in your life, whether your incubation effort was successful or not. Only after you have understood what your dream is about should you ask yourself whether it sheds new light on the incubation issue. This will discourage you from reading into your dream something that is not there, and it will help you to appreciate whatever dream you did have.

A Lawyer's Incubated Dream

Let's look at an example of a dream incubation. Judith, a lawyer for a major corporation, had grown frustrated with a job that she had once found very exciting. Yet the security and status of her job were very good, and she was unsure whether she could find a better job in the area. Judith did not want to move, and she thought she should be happy with her enviable job. She wondered whether she might have an attitude problem rather than a job problem. Judith incubated a dream with the question, "What should I do about my job?" That night she had the following dream.

> A small group of people from my high school (who are adults in the dream) are meeting for dinner. We wait in the bar for the ones who have yet to arrive. My "pair" is Jim O'Hara, but in the dream, I realize that Jim is really Tom Douglas. Everyone has arrived, and we have trouble finding places for all six of us to fit in, so we put two tables together in the bar.
> Jim/Tom takes charge in a sort of pushy-game-playing way. He dictates where we will all sit at the tables and where we will dine. The group takes on the feeling of a group of college drinking buddies with dates. Jim/Tom calls all fraternity brothers to go dine where there is lots of food and booze. I decide to leave. I feel self-confident. This is not where I belong. I have better things to do.

Asked to describe the personalities of Jim and Tom, Judith said that she had seen neither of them since high school, but that Jim was a sweet, nice guy, while Tom was the smooth, glib, good-looking leader of the pack. Asked if there was anyone in her current life who seemed sweet and nice, but who was in fact smooth, glib, and a leader of the pack, she said that her direct counterpart in another department at work, a lawyer named Samuel, was very much like a combination of Jim and Tom. Then Judith noted that just as in high school, a good deal of her discomfort with the job came from her difficulty feeling as though she fit in with the group. She said that her work group was more like a high-school clique or fraternity gang than she had recognized. Judith felt that her dream decision to leave the fraternity scene was a healthy one, and that whether or not she decided to leave her job, she should give up trying to fit in and be fully accepted by a group that simply does not suit her. Her growing self-confidence was liberating her from an exaggerated need to be accepted.

Like most dreams, incubated or spontaneous, this dream, once understood, opened the dreamer's eyes to a dynamic she had failed to adequately appreciate. Also, it did not "tell the dreamer what to do," but showed her what she *was* doing to help her make a more informed decision.

10

Fourteen Ways to Interpret a Single Dream

KELLY BULKELEY

I'm in Bosnia, in a house, on the second floor. A soldier below is firing a machine gun up through the floor, and I see bullets ripping up through the carpet all around me. I think I'm supposed to be some kind of peacekeeper; but I'm not very effective, I feel. I suddenly see lots of kids in the hallway, and I realize they're in real danger. So I slowly move them to a room that seems safe—but it's not. "Let's go upstairs," I say, and try to lead them up. But they don't follow me, and I end up only bringing their toys as I go up myself. Up above there is a big, grand living room, with beautiful old tapestries on the wall. A group of adults are sitting in plush chairs. They're in denial about the war, I think to myself. I say or do something that reminds them, though, and they get mad. Through a window I see the facades of a nearby building starting to crumble and fall down.

Kelly Bulkeley, June 24, 1995

ONE GOOD way of evaluating the many different psychological theories about dreams and dreaming is to apply each of them in turn to a dream of one's own. Such an exercise brings forth the distinctive features of each theory and allows for critical reflection on their relative strengths and weaknesses. As this book has shown, the modern psychology of dreaming has grown in large part out of people's careful, disciplined examination of their own dreams. Beginning with the pioneering self-analyses of Freud and Jung, psychologists have regularly drawn on their own dreams as one important resource in pursuing their research. This does, it must be admitted, give dream psychology the appearance of being subjective and unscientific. But the unavoidable empirical fact is that our most direct means of access to the images, sensations, and emotions found in dreams is through our own dreams. Although debate about proper research methodology continues, most dream psychologists agree that if self-analysis is combined with solid findings from other research methods, there is nothing dangerous or unscientific about examining one's own dreams. Indeed, the history of modern dream psychology has demonstrated that many of the most creative new breakthroughs have come from researchers who have taken innovative approaches to their personal dream experiences.

PSYCHOLOGICAL ANALYSES OF A SAMPLE DREAM

Background

I had the above dream in June of 1995 while staying at a hotel in New York City. Although I enjoy the cultural vitality of New York, I have always disliked its noisy, manic urban atmosphere. I was there for the annual conference of the Association for the Study of Dreams, a group in which I was playing several administrative roles, and I was very busy with the conference all week long. Two or three times during the week, while making brief visits back to my hotel room, I saw a television news report on an especially vicious bombing in the war-torn land of Bosnia. The report showed a man carrying away the bloodied body of a little girl who had been killed in the bombing. In part because I have a two-year old daughter of my own, the horrible television image made me want to cry each time I saw it.

The dream came the last day of the conference, on Saturday night (actually, right before I woke up Sunday morning). Saturday afternoon I had presided over a long, contentious meeting of the association's board of directors. One particular issue had caused deep conflict within the group, and I felt I hadn't done a very good job of resolving it. Immediately after the board meeting a psychotherapist colleague and I went out to dinner with two literary agents to discuss our proposal for a parenting-genre book on children's dreams. The agents were very encouraging and agreed with us that a book describing how dreams can help nurture the growth and creativity of children would appeal to the parenting book market. Although I was excited by the project, I secretly worried that writing a commercial book might create conflicts with the scholarly standards and ideals that had guided my other writings.

The next day I was leaving New York to meet my wife and two children in Chicago. We were going to visit and stay with relatives who live in a large, well-furnished, multistoried house. Before going to sleep I told the friend with whom I was sharing my hotel room how nervous and apprehensive I always feel before such family gatherings.

Freud

A Freudian approach to the dream would begin with these memories and associations and would use them as clues to finding the repressed unconscious wishes motivating the dream. Although an exhaustive analysis of these associations is impractical here (Freud's line-by-line examination of his "Dream of Irma's Injection" runs fourteen pages), the following dream elements seem most striking. The image of the machine gun firing upward can be seen as a classic phallic symbol, an emblem of violent masculine desire and rage. The image of the children is a condensation of many different elements: my own children, the dead child from Bosnia, the children

I will be discussing in my parenting book, my own experiences in childhood, and the child-like impulses still within me now. All of my action in the manifest dream is motivated by a deep fear that the Bosnian children are in danger. A Freudian reading might see my busy dream actions as a deceptive mask struggling to hide its unconscious opposite, a fear that *adults* are in danger—the ultimate unconscious wish behind the dream might in fact be an oedipal desire to kill my father. Such a terrible wish is too shocking to be accepted by my conscious ego, which is committed to the moral ideal of honoring and respecting my parents. So the censor has transformed that dark, repressed wish into the (superficially) less disturbing manifest imagery: casting the drama in a faraway land, where adults are all just fine and where the children are the ones in danger. But the end of the dream indicates that the struggle between the unconscious wishes and conscious ideals is threatening to break out into the open, as the nearby building's facade (the exact image Freud used to describe how the manifest dream hides the latent wishes) is starting to crumble and fall down.

Jung

From a Jungian perspective, the first step would be to amplify the dream's elements and images, seeking evidence of unconscious compensations for the imbalances of my conscious attitudes. The architectural imagery in the dream could, somewhat like Jung's house dream, be seen as a symbolic map of my intrapsychic condition. The soldier on the ground floor is a shadow figure, a deeply unconscious, unintegrated part of my psyche which my conscious ego sees as violent, destructive, and dangerous. The adults on the top floor are persona figures, comfortable in their elevated position of wealth and social status, refusing to pay any attention to the brutal warfare below. And the children trapped on the middle floor symbolize the youthful potentials and creative energies within me, the future growth of which is threatened by this terrible split between the "upper" and "lower" parts of my psyche. This dream would, in a Jungian view, be revealing to me that the exciting experiences in New York City, at the conference, and with the literary agents had combined to create an unhealthy imbalance in my psyche. Such an imbalance is endangering my ability to care for children both "inside" me (my inner potentials) and "outside" me (my own two children, the children who will be the subject of my book, the children of Bosnia). The dream tries to compensate for this excessive waking-life concern with my persona by bringing up archetypal symbols and vivid emotions from the unconscious.

Adler

An Adlerian approach would take this dream as a reflection of efforts to defend my sense of superiority and self-worth. Looking at the associations to the dream, it appears that the very difficult board meeting held the afternoon preceding the dream had deeply shaken my sense of superiority. I had tried, and failed, to resolve a bitter conflict among the board members, and I was feeling depressed and helpless about the situation. The dream, in this view, would have been formed in response to that waking-life difficulty, which my customary style of life had been unable to manage. The dream transformed my real problem (the board meeting conflict) into a fantasy problem (the Bosnian war) and thereby allowed me to use one of my customary strategies for defending against threats to my sense of superiority—the strategy of detaching myself, "rising above it all," as I do in the dream when I leave the children behind and go upstairs to the grand living room. I could not use this strategy with my waking life problem, but my dream alters the problem so that now the strategy *will* work. In Adlerian terms, the dream serves its function of preserving my sense of superiority and self-esteem, albeit without giving me any real help with the waking life problem.

Boss

From Boss's existentialist perspective dreams disclose aspects of our being-in-the-world, showing both unhealthy constrictions in our present life and wonderful potentials for our future. In this dream, the sensation of being trapped is very powerful. By focusing on the dream phenomenon itself, as Boss counsels, I see that the emotions of fear, vulnerability, and helplessness predominate. The dream indicates that this trapped mode of being-in-the-world is evident in many areas of my life (being in New York City, dealing with the board meeting conflict, writing the commercial book, going to visit my Chicago family). Boss would say that the dream is a real, genuine experience of being trapped—not a mere symbol or image, but an actual experience of that mode of being-in-the-world. However, the dream also reveals some real potentials for free choice and action. When I go upstairs and find the adults sitting in their plush chairs, I "say or do something" that reminds them of the war below; at that moment the facades start falling. This suggests that through consciousness and honest self-reflection I can break through the denial of my trapped condition, and thereby open up new potentials for the future.

French and Fromm

The Ego Psychological approach of French and Fromm looks at every dream as an attempt by the ego to solve a pressing concern in waking life, what they term the focal conflict. In this dream the focal conflict could be seen as the worries I have over writing the book on children's dreams. I'm afraid of the harm my ideals could suffer from the violent, war-like competition of commercial publishing (the soldier below), and yet I'm also afraid of the insulated, self-satisfied nature of academic writing (the adults above). My ego is caught in the middle, trying yet failing to be a peacekeeper and protect the core concern of the book, that is, the concern to help children learn from their dreams. The dream draws on many different elements from my life (the television news report, the upcoming family visit, the board meeting) in an attempt to master this focal conflict. French and Fromm would sift through my activities in the dream and distinguish the ineffective efforts to master the focal conflict (e.g., trying to hide the children somewhere on the second floor) from more effective efforts (e.g., making the adults on the third floor acknowledge the war below).

Perls

For Perls, dreams reveal holes in the Gestalt of our personalities and confront us with alienated, disowned parts of ourselves. In this dream, the soldier downstairs firing the machine gun upward appears to be the most alienated of all the characters. By experientially identifying with him, as Perls recommends, I hear the soldier say this: "I'm angry, I've been neglected and forgotten and now I'm going to make sure people pay attention to me. I know people are up there above me, and while they pretend I'm not here I'll shoot my gun until they hear me." The adults in the living room say this: "We're older, we need to rest. We've worked hard all our lives, and we've earned the right to enjoy some peace and comfort. We've built and preserved this society, and we won't tolerate rowdies who simply want to tear it all down." This is a classic example of what Perls calls a topdog versus underdog conflict. To follow this method, I would continue this dialogue between the soldier and the adults, bring in the other elements from the dream (e.g., the children, the house, the toys, the building facades), and work to understand them all as parts of myself, parts that need to be recognized, appreciated, and integrated.

Aserinsky, Kleitman, Dement

Although I did not have this dream while attached to an EEG monitor in a sleep laboratory, it was almost certainly a dream experienced during REM sleep. The dream is fairly long, with lots of visual imagery, physical activity, and emotional involvement. As I woke up early Sunday morning with this dream fresh and vivid in my mind, it seems likely that it came during the long REM period that for most humans occurs at the end of each night's sleep cycle.

Hobson

For Hobson, dreaming is activated by the random, chaotic neural activities of REM sleep. Higher mental functions then struggle to synthesize these bizarre inputs into a partly-coherent sequence of images and events. My dream certainly begins with an image of chaos and confusion, in the form of the soldier firing a machine gun upward (in his book *The Dreaming Brain* Hobson uses this very metaphor of random gunfire to describe the REM sleep neural activation that initiates the formation of a dream). The dream can then be seen as struggling to make some kind of sense out of these initially chaotic perceptions and feelings. I envision myself as being in a war, as needing to protect children; I try different strategies to get out of danger and restore peace. The dream becomes progressively calmer and more orderly as I go upstairs into the world of rational adult society, indicating that my higher mental functions are slowly gaining control over the mental chaos or "warfare" generated by REM sleep. For Hobson there is no coded message here, no deep unconscious wisdom. The dream has simply responded to the random neural inputs of REM sleep by creating a semi-logical narrative that revolves around my ordinary waking concerns with caring for children.

Crick and Mitchison

The reverse-learning theory of Crick and Mitchison holds that REM sleep works to remove negative, parasitic modes of behavior from the brain. Following their view I should just forget my dream, because trying to remember and interpret it might preserve unhealthy patterns of thought that it is the function of REM sleep to eliminate.

Hall

Hall's quantitative approach would begin by analyzing this dream into its basic structural elements (setting, characters, interactions, objects, and emotions). Briefly, a content analysis of this dream would categorize the setting as indoors, of questionable familiarity (I'm familiar with Bosnia, but not with this particular house). The characters, all unknown to me, include one adult male, a group of children of both sexes, and a group of adults of both sexes. The interactions include two aggressive ones (the soldier firing the machine gun, the adults getting mad at me) and two friendly ones (me trying to move the children out of danger, me trying to remind the adults of what's going on below). The objects include the house, the machine gun, the bullets, the carpet, the toys, the tapestries, and the building facade. And the two instances of emotion in the dream are the apprehension I feel about the children being in danger and the anger the adults feel toward me. After scoring the dream in this way, it could then be compared both to a longer series of my dreams and to data on the dreams of other people. This would enable me to determine how often in my dreams I feel apprehension, how frequently I succeed or fail in protecting children, how many known versus unknown characters appear in my dreams, and so forth. From Hall's perspective, the events, emotions, and activities in this dream are likely to be continuous with basic features of my waking life. For example, the multistoried house may be directly connected to the home of my Chicago relatives; the war in Bosnia could thus be seen as a simple mental shorthand for the emotional conflict I feel when I visit there.

Foulkes

For Foulkes, dreams carry no specific message or intent to communicate. However, he says dreams are shaped by the same logical processes of order, coherence, and association that govern all thought. In my dream, evidence of such processes can be seen in my realistic response to the danger posed by the soldier, in my verbal interactions with the children, and in the plausible, well-structured quality of the scene in the upstairs living room. These instances of rational thought demonstrate that no matter how bizarre dreams initially appear, on closer analysis it can be shown that they are shaped by the ordinary cognitive processes that experimental psychologists have found operating in both waking and sleeping mentation.

Hunt

There is a multiplicity of dream types, according to Hunt, and each different type is formed by a different combination of cognitive processes. Although my dream does not fit easily into any of Hunt's categories (it comes closest to his definition of a nightmare), it does reflect the influence of both sophisticated grammatical structures and creative visual-spatial imagery. The grammatical structures can be seen in the overall narrative coherence of the dream, with the action moving progressively from the lower to the upper stories of the house. The creative visual-spatial imagery emerges with the suddenly appearing sight of the nearby building's facade crumbling to pieces. Hunt would likely view this last image not as another bit of

REM-generated nonsense with no meaningful connection to the preceding dream action, but as a visual-spatial image that enriches and completes the developing narrative thrust of the dream: as I reach the top floor of this house and find it to be filled with an air of luxurious, self-satisfied denial, I look outside and see the facade of another building falling down.

Hartmann

I have had frequent nightmares for most of my life, usually one or two a month but sometimes as often as two or three a week. Hartmann's theory that people with frequent nightmares have thin psychological boundaries applies to my personality in a number of ways (e.g., in terms of my interpersonal relations, my gender identity, my interest in fantasy). Looking at the nightmarish qualities of this particular dream, it appears that many of the actions and emotions revolve around threats to boundaries. The bullets ripping up through the floor violently attack a boundary, the denial of the adults anxiously tries to preserve a boundary, and the crumbling facade on the nearby building show the collapse of a boundary.

Faraday, Garfield, Delaney, Ullman, Taylor, LaBerge

Popular psychologists offer a variety of practical techniques for exploring a dream's meanings. To start with, they recommend carefully studying each image in the dream. For example, using Delaney's "pretend I'm from another planet" method, I would describe toys as objects which can be played with, which are fun and make you laugh; children can make a toy out of pretty much anything. That description makes me reflect anew on the opulent yet lifeless scene upstairs in the living room. Without children to play with them, toys are mere objects; without vitality and openness (which children have in abundance), all the lovely tapestries and plush furnishings of this living room are but decorations for a tomb. Popular psychologists would also recommend trying to incubate a future dream to gain further insights into this one (e.g., by going to sleep with the question, "How can I make true peace between the soldier on the ground floor and the adults on the upper floor?"); and in future dreams they would suggest I try to become lucid, so I could confront antagonists like the soldier and find out who he is and what he wants. Finally, popular psychologists would encourage me to share this dream with other people and seek their comments and reflections. Using Taylor's "if it were my dream" method, I would ask different people what such a dream would mean to them if they had experienced it.

Such an exercise in comparative dream analysis cannot, of course, do full justice to any of the individual theories. A thorough Jungian dream interpretation, for example, would require a far more detailed probing of the dreamer's personal life and a much broader amplification of the dream's archetypal symbolism than I have provided. Likewise, an adequate Hall and Van de Castle-style content analysis would demand the careful scoring of a long series of my dreams. But the primary goal of the above exercise has been more modest than that, namely to give readers a clear and concrete illustration of how different psychological theories presented in this book would go about explaining and interpreting a sample dream.

Major Areas of Debate

A second goal of this comparative dream analysis is to highlight the major areas of debate among psychological theories of dreaming. Despite (or perhaps because of) almost one hundred years of concentrated study, modern psychologists disagree on many fundamental points about the formation, function, and interpretation of dreams.

Formation

There are at least three major debates regarding the formation of dreams. First, what is the nature of the unconscious forces that work to form our dreams? Are these forces dark and destructive (Freud), or are they positive, creative, and even spiritual in nature (Jung)? Second, can dream formation be explained without using the imprecise notion of "the unconscious"? Many psychologists (Adler, Boss, Piaget, Hall) argue that a better explanation of dream formation refers to those same basic structures of personality and cognition that operate in our waking lives. Third, what is the role of REM sleep physiology in the formation of dreams? Some psychologists (Hobson, Crick and Mitchison) assert that the neural activities of REM sleep dominate the process of dream formation, while other psychologists (Foulkes, Hartmann, Hunt, LaBerge) see a complex interaction of REM physiology and cognitive-emotional forces at work in the formation of dreams.

Function

There are three basic positions on the question of what function dreams serve. The first position (Freud, Adler) is that dreams function to deceive consciousness, masking unpleasant truths and thereby preserving our customary psychological defenses. The second position (Jung, Boss, French and Fromm, Perls, Hartmann, Hunt, all popular psychologists) is that dreams serve a variety of highly positive functions: giving deep insights into neglected thoughts and emotions, helping solve important problems in daily life, stimulating creativity and imagination, and promoting the overall integration of personality. The third position (Hobson, Crick and Mitchison, Foulkes) is that dreams have little or no psychological function beyond a modest value in diagnosing psychological disturbances. In this latter view the real functions are served not by dreaming but by REM sleep, in its role of providing routine maintenance of basic neurological circuitry in the brain.

Interpretation

Those who see no psychological function to dreams naturally have little interest in trying to interpret dreams. Those who do believe that dreams serve some psychological function approach the process of interpretation from a number of different directions. (1) Most psychologists (following Freud) insist that any dream interpretation must begin with the personal associations of the dreamer. Some (Jung) also seek amplification to the dream's images and symbols. However, others (Boss) reject associations and amplifications and say that interpretation should focus exclusively on the dreamer's experience itself. Still others (Hall) argue that even the dreamer is unnecessary, because nothing more than a series of written dream reports is required to make valid interpretations. (2) Many psychologists (Freud, Jung, Adler, Boss, French and Fromm) regard the aid of a trained psychotherapist as a valuable or even essential part of dream interpretation. Other psychologists (Hall, Faraday, Garfield, Delaney) disagree, saying that with a little practice any person can learn to interpret his or her own dreams. And for some (Perls, Ullman, Taylor), the ideal setting for dream interpretation is neither one-to-one psychotherapy nor private reflection and journal writing, but a dream sharing group. (3) Some psychologists (Freud, Hall) argue that dream interpretation can be precise, objective, and scientific in its results. Most other psychologists, however, believe that dream interpretation is more of an intuitive art in which many complex, multivalent meanings emerge out of each dream.

11

Twenty-Three Steps for Working with Your Dreams

GEORGE R. SLATER

AS WE ATTEMPT to analyze a dream we must recognize that the dream is a living thing and cannot be made into an object for study. Its meaning comes out in relationship to the dreamer's consciousness and grows as it is integrated into the dreamer's life. The dream is part of the dreamer's psychic process, like a snapshot of a river flowing, and needs to be put in that framework of a constantly evolving life. It is located in a moment in that life-flow and gains its significance in relation to the surrounding flow. That includes the events of daily life which surround it and with which it may be in dialogue.

But the meaning of the dream also involves the interpretation process itself. The dream, once landed in consciousness, has its second life, as it were, in the development that takes place through the various connections that are made to the dreamer's inner and outer worlds. It matters, therefore, when the dream is processed and in what circumstances. The intuition or perception of the moment in which it is received and studied are part of its meaning. The dream lives again and grows further in such moments of conscious participation.

In providing the format of dream analysis which follows, I want to respect this dynamic sense of the dream. Any attempt to hold it down into these categories of analysis is like a stop-action of a waterfall and will be artificial. These categories should be viewed only as a means by which the dream may grasp the dreamer. The dream must be lived.

Normally, there are four parts to doing dream analysis: the Content, the Context, the Associations, and Amplification.

The *content* includes everything that is actually given in the dream itself, the setting, all the images, any story or narrative, the basic theme, action and outcome, and the feelings involved.

The *context* comprises whatever emotional events preceded and followed the dreaming of the dream, including events and issues of the preceding day, together with the dreamer's feelings on waking.

Associations refer to any or all memories, thoughts or feelings which come in response to any individual part of the dream or to the dream as a whole.

Amplification is the process of allowing or assisting the meaning of various images or symbols to develop more fully. Dreams tend to disguise meanings by compressing them into symbols which are ambiguous. A major part of dream interpretation involves drawing out such meanings until they are full-bodied and recognizable. Only then can a dreamer sift out the meanings which best apply.

The Content

1. The Setting

Often the first words of a dream give its reference meaning: "I was wandering in the fog at night . . ." or "I was climbing a steep cliff and holding on for dear life when. . . ." suggest right away what kind of circumstance the dream may be addressing in the dreamer's life. The "fog" or the "cliff" may be metaphors for lostness or danger.

The setting may be a place that indicates in a general way what the dream is about: "We were in a mall or huge complex . . ." (which I often find may be a symbol of one's actual complex or psychological wound). It may be a place that has a special function: "I was in a school classroom . . ." or "I was in a hospital operating room . . ." which may identify that function or task as significant. Or it may be a place that is familiar to the dreamer and has certain personal meanings: "We were gathered in grandma's bedroom." (Perhaps a childhood memory being addressed.) Some settings, such as buildings, factories and machinery, because they are man-made, may indicate a memory or complex that formed under some human conflict, while natural settings may express what is "given" genetically or is being worked through with relative freedom now. Whether the setting is a house (suggesting perhaps something about the dreamer's own life or body) or is an institutional public building (indicating perhaps a collective rather than individual reference) may also be significant.

Although the setting may be associated with some experience of the previous day, it may also refer back to some earlier, childhood place. If, for example, the setting is a house familiar to one's childhood, the question is twofold: what happened in that house that the dream may be addressing, and what happened yesterday that brought that memory back? The nature of symbols is to constantly bridge between similar experiences across one's life.

2. The Images

What are the actual animals, objects, persons, or scenes? What designs, shapes or forms are depicted? Note any special colors or lack of color. All of these constitute the symbols of a dream, which can have both personal and collective meaning.

The images of a dream represent the way energy is taking form within the psyche. One can feel the difference between energy that is symbolized in the images of persons or animals, and that which is in inanimate forms, such as trees or rivers or mountains, and that which forms into stone or man-made images such as concrete buildings or a machine such as a bulldozer. The contrast here between a building and a bulldozer raises a matter that will come up again, namely the activity or power (or lack of) embodied in an object or image.

3. The Main Theme

However involved a dream may be, there is usually a common thread that runs through it. Try to express the main idea or purpose of the dream in a simple, one-sentence synopsis. Although, in the case of some dreams, it may seem almost too simple to state the theme, the significance of it may not become apparent until it is stated.

A woman once came to our first session with a dream which she had dreamed the previous night which had four distinct parts. At that time, it was very difficult to see any connection between them and if pressed to state a main theme all she might have said was that she had had a dream in which four different vignettes or views were presented. However, in the three years we then worked together in her analysis, it became clear that that original dream was laying out the four basic issues that she had to deal with in her analysis. Then the theme could be stated as "these four cameos show the struggles of my life."

Where the content of a dream does not involve a story or action sequence, the theme may be to portray a scene, a relationship, an image or a feeling.

4. The Action or Effect

Where there are events taking place as in a story sequence, observe the effect or outcome of the action. Is there a movement, a resolution, in the dream? What is accomplished in the dream? Attention to the action or movement taking place within a dream will often reveal where the energy is flowing (or blocked). Energy flow may also be evident when persons or materials are transformed in a dream. For example, when one person is replaced by another during a dream or when a substance changes state, as in a fire, explosion or chemical reaction, it may indicate a shift of energy or attitude within the psyche of the dreamer. The death of a person in a dream is a clear indication of energy going out of that symbol. One needs to ask where the energy or value that resided in that person has gone. Frequently another form will be assumed by something new appearing as a transformation of that energy, for example, a baby might be born or a new relationship begun in a dream. Babies often symbolize new beginnings.

5. The Feeling Tone

A key to understanding our dreams lies in noting the feeling tone in the dream; that is, while you were dreaming the dream what were your emotions? This will normally be the feelings of the dreamer. The feelings of the other characters in the dream are important, too, and may be noted as expressions of attitudes that might be quite different than those held consciously by the dreamer. The dreamer's own feelings are helpful, both in relation to the feelings of others in the dream and in contrast to the dreamer's waking feelings.

Although I have spoken of feelings here in terms of emotion, the more important factor is to identify the feelings in the dream in terms of the worth that is attached to certain persons or objects. What are the feelings of value present in the dream?

THE CONTEXT

6. The Feeling on Waking

Often the contrast between the conscious and unconscious minds will be felt as the dreamer emerges from a dream into consciousness. It may be a sense of great relief, if the dream has been frightening, to discover it was only a dream. Whether comforting or not, the felt difference between the attitude in the dream and the conscious attitude is of great importance. It makes a person aware of the range of his own attitudes and may indicate that an attitude different from the conscious attitude is emerging into consciousness and there may be a need to integrate the two by a shift in consciousness. Insofar as the felt difference between the feeling on waking and the feeling in the dream represents the challenge to accept new contents into consciousness, holding it in consciousness may be met with resistance and the dream might be forgotten as a way of avoiding the challenge of facing the feeling difference.

7. Previous Day's Events

Freud believed that dreams responded to the previous day's events. Jung, while not so narrowly focused, regarded dreams as the dialogue which the unconscious carries on with the conscious mind, usually in the light of recent events. He viewed the human mind as a self-regulating mechanism in which the unconscious seeks to bring balance, healing and wholeness to the consciousness.

The context of a dream, then, would take in the whole emotional, relational life of the person prior to the dream and would be just as important to understanding the significance of a dream as a witness' testimony is at a trial. The events of the previous day or so, especially those that had a priority impact on the dreamer, could be relevant.

8. Emotional Landscape

Any particular problems, stresses or emotionally charged thoughts of the dreamer similarly would be important to consider. Had the dreamer been seeking a solution to a problem or specific need? What had been the most important relational focus just prior to the dream?

Equally, the emotional landscape includes emotionally charged issues either before or after the actual dream. Dreams may be in response to, or in anticipation of, such issues that claim one's emotional attention. All of this addresses the context to which the dream might be speaking. Establishing the connection of the dream to the surrounding conscious experience of the person is of major importance in interpreting a dream.

ASSOCIATIONS

Associations are anything that comes to mind in connection with a dream or its parts. However foolish or irrelevant they may seem to our conscious mind, they have their own way of relating to a dream.

Therefore, it is important to note any associations you have to anything in your dream, however unreasonable or absurd they may seem. So-called stray thoughts or images often make a very definite connection once we let them flow.

9. **What associations do you have to any of the images in the dream?**

10. **What in your life is similar to elements in the dream?**

11. **What memories does the dream bring back?**

12. **What similarities does this dream have to other dreams you've had? To religious or secular stories, legends or fairytales?**

AMPLIFICATION

In the process of making the dream material more fully conscious, it is necessary to expand the message which has been compressed in the dream symbols. Meaning that is held in the unconscious is communicated through dreams in the form of symbols which partially hide its true meaning from consciousness. Disguised in this way, in the form of symbols, the messages are partial, ambiguous and fragmented. In order to be understood and received into consciousness, the meaning needs to be drawn out or amplified. The following are some methods of amplification.

13. Balance

The unconscious may be seeking to compensate the conscious attitude or situation according to a principle of balance. How is the dream different from my waking attitude or values? Here it is helpful to compare the feeling or attitude in the dream (#5) with the feeling on waking (#6). Reentering consciousness after a dream often brings the awareness of how different the two worlds are.

The contrast may be instructive in a variety of ways: the unconscious position as expressed in dream symbols and experienced by the dreamer as a particular attitude or feeling may be offering a potential way of growth, or suggesting a helpful adjustment, if adopted into one's conscious life. Take, for example, the born-again Christian who lived a moral life and was shocked to wake up from dreams in which murders and violence were an accepted commonplace. When these violent crimes, usually against men, became the theme of recurrent dreams, she began to ask what that very different attitude in her unconscious might mean. Studying the contrast led her to realize how completely she had repressed her anger about her former husband and how she had to acknowledge that anger consciously before she could go forward with her life. As she began to claim those angry feelings, she became aware that the difficulty went beyond her relationship with her former husband. She saw that in her relationships, in general, she had been self-effacing and timid about confronting others with her true feelings. The dreams were leading her to balance her former inhibited way of relating with a more forthright self-expression.

The unconscious often functions in dreams to show us the dark side of ourselves, that part of our personality that is opposite to our usual conscious position. In this way, it seeks to add to, enrich or adjust our conscious attitude. A good question, to ask, therefore, in analyzing a dream is: What does this dream correct or add to my usual way of living or thinking?

14. Active Imagination

In waking life, go back into the dream and dialogue with any of the persons in the dream with whom you feel comfortable. It is quite possible to enter into a discussion with these dream figures and to become familiar with them. Ask them whatever you wish and be prepared to have them ask you, too. Learn to wait and listen.

Caution: It may be unwise to open yourself in this way to evil or dangerous characters. Let your feelings be the guide. Don't force yourself to face figures that terrify you.

Active imagination is a potent exercise. To avoid slipping too deeply into the unconscious, it is important that you not do active imagination when you are alone. Arrange to have a friend present who can remind you of the real world to which you belong.

15. Gestalt

This refers to the ability to see things in different perspectives and thus have a sense of the whole. The dreamer, or "dream-ego," normally stands for that part of the unconscious that is most closely like the conscious personality. However, other parts of the unconscious personality may be present in the dream in other symbols. All characters, animals and objects in a dream may express different aspects of the dreamer. Allow yourself to be any of the objects in the dream and feel into those various identities. What is their point of view? How am I like the persons, animals or object in the dream?

Making a mask which represents a character in one's dream can be an effective way of getting in touch with the meaning embodied in that dream character. There is a great value in the process of creating the mask itself; in conceiving it, shaping and forming it. Even if it is only a paper bag with eyes, mouth and nose cut out and colored with crayons or markers, it is a work of intuition and imagination, which connects with the unconscious from which the dream flowed. Usually insights and feelings begin to flow as one works on the mask itself. More elaborate creations can involve papier-mâché or plaster of paris materials. Then in the putting on and wearing of the mask the dreamer steps into the role more completely and may experience the energy and inner reality of that dream character. After working through the feelings evoked by the mask, a dreamer may want to keep the mask and display it as a reminder of that meaning and the reality it has as a part of the dreamer's life.

Acting out one's dream in a group format as a kind of psychodrama can be a particularly powerful form of gestalt. It requires, however, having a willing group of participants or friends who will allow your meanings to emerge and not impose their own.

16. Draw or sculpt the dream images

Drawing, painting or sculpting images or whole scenes from a dream can be a helpful exercise. In this way, images become more concrete and may expand in their richness; and relationships between participants and objects in the dream may become more clear. Forget artistic values for the moment and focus instead on giving a reflective, even meditative, expression to the images, shapes and characters in the dream. As the images take shape, they may come alive with their own meaning and begin to reveal connections which had been hidden. In this way, a dream may continue to unfold its meaning.

17. Confront your monster

Dreams such as nightmares, where monsters or terror presents itself, may be offering the opportunity of coming to terms with some deep fear. Facing that terror in active imagination may help it to transform. Giving the monster a friendly name, asking what its purpose is in your life, or telling it that you want to be friends, may serve to integrate it and free that energy for more constructive purposes. This is the practice of the Dream People of Malaysia who teach their children to do precisely these things in confronting dream monsters, believing that the monster symbolizes a part of reality which they need to befriend and win over.

In view of the caution noted above (#14), a good test is to ask yourself if you are willing to risk confrontation in each particular case and get your gut reaction. It may make a difference if you confront that dream personage when you are in the safety of a therapy relationship or with a trusted friend.

18. What question might this dream be answering?

Since a dream may be understood as a response to one's conscious life, daily experience is often the setting to which a dream speaks. A dream may sometimes be seen as an answer to a conscious question or problem, or a comment on one's situation in life, or a form of questioning or warning about some conscious decision or action. One way of trying to assist the process of dreaming is to ask a question before falling asleep at night. Whether that is put explicitly or not, a person's life may frequently be seen as expressing a question or need. A dream may be a visible answer to such questions.

19. Intervention

When working with dreams of danger, perplexity or abandonment, invite a religious figure such as Jesus or a trusted friend to come into your dream. Using active imagination, see that figure in your dream and watch what he or she does with the situation.

A woman, who had suffered sexual and verbal abuse from two husbands and other trusted men and was subject to severe depression, told me her dream of a huge scorpion that came after her. Instead of stinging her, it exploded all over her face and neck. Telling the dream, she was almost sick with her terror of scorpions. Because she had already indicated her Christian faith to me, I suggested that she ask Jesus to come into the scene and for her to simply observe what he did. Almost at once, she saw him come into the dream scene of the scorpion which had just exploded over her. She saw him turn and come to her, gently wipe the scorpion pieces from her face and then take her by the hand. There was a noticeable calming following that encounter and, as she opened her eyes again, she felt strengthened within herself.

20. Completion

How does the dream end? Some dreams are incomplete and need an ending, others end in ways that are terrifying or troubling. What resolution or completion would you like to see to the dream? What completion can you believe is possible or likely? As in active imagination, go back into the dream, in a waking state, and imagine the ending you would like or the one that seems to fit at that time.

A man who was facing financial cutbacks, and who usually dealt with life by denying his feelings and thinking his way through, had a dream in which he was carrying a young boy on his shoulders just as a sixty-foot dinosaur turned toward him. As he looked in terror, he saw that the dinosaur was not real. It was like the toy model his son played with that was made of strips of interlocking wood. But it was sixty feet long and as he looked its neck moved and its great head swooped down toward them. In sheer terror he ran with the boy on his shoulders to find some place to hide from the monster that was pursuing them. Somehow he knew that the monster could not attack if someone saw him. He took refuge in a betting shop where a friendly man behind the counter welcomed him. The man knew all about the dinosaur but wasn't the least bit afraid. The dreamer asked why the man wasn't afraid and he said, "There's nothing to be afraid of. He's inside you." The dreamer went over to the window of the shop and looked out to see where the dinosaur was, as the dream ended.

Later, in working on the dream, the man realized that the dinosaur represented his fears of financial woe. He also recognized that the betting shop indicated the need to take some calculated risks in facing his fears. He set about making a plan of action in dealing with his financial situation and a list of alternative outcomes, if the worst happened. Then, in active imagination, he reentered the dream scene to talk with the betting shop man. What could he do to overcome the dinosaur? "Just face him." Still carrying the boy on his shoulders the man stepped out of the door, looked squarely at the dinosaur who still stood there, and in a loud voice he shouted, "Go away!" To his astonishment a shudder when through the dinosaur. It began to tremble and shake and then collapsed on the ground like a pile of matchsticks.

21. Archetypal identity

Many of the symbols in dreams give expression to our complexes, those unique bundles of experience marking our fears, conflicts, dependencies, and distorted views of reality. Each complex corresponds to and is rooted in an underlying healing image, called an archetype. . . . The personal mother complex, for example, is rooted in the Great Mother archetype, the ego is rooted in the Self archetype. The collective unconscious has the ability to produce symbols from its depths which are able to reconcile and transcend the distortions and conflicts of the complexes. This ability is called the "transcendent function" whereby complexes and conflicts are not denied but outgrown and integrated into a larger whole.

In doing dream work, it is essential that archetypal symbols be recognized and responded to consciously. They usually manifest with power, clarity and wholeness; there may be a sense of breakthrough, the resolution of conflict or emergence into freedom. Paramount among archetypes is the Self which may be expressed in symbols of wholeness, such as mandala (magical circle) forms, a wonder child, or divine figure. Note any archetypal symbols or feelings that accompany archetypal expression and observe the effect on the symbols which express your complexes.

22. New Knowledge

Those who work regularly with dreams know that there is a purpose to our dreaming. Something is being revealed that we need to bring into consciousness. We can assume that every dream contains some new message that we have not previously heard or acted upon. What does it tell me about myself or others that I did not know before? What does this dream add to my understanding?

23. Conscious Response

The focus of the foregoing analysis is to form a conscious response to the dream. On the basis of all that has been gleaned from each of the various categories covered, what action, question or decision do you make in response to the dream? If dreams truly offer to add to our knowledge, then it is important that we carry that knowledge forward to some beneficial result. Make a decision, do something, in response to the dream. Not to act on a dream that has given a clear message is to discourage further dialogue.

You may need time to digest the import of a dream. Sometimes it helps to distance from it for a day or two. Then, on returning, it may be seen with more objectivity and perspective. Also, dreams are seen in different light when put in the context of a series of dreams, where repeating themes and symbols may form meaningful connections. Furthermore, when one has moved forward in time and then goes back and reviews dreams that occurred sometime in the past, there may be fresh nuances and connections because the dreamer has moved further on in understanding. In short, one can continue to reflect on past dreams and to formulate a fuller response.

12

Working with the Metaphors of a Dream

EUGENE GENDLIN

HERE ARE some small dream-bits, to accustom you to the metaphoric language of dreams. You don't know the whole dream nor the associations. Therefore you can *conclude* nothing. The things and the bit of story can give you a general sense for the *kind* of thing it *might* mean. Such a general sense helps in working with a dream. You would let your associations and what comes in you modify and change such a general sense.

To give you some practice, I tell my versions afterwards. First ask yourself: As a universal way of speaking, what might this story say?

1. I was lying in a room off the kitchen with no door.

2. Our house was swept clean, not a bit of clutter anywhere. All the chairs were covered with muslin dust covers, like a summer home readied for the owners to leave.

3. I put some of the flowers in a cheap little glass that I have kept to use as a vase, but the top is too narrow, so I transfer them to a similar one with a wider top, which is perfect.

4. Just as I had gotten on the bus and paid, I saw my grand-mother walking toward another bus. I immediately got off my bus and boarded hers.

5. I became mesmerized by the beautiful, vast, enormous snowcapped mountains appearing from the clouds.

6. There was an old granite building. The stone work looked very strong. The building appears to have withstood a great deal of harsh weather without any visible signs of damage. I feel a strong desire to explore the interior of this building.

7. Two girls were putting a cast on my leg. Then they said I needed a full body cast. I jumped up and started shouting. The doctor came and ordered them out.

8. There was a line sheep waiting to get through several gates. I was helping them through, and I hugged this one black sheep with my whole body.

9. My brothers got very mean and took all the buttons off the phone and the doorknobs off the doors.

10. My father was building something and teaching me about it and my feet were naked and I am getting dirt and grease all over them and it's squooshy.

11. Dick and I had our cars linked together. We were in the one in back. The cars were going backwards so fast I had to brake hard to stop them.

12. My parents were going to that crater in Hawaii. I emphasized to them that they must go all the way down to the bottom and through it.

13. Sharon let a bull into the stable where I was, and the bull charged me. I was real angry and I climbed up the wall to protect myself. I didn't get hurt. Instead I ended up in the next room where there was a banquet.

14. I pulled out a very underdeveloped baby from my body. The baby was perfectly formed but I pulled it out of the womb too soon.

15. I was cooking two babies in a stew. My mother said she was given a psychological test that showed she was strong enough to handle the situation. Then I was taking care of a strong baby.

16. My grandmother said, "Now I can give you all my money," and her money was under her head in her pillow and she pulled it out.

17. I'm up on a bridge but it stops in the air. I have to go down and get across a lot of mud. I follow some track and get across.

18. Jenny [her baby] has a big shit. As I clean it up it's also mixed with my shit, and there is more and more of it. I can't clean it all up. Then a girl comes, with dark, curly hair. She has a sore on her leg. She says she doesn't mind the shit, it might even heal her sore.

POSSIBLE METAPHORICAL MEANINGS

Yours may differ from mine and be just as right. Add mine and let them expand your "general sense," which you would try out.

1. *Kitchen*—cooking, food, nourishment, taking something in; what is a kitchen? what goes on there?
   No door—open to whomever, defenseless, no control? What is a door?
   Lying down—Defenseless, passive? Childhood experience with kitchen, with taking in, with lying down? Maybe open to what's cooking, to being nourished?

2. *Leaving some place*—too clean, not usable, not actually living in it? Is something so protected from dirt that it can't be lived in? Something is being put away for safekeeping?

3. *Cheap little glass*—not enough energy or care for this? Or, it looks cheap, but it's perfect
   Flowers—something living and beautiful
   A vase—the female sex organ? A little more room to put something living in? Something long kept and not used?

4. *Bus*—takes you to some destination. You aren't now going your own way, having your own destination?
   Grandmother—You're now living some traditional way, an old way? Or is it wise and better first to go that old woman's way?

5. *Vast, high mountains, beautiful*—spiritual, cosmically meaningful, big opening, large vision? What comes just before this? How did you get there? What is associated with this? Whatever this stands for is of great value. In the clouds, perhaps not quite grounded yet?

6. *Building*—perhaps you. You've gone through a lot, withstood a lot?
   No visible damage—it doesn't show?
   Desire to explore—explore the inside of it, your own inwardness?

7. *Cast*—*part or all of your body could be made rigid.* No feelings there where the cast holds it in?
   Doctor—a wiser part of you throws out what makes you rigid. (Can you sense something in you that would throw them out? Be that a while.)
   Girls—make you "rigid"? Erection? Tense? A female part of you? A young part of you?

8. *Sheep*—warm, good animal side of you.
   Black sheep—it has been disapproved of in the past
   Gate—it's coming through what used to be a barrier?

9. *Telephone*—you hear from unseen source, from the unconscious?
   No buttons, no knobs—isolation, can't communicate, can't go out
   Brothers—childhood abuse? Good brothers? Keep you in this spot for your own good? Part of you isolates you?

10. *Father, building something, teaching me*—good father roles
    Getting feet dirty—in earth, real stuff
    Squooshy—sexual, mucous, sense of body and earth

11. *Cars*—going somewhere. Maybe physical, sexual being.
    Backwards—sliding back, to where you've been? Going back? Perhaps something with your backside?

12. *Crater*—deep into the earth, unconscious, deep down
    Volcanic crater—anger, explosiveness

Parents—related to the origin of some of your personality; your childhood. Their problem is in you some way.

To the bottom—get to the bottom of it (the dreamer, added, "especially about the trouble between them"). Face it. Trouble in the ground; something stands in the way of getting grounded.

13. *Bull*—sound animal instinct, can be strong

   The bull charged . . . I was angry—anger; some of it is still coming at you? Is something out of control in your life?

   Climbed the wall—You take care of yourself, protect yourself? Had more feelings than you could stand ("climbing the walls")? At first it seemed too much for you? You tried to climb the walls to get away from it?

   Banquet—eating, taking in, digesting, integrating, nourishing, expanding. So it seemed too much for you, but afterwards you made it part of you and you felt larger. Does that fit?

14. *Baby*—new life, vulnerable, new development

   I pulled it out—are you doing something, insisting you should be further along than you quite are?

   Womb—vagina, sexual, creative spot where something is developing

   Too soon—it's developing perfectly, but it's too soon now to take it out

15. *Stew*—something eventually eaten, taken in, integrated; a unity of many things cooked (processed) so they go together

   Two babies—two still vulnerable, very new developments

   Strong baby—strong new way of being

   Psychological test—something wise and knowing says . . . (only in dreams are psychological tests to be taken that way!)

   Mother—Your actual mother is strong enough to stand it. (When you were little, did you have to take care of her?) The part of you that is your mother is strong enough to stand it.

16. *Money*—value, energy, power. What did your grandmother have that's of value? What was she like?

Her *head*—thinking? insight? concentration? will power?

Under her head—she kept it safe and out of sight with her head, but not in her head

Now I can give you—What did she have that you're only just now ready for?

17. *Bridge*—way to get across

Mid-air—up high, thinking, not grounded, skipping over

Mud—earth, concrete reality, muddy, unclear, slow going. You wish you could skip over a lot, but you might have to go through it. Feelings? Actual experience? It's muddy, earthy, the ground, feet on the ground. Seems there is some track to follow and you do get through O.K. What are you hesitant about getting into in your own development now? Perhaps the dream says you can actually go through it.

18. *Baby*—new life, new development, your actual baby and your growth

Shit—natural stuff, organic bodily matter, left over from digestion

Clean it up—eliminate smelly, earthy stuff. You think it is shit and has to be cleaned up but, actually, it can heal something?

Girl—the sensitive, receptive, emotional part. It can heal that part of you? Healing her has to do with your new development, perhaps also with Jenny.

Of course we need the whole dream, the associations, and what the questions would bring. Without these we cannot know whether such symbolic meanings apply. Sometimes we can think of opposite possibilities. But the symbols and metaphors do give us something to ask about.

13

Active Imagination:
Returning to Dream Reality

ROBERT BOSNAK

A VITAL ELEMENT in dream work is the return to the reality of
the dream. The dreamer moves into the inner space of the dream
to the extent that the images can be recalled. In this remembered
dream space, the dream events reoccur. This is an essential component of dreamwork. In particular, fresh dreams that are retained
as spatial dream images and survive as real events, not just as a story,
must be approached as much as possible through their spatial details.
Fresh dreams are usually those of the previous night or dreams that
have left behind a particularly strong impression. Some dreams
remain fresh for days.

The activity of entering the dream world by way of daytime
consciousness is a discipline of the imagination. In contrast to passive daydreaming, during which images are merely perceived, in this
disciplined imagination an active interaction with the image world
takes place. The faculty of memory is actively used to reconstruct

the dream reality. . . . After this reconstruction, which often begins with the vague remnants and ruins of a dream, it is possible to continue dreaming the dream. This art is called *active imagination*.

The following dream can serve as an illustration. The person in question is a stiff white professor in his middle years who came into analysis because of dependency, after prolonged psychiatric treatment, on a whole arsenal of medications. He dreams the following dream.

> *I'm walking through a run-down black neighbor-hood. I'm right by the bridge that will take me to the white neighborhood. I don't feel completely at ease, although I'm not frightened. I stop near a tall young black man. He is hanging on the jungle gym in a playground. The bars are really too low for him, but he keeps his feet off the ground by swinging his legs around in a counterclockwise motion. His feet touch me. I move back. But the farther back I move, the farther he swings out. He keeps on touching me. I walk calmly away. He comes after me. I get angry at him and curse him out. I tell him that he has to leave me alone. He stays back but still throws a stone at me when I'm on the bridge. He doesn't hit me.*

The dreamer's first reaction in telling the dream is an undertone of pride that he didn't run away from the young man but rather defended himself.

We go back to the dream, and he says that the young man is very limber. He describes the jungle gym and the surrounding houses. It all makes quite a run-down impression. It becomes clear how much the dreamer fears the black man. At the same time it appears that the young man wants to come into contact with him; he keeps trying to touch the I-figure. This irritates the professor immeasurably, and he gets angry. At this point I ask the dreamer to describe the whole dream environment precisely. I also ask him what the young man looks like now. Then I ask the professor not to be so aggressive toward the man this time around. Now it comes out that the black man has no malicious intentions. What is frightening the dreamer is his own prejudice regarding blacks. This specific black man appears to be different from the way he is in the dreamer's prejudiced view. In dreams, just as in daily life, we frequently react to the figures we encounter from the standpoint of all kinds of prejudices. When reliving a dream, it can be useful to suspend this prejudice and let the dream figure speak for himself. I suggest to the professor that instead of the tirade he aimed at the young man, he should ask what he wants from the dreamer, why he keeps touching him. The dreamer does this. The young man answers immediately, spontaneously, "Don't be so uptight, man! Hang loose!" The black man starts to laugh. "Relax, man, relax. Don't be so tense."

This short dialogue brings out a characteristic of the young black man that was present in the image: he hangs loose. He is a relaxed figure with whom the terribly tense professor has little affinity. Through the dialogue, a relationship develops between the dream figure and daytime consciousness. It is now possible for the professor to consult the young black man from time to time when he feels particularly tense. At such moments, he can evoke the black neighborhood and have a further conversation with the young man. The stressed-out daytime consciousness can learn relaxation from this dream figure. This is not a relaxation imposed from the outside by medication but one that arises from within, out of an independent inner need. In the dream, habitual consciousness remained ultimately untouched by the relaxed young man ("He doesn't hit me"). The active imagination, however, does not let itself be carried away by the resistances that the stiff professor (the figure with whom the "I" identifies) has toward the relaxed man who hangs loose. Thus, the active imagination can establish contact between the dreamer and relaxation. This diminishes his identification with what makes him into a stressed-out, uptight person.

The concept of active imagination comes from C. G. Jung. He describes his discovery of active imagination in his autobiography:

*. . . I let myself drop. Suddenly it was as though the
ground literally gave way beneath my feet, and I plunged
down into dark depths. . . . But then, abruptly, . . . I
landed on my feet in soft, sticky mass. . . . I caught sight
of figures, an old man with a white beard and a
beautiful young girl. I summoned up my courage and
approached them as though they were real people, and
listened attentively to what they told me. . . .*

In an ordinary dream, the I-figure sees the other dream figures
as ordinary people. The dream reality and the daytime reality are
usually indistinguishable. In active imagination, your sense of reality is different from what it is in an ordinary dream. There is a continuous awareness that you are dealing with a reality distinct from
daytime reality. That is why Jung says in his description that he
"approached them *as though* they were real people."

In active imagination, you are aware of this difference in the
nature of the figures you encounter, yet at the same time you regard
these different entities as *real*. They seem to be real beings who
behave autonomously in the same way that dream figures behave
entirely independently of the I-figure. Active imagination assumes
that, just as in the dream world, many different bearers of consciousness exist simultaneously and that the I-figure can make
(renewed) contact with these dream beings through disciplined
active imagination.

It is advantageous to begin a process of active imagination with
a dream image, because the sharpened memory of the dream reality can change naturally into active imagination. Take, for example,
this dream told by a nurse:

*I'm on the night shift and have to make my rounds.
The room where I find myself is brightly lit. First I go to
Room 1. It's dark in the corridor. I go into the room.
Here it is very dark. Vaguely I see an old woman
standing with her back toward me near her bed. I switch
on my flashlight. I see that she has a big black-and-blue
mark on her neck.*

We start our work on this dream with the nurse's room. The light is bright, almost glaring. The desk she is standing next to is white formica. It reflects the neonlike light. The room is rather small. The corridor has a grayish floor covering. The dreamer cannot clearly see where the light is coming from; it is rather dark. The door of Room 1 is bare wood. The doorknob is to the right and is silver-colored. Inside it is pitch dark. There is a hospital bed and a night stand, but nothing is clearly visible. Once the flashlight is on, the dreamer sees the old woman at a distance of about eight feet. The old woman is thin. She's wearing hospital pajamas. The nurse does not know the woman. From that distance she clearly sees the black-and-blue mark on the woman's neck. At this point the dream memory ends. The dream memory has led her to an image that feels very real.

Now the active imagination begins. The transition from dream memory to active imagination is hardly noticed by the dreamer. She begins to move toward the woman. The black-and-blue mark is now extremely clear. The old woman is still standing with her back toward the nurse. The nurse is now so close that she can touch the woman's neck, which she does. Then the old woman turns around. Her face expresses endless sorrow. The old woman and the nurse gaze at each other for a long time. They both stand without speaking and feel the sadness.

In doing active imagination it is important first to alter our state of awareness into an image consciousness. We can accomplish this through the very detailed recall of a dream image. Through this, the sense of reality of the image world intensifies and the I-figure can begin to move *through* the space of the image.

If you do not begin active imagination in such a state of consciousness, there is a chance that you will just fabricate stories, which produces a sense of unreality. In active imagination, you don't have the feeling of unreality; it is rather as if you participate in two equally true realities simultaneously: the world that is actively imagined *and* the world in which you know that you are involved in active imagination. By contrast, during the dream it feels as though you are participating in one reality, the dream world. Thus, active imagination is a state of mind that is distinct both from that of making up a story and that of the immediate dream experience.

The work on the nurse's dream shows how we pass from dream memory into active imagination and how the dream world itself creates new images spontaneously.

14

Dreaming About Family Members

PHYLLIS R. KOCH-SHERAS AND PETER SHERAS

IN FAMILY dreamwork, the family becomes a dream unit in itself, sharing dreams, discussing unresolved problems, and creating new visions for the future. You can work on dreams and visions directly with your parents, siblings, or children if they are willing to listen and join you in letting go of old patterns and beliefs in search of new ones. You can also work on your dreams on your own and then share the results or apply them to your family interactions in waking life. Exploring new possibilities and taking risks can pay off in personal growth and richer family relationships. This kind of mutual sharing of wishes, thoughts, and feelings from the deepest unconscious mind increases intimacy and trust between family members sensitively but quickly—something we need in our busy lives.

Sharing dreams and visions regularly can create a thoroughly supportive family environment. . . . [T]he Senoi Indians of Malaysia reportedly shared their dreams each morning in their family circle, creating a cooperative lifestyle in which each person contributed to the common good of the family. Any negative feeling or interaction involving a family member that came up in a dream was shared and transformed into a positive image or gift to that person. By resolving conflicts and fears symbolically through the dreamworld and dream sharing, the Senoi supposedly lived in harmony for generations. Although we are not likely to follow such strict regimens in our lives today, we can use the story of the Senoi as a model of what a family committed to dreamwork can do to learn about and support one another.

As you start to pay attention to dreams about your family members, you will notice that your parents, siblings, or children may not always appear literally as themselves. Often they will appear in some symbolic form, as a stranger, casual acquaintance, animal, distinctive object, or archetypal figure such as a wizard, witch, clown, king, or queen. Such was the case for one young woman, Marilyn, who had just learned that her mother had contracted a serious illness. She was alerted to the need to deal with her feelings about it by the following dream.

The Onions and the Shoes

I'm buying some shoes. A friendly woman waits on me. I notice someone trading in an old pair of shoes for a new pair. I ask the saleswoman about that, and she tells me that I can make a trade-in, but I have to put an onion in each shoe. I decide to do that and return the pair I just bought. I feel very sad as I leave the store.

Marilyn's mother loved shoes, and she often bought several pairs for herself and her daughter. After having this dream, Marilyn realized that the shoes pointed to her feelings about her mother's mortality that she really had never faced before. "I would need to deal with these issues like peeling an onion," she said, "a layer at a time. I would have to 'trade in' the old pair of shoes, that is, my old image of my mother as immortal, for a new one—an image that included her illness and mortality." Marilyn also saw that the onion in the dream pointed to the need to let herself cry (as when cutting an onion) and release the tension and sadness she felt about her mother's medical condition, something she had not yet done.

As "The Onions and the Shoes" dream shows, the feelings that come up during or at the end of a dream can be the main clue to the associations you make. When you have an intense emotional reaction to a dream character or object, it often relates to a family member to whom you have a strong attachment or with whom you have an unresolved conflict. When authority figures appear in a dream, they usually have some connection to our attitudes toward our parents. Think about these associations, and work with whatever comes up. You may find the results worthwhile for years to come. Marilyn used the images and insights from her dream to work through her issues about separation and loss over the next ten years of her mother's illness and subsequent death. She reports, "The idea from my dream of going through the layers of grief helped me to manage the intense periods of sadness I felt and to trust that there would be an end to it just as with peeling an onion."

In addition to your parent figures, check also to see what part of yourself is represented by a particular family member who appears in your dream. You may learn a lot about the mother or father parts of yourself, for example, by using dream language and owning their characteristics in your own behavior. Even though we may not like some of the things our parents did, we often repeat their mistakes. Paying attention to your dreams can alert you to how you may be carrying those old patterns into your current behavior. You may also instill your mother or father with positive attributes that you may not see in yourself; owning those parts of yourself in a dream can help you recognize and develop those strengths in your own personality. In addition, by exploring the world from your dream character's perspective, you may gain an appreciation of a different point of view. That is what happened to Carolyn as she explored the meaning of the following dream about her father.

Taking Care of Me
I'm taking a test in a glassed-in room. I can't concentrate or answer the questions. My son is there

*with me, distracting me. I'm getting more frustrated,
angry, and upset. I give the exam to the professor. I
notice that my dad is standing next to me. He explains
to the professor that I just had a baby recently, and that
I am not functioning well yet. I feel foolish and stupid,
but at the same time I feel warm toward my dad for
taking care of me.*

Carolyn had this dream shortly after delivering her second child. She was feeling tired, isolated, and vulnerable ("glassed-in") at the time. She wasn't at all sure that she cold pass the "test" of taking care of a house and two children. Her father had offered to pay for some household help, but she had resented his thinking that she couldn't take care of herself. After role-playing her father in this dream, she said, "I could feel the love and concern that was motivating him, and I changed my mind about his offer. I called him, shared the dream, and thanked him. I could also own the father part of myself that could be kinder and more nurturing in meeting my own needs, rather than constantly putting myself through a 'test.'" Carolyn then created a visioning statement for herself of "I take good care of myself." She repeated it every day, and it helped her get through this challenging period of her life. . . .

DREAMWORK WITH AND ABOUT PARENTS

Other than couples, the relationships that generally bring up the most intense feelings are those with our mothers and fathers. We share an intense bond with the people who created and raised us. No matter how long that connection lasts, it has a lot of history behind it that shapes our development and future. We received, directly or indirectly, many early messages from our parents about who we are and how we should behave. Many of these were positive, helping us to grow and encouraging us to develop our strengths. Some of these messages, however, were limiting and blocked our awareness of our own assets and virtues.

Fortunately, as an adult you can rework the negative injunctions into positive notions that can serve as stepping stones toward a more confident and flexible image of yourself and an improved relationship with your parents. Your dreams can bring to light some of these powerful messages hidden in your unconscious. They can inspire both you and your parents to address the issues from the stance of a dream story. This may give you the courage to bring up sensitive topics with them, and allow your parents to be open to listening without feeling attacked. You can then go on to create a joint vision with them that improves your relationship. The following example shows how a dream gave Denise the resolve she needed to improve a strained relationship with her mother.

Holding My Mother

It is night, and I'm trying to find a place to sleep. I go outside. My mother is there. I sit just behind her, putting my arms around her and resting my head on the back of her neck. There is something beautiful and strong about her. I go to sleep with a feeling of peace and security.

The communication between Denise and her mother had been strained for a long time, something she felt sad about but too intimidated to try to change. She had this dream shortly before going to visit her parents. She was so moved by it that she resolved to make a special effort while there to let her mother know "how much I love and admire her despite our disagreements." She followed through on this, and their relationship has improved steadily ever since.

Even if you don't share your dream with a family member, your own dreamwork related to your feelings about that person often leads to new insights and improvements in your self-image and in the relationship itself. Such was the case for Arthur, who had an abusive upbringing.

The Coins

I'm walking through a store that my mother owns. I find some sandwiches and cakes. I take little bites, then

> *wrap them up again so no one can tell they were*
> *opened. I decide to buy something. As I'm counting my*
> *change, I realize some of the coins in my hand have*
> *greater value than their face value. I keep these and*
> *spend the ordinary ones.*

As a child, Arthur's mother often spanked him severely and showed no consistency in punishments and rewards. In working on "The Coins" dream, he noticed that he was beginning to nurture himself (with food), even if it was only surreptitiously and in "little bites." In keeping the valuable coins, he came to see himself as being open to extracting something useful from his childhood. He saw the change in his hand as representing his desire to confront and deal with his past, so that he could "change" himself and his life for the better. Arthur's father is a coin collector, and the dream helped Arthur to recognize the things he learned from him that held meaning beneath their "face value." Arthur said, "This insight created a new possibility for discussing some of these issues with my parents and for acknowledging them for the 'extraordinary' value they contributed to my life." Arthur could add to this insight a vision statement, such as "I value my parents," to empower his taking action to follow up on the dream. Without some kind of resolution, the most significant insights can be relatively useless. Creating a vision and restating it can often get you to say or do something that might otherwise just remain a "good idea."

DEALING WITH DEATH

Having an intimate discussion with your parents is not always easy. But if you are willing to risk shaking up the old patterns of communication within your family, dream sharing can lead to greater closeness and understanding at many levels. That was the experience Justin had when dreaming about being at the funeral of his father, who, though ill, was still very much alive in waking life.

My Father's Funeral
> *I'm somewhere in Eastern Europe. I walk into a*
> *room that I come to realize is a synagogue. The rabbi is*

*elevated above the congregation. There is a wooden
pulpit and a sounding board above the dais. I realize
this is a funeral, and the rabbi is eulogizing the person
who has died. The scene changes to a party. There's
music and violins, and food everywhere. People are
laughing and crying. I feel everything from euphoria to
grief. The scene changes again. All I can see is my feet.
It looks like I'm walking in a cloud, with smoke and
blackness all around. Slowly into focus in front of me, I
see a man walking toward me, wearing a Western-style
business suit. He's carrying his jacket over his shoulder. I
get behind him and say, "Excuse me." He turns around,
and it's my father. It hits me that I've just been to his
funeral. I say, "But Dad, I'm not ready for you to be
dead yet!" I wake up sobbing uncontrollably, thinking
my father must be dead.*

Justin shared this dream with his wife in the middle of the
night. At 6:30 in the morning, he called his father. His father
answered the phone, and Justin blurted, "You're not dead!" After
telling him about the dream, Justin told his father that he loved him
very much. His father then told Justin that he loved him. It was a
very moving moment for both of them that, a year later, Justin still
describes with intense feeling. His father, whose Jewish heritage
Justin has not followed, remains ill, and Justin waits for that eventual phone call that everyone dreads. In the meantime, both men
have had the experience of facing the reality of death through Justin's
dream, and of expressing their love for each other before it was too
late. To make good use of the lessons of this dream, they could make
a proclamation, such as "We express our love for each other," or "We
are a loving family." This statement could continue to serve as a
reminder of the power of Justin's dream and of the expression of love
that came from it.

DEALING WITH DIVORCE

As Justin discovered through "My Father's Funeral," dreams can often alert us to unconscious fears or desires about our parents that we may be ignoring or avoiding, and which, if expressed or acted on, can lead to increased closeness. This is often the case when divorce is involved. Thirty-five-year-old Bruce had the following dream nearly twenty years after his parents' divorce.

> ### Parents' Day
> *I am back at the camp I went to as a child. One of my friends tells me that it's Parents' Day. I see my mom and dad arriving into the parking area in a new car. Even though I am an adult now, I'm so happy to see them. I rush up and hug them, feeling excited and happy. My mom looks very beautiful, and my dad looks very handsome.*

Bruce's parents had divorced when he was a teenager. When he awoke from this dream, he said, "I remembered how much I missed seeing them together and having contact with my dad, whom I rarely saw or even spoke to on the phone. I saw that I had been blaming my father for this lack of communication all these years." Out of this dream, Bruce realized his own responsibility for being out of touch and decided to do something about it. He told his wife about the dream, and they created a proclamation of "We are a close family" that motivated them to act on their vision. They immediately arranged for the whole family to visit his father and stepmother. These visits continued on a regular basis until his father's death about ten years later. Bruce and his wife were also able to maintain a close relationship with his stepmother afterward, thanks to the foundation they had already created out of their vision. One wonders what would have happened to that relationship if Bruce hadn't paid attention to his dream.

DEALING WITH IN-LAWS

In addition to divorced parents and stepparents, couples often have difficulty dealing with their spouse's parents. In fact, problems with in-laws is one of the most frequent complaints that couples bring into marital therapy. It is often hard enough to work out the relationship with our own parents, let alone adjust to someone else's. To make matters worse, this often creates added tension within the marriage, and the couple ends up fighting with rather than supporting each other. There is not much guidance readily available for how to work out these conflicts. That is where dreams and visions can be invaluable in creating new possibilities with in-laws. One couple, Jennifer and Mitchell, who have been happily married for twenty years, had been arguing about his parents ever since they met. They were having little success changing the situation, as reflected in Jennifer's dream, which alerted both of them to the seriousness of the matter.

> ### My In-laws
>
> We arrive at the house where Mitch grew up. We go in the house, which is crowded with people. More and more people are arriving. There are children and toys all over. I go from room to room, tripping over balls, dolls, and teddy bears. Everyone is laughing and talking so loudly that the sound has become one big roar. My head hurts, and I feel dizzy and exhausted. I lie down on the couch and place my hand, palm up, on my forehead, looking like a Southern belle having a fainting spell. Mitch sees me and asks if I am all right. I say, "Yes, but I have to rest now," and I proceed to go to sleep.

The visit Mitchell and Jennifer made to his parents in Georgia shortly after this dream closely resembled what took place in the dream story. The memory came back to Jennifer when it came time to plan the next trip there. She shared her memory and the dream with Mitchell, and they decided to heed the warning this time and create a visioning dream for their visit. The vision they wrote out and took with them goes as follows: "We are soul mates on vacation in Georgia, being ourselves, taking care of each other, having a great time, creating a space for genuine acceptance, appreciation, and love for family." They felt much better about the visit afterward. Mitchell's family eventually accepted that this trip was different from earlier ones and supported them in their new vision, including their staying in a hotel instead of at his parents. They had a great time and are now looking forward to future visits.

You don't have to wait for a special occasion to create a visioning dream of the kind of relationship you would like to have with your parents or in-laws. A vision can change your everyday interactions if you make use of it. This is what one man did who had been having trouble getting along with his mother-in-law for years. He asked a friend for some coaching to deal with it. When his friend asked him what he would like his relationship with her to be like, he said, "I want to have the kind of mother-in-law I could go out to lunch with and talk to like a friend." His coach told him to proclaim that as a vision and to start acting on it now. He took his mother-in-law out for lunch the following week, had a great time, and continued to do so regularly until she passed away.

DEALING WITH SICK OR DYING PARENTS

Visioning dreams can be particularly useful in dealing with our parents in the last days of their lives, when they are ill and dying. These can be poignant and intense times, and it is often difficult to know what to do. They can be either positive or negative experiences, depending on how we handle them. Creating a visioning dream for your couple or family can provide some structure and help keep up everyone's spirits.

We found this to be the case for our family in dealing with the terminal illness of Peter's father. When we heard that he was losing ground rapidly, we decided to plan some visits to go see him with the children. Instead of a sad occasion, we wanted to make the visits a celebration for our whole family. We wanted Dad to see us enjoying ourselves rather than being in mourning. So we rented a nice car, arranged interesting things to do between visits to the hospital, and shared with him our pleasure visiting him. Our vision and positive attitude allowed us all, including him, to have a good time and to have fond memories of his final days of life.

REMEMBERING OUR PARENTS

It is fortunate that our dreams can alert and motivate us to do something about our relationships with our parents while there is still time to act on them. But the utility of dreams in helping us to work through these significant relationships doesn't end when our parents die. If anything, dreams about our mothers and fathers become even more frequent within the first several years after their deaths. Perhaps this is a way that our mind lets us know there are some important things about our parents to resolve in ourselves. Once the funeral is over, there usually isn't much opportunity or structure for resolving the grief or issues that remain. Dreamwork can provide both. In fact, we can get even closer to our parents in our dreams after they're gone, without that pesky waking reality to get in the way of increasing our intimacy. Our parents can be dead and alive at the same time, and our relationship with them can go on as long as we would like in our dream life.

Like the sixty-three-year-old woman in the following dream, you may find yourself finishing arguments and coming to terms with your father or mother through your dreams in ways that you may never have done while they were alive.

Mother Listening

I'm with my mother, explaining things to her. She's listening. I tell her. "I hope you understand why I did all those things."

Following her mother's death, this woman had had many dreams about her. After this particular one, she described feeling at peace about their relationship as she never had before.

In "Mother Listening," just recalling the dream seemed to be enough to help the dreamer come to resolution about her mother's death. Although not many dream experiences end up with such immediate and direct results, they can give important clues about what is needed to reach a feeling of peace. We found this to be the case when Phyllis had the following dream about a year after her mother died, and it helped her deal with the loss of both her parents.

Letters at the Health Spa

I'm at a health spa with my sister. I follow a woman I know to her room — many toys in it. I invite her to join us for dinner. She says she can't come. I'm disappointed. I go to my room to pack to leave. There's mail by the door — six airmail letters from my mom and a big package. I ask at the main desk about why I didn't get them before. They say it was unclear whom they were for. I'm angry, but see that the address was on the wrong place on the letters. I feel sad.

Phyllis . . . came to realize she recently had had feelings about missing her mother while at a health spa with her sister. They had become friendly with two sisters who were there with their own mother, and had noticed several other mothers and daughters in attendance together. Phyllis had been blocking the sadness until she worked on this dream a few weeks later, closer to Thanksgiving and her father's birthday. It occurred to her then that it was the tenth anniversary of her father's death, and that she was missing them both very much at this holiday time. Not getting the letters, represented to Phyllis her "missing" communication with her parents. When she saw this, she cried and felt a tremendous physical release. She made a proclamation of "I am in touch with my parents" and took specific action around that. She wrote a letter to herself as if it were from her mother: "We miss you . . . We're glad you two girls are together. Get some rest and don't work too hard!" Then she wrote a letter back to her parents: "Thanks for persisting in getting through to me. It feels so good to hear your words . . . I love you and miss you both." Inspired by the dream and the letters, Phyllis later wrote a poem about her mother's death, entitled "Just Wait," ending with the following stanza:

> I missed something important:
> Being there with you at the end.
> Maybe it's not "the end" for you though.
> Maybe you're still here with your glow—
> Perhaps I only need to just wait for it to show—
> Just wait and we'll be together . . .
> Now I know.

As you can see from so many of the dream experiences above, perhaps no other event in our adult years has the emotional impact on our evolving self-image as the final separation from our parents—their deaths. Difficult as this loss is, however, it can provide the impetus to turn to your inner strengths and resources and develop a new and deeper trust in yourself. Dreams and visions can help on this difficult and sometimes lonely journey to discovering your own strength by helping you understand your feelings and giving you a way to make sense of the confusion and pain. Lynette experienced this through the following dream, which she had the night after her father died.

The Key
I am standing outside with my mom and dad. It's a bright, sunny day. My sister is sitting in a car off in the distance. My dad hands me a large gold key, and then walks off carrying his briefcase through a doorway, down some stairs, and disappears into a bright light. I feel sad and anxious.

Lynette worked on this dream on the plane while flying to her father's funeral. She had always looked to her father for guidance and respected his advice. Now she experienced him taking his wisdom (in the briefcase) with him into heaven (the light). She felt anxious but saw her father passing her the key as a statement of his confidence and trust in her to carry on without him. "I need not stay in the background like the sister part of me," Lynette says now, "and wait to be driven or guided around by my father or anyone else any longer." To solidify this insight, she drew a picture of the dream depicting the passing of the key. This image stayed with her through the funeral, and she still remembers and thinks about it to this day.

Dream-inspired creative expression: Drawing a picture of your dream, as Lynette did, can reinforce and add to what you learn from the dream. It was in making the picture, in fact, that Lynette first came to realize the symbolic significance of the key, which had greater and greater prominence as she drew it. Creative expressions, such as Lynette's drawing or Phyllis's poem "Just Wait," often flow naturally out of doing dreamwork. Dream thought is similar to creative thought; it occurs relatively free of inhibition or the fear of judgment.

Re-dreaming: Another way to add something to your dream experience is to finish or change the dream in waking fantasy. Such an exercise can clarify or complete issues it brings up. In the case of dealing with the death of parents, re-dreaming can help you complete the grieving process in a concrete way. The following dreamer, Sharon, was able to do this a year and a half after her mother died.

Let Her Go

I'm at a large meeting. I see Mom there. She is leaving, being hoisted up in a wheelchair into a van. I think she could come to lunch with our family before she leaves. I feel ambivalent, but I go ahead and ask her. She says, "Of course," and she is lowered back down. I go to get her, and wonder how I'm going to manage it all. I feel anxious.

Sharon had been very close to her mother and was having a hard time coming to terms with her death. After having this dream, she realized she was ambivalent about letting her go. She could see from the dream how she was causing herself and her family anxiety and added difficulty by pulling her mother "back down" into their lives, when perhaps she—and even her mother herself—was ready to "leave." She saw that she didn't have to take care of her mother anymore, that she could "let her go." Sharon changed the dream so that she could see her mother ascending to heaven, looking radiant and saying, "I'm ready to go now. I love you. Be well, my darling daughter." Tears came to Sharon's eyes as she said out loud, "Goodbye, Mother. I love you. God be with you." Sharon continued to think about and miss her mother, but her grief no longer consumed her. She cold let go of the sadness and anxiety and replace it with a beautiful image from her dreamwork.

15

Dream Lovers

JENNY DAVIDOW

MANY PEOPLE get very worried if they have a dream, fantasy, or impulse in which they are attracted to someone other than their partner. In a dream, if they make love with an exciting new person (who may or may not resemble someone they actually know), these people may feel guilty, as though they have been unfaithful to their partner. Or they may take their attraction as clear evidence that they are no longer interested in staying in their relationship. None of these interpretations may be true. Your new attraction may be a symbol for a valuable part of you that is seeking expression.

Dreams, fantasies, impulses, and real experiences in which you are attracted to or sexually involved with someone other than your partner have much to say about the subconscious influences at work in you—and in your relationships. If your subconscious is bringing a problem in your real-life relationship to your attention, you will be in a better position to deal with it effectively after you have done an Inner Dialogue.

What to do: Choose a dream, fantasy, or real-life experience in which you are attracted to someone who is not your partner. In this exercise, you will speak not only as yourself, but also as the other two parts of the love triangle: the new person to whom you are attracted, and your partner. You will speak to each of them about what you like and don't like about them, and then let them respond. You may discover attractive aspects of yourself that you will want to reclaim. You are also likely to gain insight as to how your subconscious influences feelings of attraction to certain people in your life.

Find a quiet place for fifteen minutes to do an Inner Dialogue, a process that lets you give a voice to the people and feelings you need to explore. Inner Dialogue enables you to shift from your normal conscious perspective into a state of mind that includes the perspective and wisdom of your subconscious. You may wish to write your Inner Dialogue in your journal as it unfolds, so you will have a record of it to reflect on later. After you have completed this process, you may want to share part or all of it with your partner. In your imagination:

- Speak as the person you are attracted to, describing yourself as him or her.

- Speak as your partner, describing yourself as him or her.

- Speak as yourself: dialogue with the one you are attracted to, and then with your partner.

- Tell the person you are attracted to, and then your partner, what you like and don't like about each of them. Let each of them respond.

- Notice in what ways the two people are different, and in what ways they are the same.

- Think about the qualities of both people as qualities you need to be more aware of in yourself—both positive and negative.

- Negotiate an agreement between you and your partner, as well as between you and the one you are attracted to. Think about each pairing and the ways in which the qualities or energy belonging to you and the other are complementary, two parts of a whole. Enter into an alliance with each that gives both of you room to express a little more of yourselves.

- Consider some ways in which you could benefit from using the qualities each person represents (even to a small degree). Imagine expressing those qualities with good results in a particular situation in your life.

16

Dead-end Dreams

FRED OLSEN

SOME NIGHT dreams are what I call dead-end dreams—dreams that have an undesired outcome or reflect a destructive path being followed by the dreamer in life. One way to work with such a dream is to focus on what takes place *before* the destructive event occurs, even if the preceding event was not remembered or did not appear in the dream. Often, important clues can be discerned that can be used to facilitate a different outcome or choice.

Here is an example of how one person reframed a dead-end dream. While I was speaking to a group of high school students at a church conference, a young woman asked me about a recent dream. "In one scene," she said, "I am drifting on my back on the bottom of the sea. My body is full of seawater and shifting among the kelp plants. I am dead." She then mentioned a recurring dream: "I am in my kitchen and parts of my mother, my sister, and myself are cut up and spread around. There is blood everywhere."

After exploring various avenues related to the symbols in the dream, I asked her to tell me what was happening just before the scene in which she found herself at the bottom of the sea. Although she had not recalled this scene in her night dream, she immediately found herself in a scene with her family. They were in a high-speed powerboat running out of control. They were headed directly for a reef. Her father was at the helm and unwilling to listen to their warnings. She, her sister, and her mother were sitting in terror and felt powerless to intervene. She wanted to jump out of the boat or stop her father, but was too terrified to do either.

I asked her if anything was going on in her life that felt like that. She reported that her father was an out-of-control alcoholic who was progressively getting more abusive and dangerous. I suggested to her that she take the dream very seriously: that it might portend a serious or violent altercation at home if she did not pay attention. I then asked the church counselors at the conference to follow up with her.

The dreams in the kitchen and at the bottom of the ocean indicated the outcome of a dead-end situation: the dream could not move forward from there. By going backward to the preceding scene in the dream (or using one's imagination if there is no memory of a previous scene), the dreamer can discover the causes to a personal problem and thus devise alternative actions that may lead to a better outcome in life.

17

Recurring Dreams

KATHLEEN SULLIVAN

GRASPING REPETITIOUS dream images feels like trying to capture fog as it moves through a dense forest: no image holds steady long enough to make an imprint on my mind's canvas. But finally, repetitive wisps begin to etch themselves into a pattern. I awaken from a dream with a feeling of familiarity. Even within a dream I begin to remember that I've been here before, felt this over and over, or seen that same symbol many times.

Most dreamers are fascinated by repetitive dreams and the questions they stimulate. Why do we have them? What do they mean? Why would one particular dream symbol continuously reappear for many years, on important anniversaries or at crisis points in our lives? What are we telling ourselves, over and over? What is the intent of this persistent dreaming self?

A variety of dream elements may repeat: a theme, a symbol, a character, an emotion or even a vague sensing. In whatever form, repetitive dreams clearly get our attention. Just as we need to repeat any experience — in relationships, at work, or in any aspect of our lives — in order to become aware of the existing dynamic or forming pattern, it seems that dream images need to repeat before we can perceive our psyches' focus and intent.

To illustrate the movement of this repeating energy, here is a series which occurred many years after my parents' deaths. . . .

Approximately thirty of my dreams presented the repetitive symbol of *plants needing care*. The dream environment, different in every dream, always was identified as my parents' home. At first, the dream's settings were dimly lit shacks. Over the years the shacks evolved into cottages, apartments, and eventually one lovely condo. The final dream of this series takes place in a stunning top-floor apartment.

In nearly every dream, dream ego (the "me" in the dream) became anxious as soon as I realized that I was in my parents' house. Then I felt extreme distress about the responsibility for the care of many potted plants in my parents' living environment. I knew I must face the plants' condition and that it was my frustrating job to care for these neglected living things.

In most of the dreams, dozens of plants hung from the ceilings, sat on counters, or were supported by free-standing planters. In the beginning, all of the plants were desperately needy, often confined in dark, dingy rooms. Most were dehydrated and near death. The hanging plants had leaves or fronds that had been dead for many years but never trimmed. Some plants sat in smelly, stagnant water, in obvious danger of death from drowning. Others had only two or three healthy leaves.

For the first three years of the series a frantic person — sometimes a girl, sometimes a woman — charged around, trying to rescue and revive these pathetic dying things. Sometimes she cried in frustration, exhaustion, or worry. Occasionally, fury showed on her face as she judged her parents' neglect of these living, growing things. At times the woman sat in despair, apparently feeling it was too late, all was lost.

Toward the end of the third year of this series the images began to change. Many plants were trimmed and tidy. Though some were still over-watered and others thirsty, many looked vibrant in rooms well lit by clean windows. The woman tending the plants appeared more calm, less concerned as she moved from plant to plant, doing what she could.

During the last year enormous changes were obvious. A wide variety of health plants were well pruned and tended. The parents often were doing the work, sometimes helped by other people as well. The original caretaking woman was clearly relaxed, even serene as she observed the bountiful, lush beauty that had been nurtured by her and others.

In this series' last dream, dream ego realized she was going to visit her parents' house. The automatic feeling of dread was quickly replaced by cautious anticipation as she recalled that her parents had *hired a full-time gardener*. As she entered the luxurious *upper-level* apartment in which her parents now lived, she saw a bounty of beautiful plants, some exotic and some commonplace, all sizes and types, enhancing every room. In the kitchen, dream ego met the gardener who said, "There is a huge compost pile in the corner by the stove." Clearly everything was now being processed and cared for without the woman's intervention.

To understand the significance of this Plant Series a short family history is necessary. My dreams about being the desperate caretaker accurately express the panic I felt when I was an adolescent responsible for my severely ill mother. Mother's precarious physical and emotional problems began ten years before my birth. To deal with a sudden weight gain, so the story goes, she fasted while drinking only soft drinks and smoking cigarettes. After several weeks of this weight-loss regime, she suffered her first "nervous breakdown" at the age of twenty-five.

During all the years I knew her, Mother rarely ate a normal meal, fearing that she would become fat. She drank at least one six-pack of 12-ounce soft drinks every day and smoked continuously until she died. For the many years that my father managed a bar, she added gin to the Pepsi by early afternoon. In the beginning mother's alcoholism, which relieved her nervousness and depression, was a blessing to me. Violent rages soon replaced that short-lived serenity, including many incidents of throwing cast iron skillets and other objects at my father.

In her early forties Mother's spine began disintegrating, resulting in a series of unsuccessful major surgeries. With the onset of her back problems Mother's chronic "nervous condition" moved into severe clinical depression. For three months she experienced extended catatonic periods which were not alleviated by electric shock treatments. Mother's alcohol addiction was superseded by sleeping pills and morphine after her first surgery.

Except for the times that she was hospitalized, I was the primary caretaker for this desperately unhappy woman in constant physical and emotional agony. I soon began to live in terror of what I might find when I entered the house after an absence. Three times I opened the door to the throat-clenching odor of blood and the sight of Mother's unconscious body and large areas of her bedroom and bathroom stained red. In two of these cases, Mother had sustained head and body gashes from drug-induced falls; in the third episode she slit her wrist, using small sewing scissors. In all three cases, doctors arrived in time to bring her back to a life she clearly felt was not worth living.

After eighteen months of severe mental problems, Mother somehow found her way back to the mind she had lost. However, her connection to it remained tenuous. Three years later, after a total of three ineffective back surgeries, she successfully planned her death and died of an overdose of pills. I was nineteen years old.

In light of this history I hope you can see the obvious metaphors in the Plant Series. Despite my inability to repair her back or to keep Mother from abusing her body through addiction, I was compelled to clean up the messes her illnesses created. I was expected to keep the "dying plants" alive and vital. During Mother's disintegration I had no choice but to assume the futile role of frustrated heroine in a tragic melodrama. I could clean up the blood, but I couldn't stop the falls. As seen in the dream series language, I could water the plants, provide new soil, prune, and feed, but I couldn't control the forces that were perpetually destroying the plants.

I felt a strong need to do more than keep my mother alive physically. I decided I was also responsible for making her happy, for giving her reasons to live. Providing stimulation for a catatonic is as impossible as forcing a drunk to put down the bottle. The desperate needs I felt as an adolescent created a lethal pattern of trying to fix the unfixable. As a youngster I couldn't know the futility of my attempts. As an adult suffering from my own illnesses, my very survival depended upon recognizing this pattern.

What is the meaning of the healthy movement we see in this four-year dream series? Clearly the plants are being effectively tended as the years go by. Since both my parents were dead at the time of the series, the dreams are speaking of progress within *me* and the ways *I* was healing the patterns from childhood. The Plant Series represents a shift in my behavior with others. This learning continues to this day. Gratefully, I have never suffered a relapse severe enough to reactivate the Plant Series.

A dream series of this magnitude has many levels of meaning. Beyond my reactions to others I was learning to "parent" and nurture myself (the plants) in ways that neither of my parents had been able to model for me. This was happening at the physical level (the proper watering, trimming, transplanting) and the spiritual/mental level (movement from dark, cruddy shacks to the sunny top-floor environment).

18

Working with Dreams in Therapy

GREG BOGART

DREAMS ARE like icebergs rising out of the deep waters of the unconscious. Some are icebergs of the past, helping us understand past traumas and undigested memories, and thus are *retrospective*. Dreams are *integrative* in that they enable us to perceive and reconcile our many conflicting subpersonalities. They also are *prospective* or anticipatory, icebergs of the future, depicting what is emerging, images of what the individual potentially can become. Looking backward and forward simultaneously, the dream's essential function is always to expand the aperture of consciousness, the circumference of perception, the sphere of identity.

The main dreamwork technique I utilize is a willingness to inquire with open curiosity into the current significance of every character, place, and action in the dream—each of which refers to the dreamer's intrapsychic condition and current life situation. The often humorous and paradoxical messages revealed by dreams jog loose new perceptions. Reflection on the dream's mystery evokes a feeling approaching religious awe; we become filled with amazement at the psyche's capacity to portray its own condition.

In this chapter, I recount some examples of how dreams can influence the therapeutic process, evoking central themes that become the focus of treatment. For example, Bob, a man in his mid-forties, had this simple dream: "I am six years old and I am with my mother. We are cleaning out the closets." I was immediately drawn to the emotional significance of the events in Bob's sixth year and his need to sort through whatever was hidden in the closet. Many family secrets were brought out of hiding in subsequent therapy sessions, and I learned about the domestic violence and alcoholism that were central features in Bob's family environment.

Bob was currently in a deep depression after the breakup of a relationship. As we began to examine his underlying anger and sadness, he reported the following dream: "I am on my hands and knees in front of my bed, potting a cactus plant." The cactus plant, Bob suggested, represented his prickly personality. When asked what the further significance of a cactus might be, he said, "A cactus can live in a desert for a long time with very little water, and it finds its juice within its own body." The cactus thus became a symbol of his need to find sustenance and satisfaction within, rather than turning to women for establishing a sense of self. Bob had to learn to live with and care for himself. When Bob contemplated the image of being on his hands and knees, he felt that it indicated a need for humility.

A simple dream often carries deep emotional meaning, as we can see in the following dream of Jill's: "I am in the store where I work, counting a stack of money, but a bunch of money is missing." Being robbed in the dream reminded Jill of her unhappy childhood. "I never got a chance to be a kid, to be cared for and pampered and loved. I was short-changed and robbed of the joys of being a kid." As we explored this theme, Jill recounted how she had been "parentified," being forced to function as an adult in her family when she was quite young. Through the metaphors of her dream, she began to understand more clearly how much grief and anger she still carried from her lost childhood.

Tanya, a woman in an asexual marriage, dreamed that there was a massive wall between the living room and the bedroom of her home. For her, the wall symbolized her resistance to sexuality and her need to maintain boundaries in order to defend against the possibility of physical and emotional injury. Contemplating this image and sharing it with her partner proved helpful not only to Tanya but also to James, her husband, who was able for the first time to understand the depth of Tanya's fears of intimacy. Dreamwork helped Tanya to recognize how her body had become frozen in fear, creating an impenetrable barrier to any sense of closeness, and it also enabled her to begin the process of dismantling the barriers between her husband and herself.

An ex-priest once dreamed that he entered a cave in which he found an altar, in front of which lay a sleeping wolf. As we explored the dream, he came to see the wolf as a symbol for being alone—a "lone wolf," as he referred to himself—and having to fend for his own survival without the support of the Church. But he also saw in the image of the wolf his long-dormant (sleeping) animal nature, his sexual desire, and his hunger for an embodied, passionate life.

Dreams also provide important insights about the therapeutic relationship. A fifty-year-old woman named Ann, an incest survivor, presented numerous dreams that referred to her feelings toward me as her therapist. In one example, Ann dreamed that she was sitting in the back of a large room filled with people as I gave a lecture. She could not decide whether to stay or leave. We talked about her ambivalence about the therapeutic process: should she stay or flee? Her dream made me reflect on my own style of interaction. Was I, perhaps, being overly intellectual or preachy, lecturing her when she really needed listening and support? In another dream, her therapist unexpectedly disappeared, reflecting her fear that I, and any other man, might abandon her.

Cindy, another incest survivor, shared the following nightmare with me:

My mother was accused of several grisly murders.
Part of her ritual in these killings was taking pictures of

> *the bodies. I was looking through the pictures. I didn't*
> *know the people. Out of the corner of my eye I saw a*
> *poorly exposed photo of a bloody face wearing a football*
> *helmet. I looked at her and said, "Mama, did you do it?"*
> *I shook her. She didn't answer me.*

The grisly murders and bloody faces reflected how Cindy felt: that she had been bludgeoned emotionally as a child. The dream initiated a process in which she was able to talk about her troubled relationship with her mother, one that was filled with buried rage. Cindy had previously explored her relationship with her stepfather—the perpetrator of sexual abuse—but this dream clearly voiced the question, "Mama, did *you* do this?" In other words, What was your role in what happened? This dream brought to the surface the depth of Cindy's feelings of being abandoned, of not being able to trust someone who supposedly loves you and takes care of your needs. With the help of her dream, Cindy could begin to verbalize her core disappointment: "that my mother abandoned me and left me in the hands of this terrible man."

Dreams also can help us understand the complex developmental challenges of a particular stage of life. Here are two dreams of a forty-year-old man who was struggling with a midlife crisis. A longtime student of meditation, Karl yearned to pursue a contemplative lifestyle but felt restricted due to the responsibilities of fatherhood and work. He sought psychotherapy to address his marital and sexual problems and an obsession with pornography.

> *A woman is sitting on the floor meditating. A guy*
> *with a reputation for being inconsiderate of others is*
> *there making a lot of noise. I tell him I'll beat the crap*
> *out of him if he doesn't stop. Teenagers are playing a*
> *sound system really loud, playing CDs of contemporary*
> *teeny-bopper love songs, full of teenage angst. I wonder*
> *how to change this music to make it better for*
> *meditating. Then I crisscross a river and see a shelter*
> *where I find two guys in their early twenties. They look*

worn, as if they've been homeless for many years. Then a group of people in a room discuss how to care for the sick and elderly. They want to help but are afraid of not knowing what to say. They might offend someone or say something taboo. What if they make the person feel worse? What about diaper changes for the dying person, or what if they had to watch the dying person go through something deforming or disabling? Someone presses a button and an electronic Tibetan bowl starts to make a sound. It is meant to relax everyone, to get their minds to quiet down. The sound changes; upper harmonics gradually fade in. The overtones are opening. I go deeply into the sound, which takes me into a deep trance. I lose the sense of the room. As I come out of the trance, the people in the room are still in a quandary about what to do about the dying person. I suggest that they go and simply express their love. I realize I haven't visited my sick uncle in over a month. I feel bad about not visiting and decide to do so as soon as possible. Then I wake up.

When asked about his associations to the various dream figures, Karl replied, "The woman meditating represents my desire for spiritual exploration and inner freedom." Indeed, the dream itself provides a taste of release (the trance state), but it also may reflect a desire to enter altered states to avoid painful feelings.

Karl continued, "The inconsiderate man reminds me of a part of myself that snaps at my kids or wife. It's my temper when I'm reactive and inconsiderate, my way of being demanding of others, coming across as harsh and unpleasant." Here the dream focuses on the integration of Karl's shadow material related to anger. Then Karl noted, "My statement in the dream that I will beat up this man reminds me of how I beat myself up for snapping at others, for wasting time, watching junky TV, staying up late, not getting enough exercise, and not being romantic enough with my wife." We had uncovered a hostile inner critic.

The teenagers in the dream reminded Karl of his twelve-year-old son and his peers, and of the noisy, disruptive quality of adolescents and adolescent culture. Asked about the homeless young men in the dream, Karl said, "They don't want to work hard. They have a degenerate quality I don't like, and it reminds me of the degenerate quality of how I fritter away time looking at pornography on the Internet or watching crappy TV shows." When asked about what part of himself felt worn, Karl replied, "From carrying around my baby girl." Karl and I were now able to identify the pressures and fatigue of parenting (changing diapers) as central themes in his life, quite in contrast to the blissful pursuit of meditative trance and inner journeys.

Karl is feeling the weight of the earth, both in the responsibilities of caring for children and his awareness of the need to care for the dying: "I haven't wanted to deal with the fact that my uncle is going to die soon. And I wonder, is it OK to talk with him about his own death?" As a man in midlife, Karl is both caring for new life and confronting the end of life. In the midst of it all, he is surrounded by teenagers, full of sexual energy and longing. The theme of adolescent sexuality is further addressed in Karl's next dream:

> *I leave a business meeting and go into the bathroom.*
> *I find a* Playboy *magazine and start getting really*
> *excited. Then a woman walks through the room, a*
> *prostitute who is just getting off work. She is holding her*
> *child and is taking him upstairs to go to bed. Another*
> *woman comes in and I pay her $20 to remove her*
> *clothes. I see she has terrible surgical scars on her body*
> *and then I am shocked to see an erect penis. She is, in*
> *fact, male, a transsexual. I am horrified and repulsed.*
> *Then I realize I've been absent from the business*
> *meeting for a while. My wife, Jane, shows up and ushers*
> *me back to the meeting. How will I explain my absence?*
> *Inside the meeting my colleagues are sitting at a great*
> *round table. They are all older, in suits, with gray hair,*
> *and are discussing their need for city planner.*

The dream shows how Karl's pornography obsession had been distracting him from his work. It highlights the conflict between an adolescent type of sexual excitation by pictures and Karl's efforts to love a real woman with a child. When questioned about his feelings toward the prostitute, he said, "I feel compassion for her. She's a hardworking person trying to raise her child on her own. But the fact that she has a child makes me less interested in her sexually." The figure of the prostitute-mother is a symbol of woman as both whore and madonna, a sacred image of unified opposites. Karl quickly makes the connection between this dream image and his ambivalent feelings toward his wife. By facing his feelings through the dream, Karl could begin to feel how deeply he loved and respected his wife and how much he appreciated her as both mother and lover. He also was able to reach a moment of profound honesty and insight: "There are aspects of my sexuality that are not about the emotional connection. Getting off with pictures of Playboy bunnies is more like play; there is no attachment, no pressure to attend to a partner's feelings. I realize that one of the problems I have with our sexual relationship is that I feel like I have to constantly prove that I still love her by being sexual all the time."

Here the image of the transsexual was crucial to my exploration of this dream with Karl. I asked him if he ever felt an aggressive, phallic quality in his wife or her sexuality. Karl replied, "Yes, very much so. I find it totally intimidating. Sometimes it is a turn-on for me when she is sexually aggressive. Other times, it is just too much." Working with this dream helped Karl explore a full range of feelings and perceptions about his wife and their marital relationship.

The older men in Karl's dream symbolize the *senex*, the archetype of age and maturity, which often carries with it a sense of being trapped by responsibilities and obligations. These figures contrast with the dream's *puer* imagery (the archetype of eternal youth) in the bathroom with the magazine. In our discussion, the men sitting at the round table suggested Arthurian knights, which introduced a mythic dimension to Karl's need to accept his role as a mature, stable man, a provider or "city planner"—an image that Karl believed symbolizes his need to plan for his family's future.

These dreams illuminated a number of opposing elements in the psyche that ultimately became unified in Karl's awareness: madonna/whore, mother/lover, young/old, male/female, birth/death. In these potent dream images, Karl discovered material enabling him to embrace a more spiritually meaningful life, one lived in the conscious tension between apparent opposites and in the awareness of how they are eternally intertwined. Dreamwork helped Karl understand some of the complex emotional and interpersonal challenges of his current stage of life, and led to noticeable gains in his capacity to find satisfaction in his work and family relationships.

I have found dreamwork to be an essential tool in my therapeutic work, portraying my clients' central concerns, deepening access to their most emotionally charged material, and leading directly to increased self-awareness and personal integration. Dreams are like a fountain flowing from our inner depths, of inestimable value to psychotherapists and their clients.

19

Creating a Dream Appreciation Group

DEBORAH JAY HILLMAN

IN THE CONTEXT of the current dreamwork movement, we view as grassroots efforts all community-based, nonclinical dream groups organized by and for lay people (in the traditional sense). These run the gamut from informal, leaderless groups that are free to groups offered by the "new" dreamwork professionals, for a fee. Excluding from the "grassroots" designation groups run by clinical professionals does not deny the role some clinicians have played in furthering the grassroots cause.

Among clinical professionals encouraging and inspiring the grassroots movement, Montague Ullman, in particular, stands out. His systematic and popular approach to dreamwork is touched upon here.

GRASSROOTS DREAM APPRECIATION GROUPS

There are so many variations in the structure, composition, settings, goals, and methods of dream groups that it is possible to say, "a dream group is not a dream group is not a dream group."

Composition. Dream groups vary in regard to such factors as size, age and gender make-up, and the nature of members' relationships to each other. The patterning results in varying degrees from both circumstance and design, especially since "groups can come about in a number of different ways. Natural groups can spring up among friends, members of a family, people at work, or even among strangers who find they share a common interest in dreams." And while some groups arise spontaneously or are assembled through personal networks, others develop by means of organized efforts to recruit members. This is done under the auspices of community organizations like churches and schools or simply by advertising in local newsletters and meeting places. In addition, the *Dream Network Bulletin* lists in its classified section both regional dreamworkers' organizations and local dream groups seeking new members.

Dream groups range in size from three or four people to upward of fifteen or twenty. Sometimes they form on the basis of a particular shared core of experience, whatever similarities and differences might characterize their members in other ways. There are artists' dream groups and women's dream groups, for example, and not long ago the *Dream Network Bulletin* advertised a dream group for "12-Step People," meaning those involved in recovery programs modeled after Alcoholics Anonymous.

Some dream groups have a long life and fairly stable membership; others function with a high rate of turnover. Testimony to the former can be found in Jenny Dodd's warm account of the "mothers' dream group" she organized in her suburban community. Originally seven women, they had grown to nine and after four years still managed to meet weekly. In contrast, I talked with a dreamworker who left a group after several sessions because, apart from a common interest in dreams, "there didn't seem to be any other thread."

Settings. Grassroots dream-appreciation groups take place in a variety of settings. Some are held in such community spaces as recreation centers, libraries, churches, and schools; others gather in the workplace. But the most common site for dream-group meetings is in participants' homes. Some groups, like Jenny Dodd's, rotate the role of host; others meet in a single, fixed location. Occasionally groups come together in more ritualistic settings, such as a special tepee designated as a "group dreaming space." Here, members not only relate their dreams to each other, but actually *dream* them together.

Goals. Individual dream groups do not necessarily articulate their goals, apart from "working on," "talking about," "getting in touch with," or simply "sharing" dreams. But a host of reasons for engaging in dreamwork have been expressed by the dreamwork movement, and they exist as motivations within the grassroots sphere.

Broadly speaking, the goal of nonclinical dreamwork is to foster an appreciation of dreams and to make them more available as useful resources for waking life. Differences exist in the ways that sense of appreciation is engendered and in the waking domains to which the dreams are most assiduously applied. Generally, it is the psychological and spiritual dimensions of the dream that receive the greatest attention. For although dreams contain a wealth of social and cultural information, these aspects are rarely explored in dreamwork settings, at least not explicitly.

Along with the more generalized dream-appreciation groups, there are those with a specific focus on a particular aspect of dreaming or way of applying dreams. Some groups, for example, concentrate on the experience of lucid dreaming (a state of consciousness in which the dreamer is aware of dreaming while it is actually occurring). Others are devoted to exploring the purportedly psychic dimension of dreams, and still others to using dream images as inspiration for creative art.

Methods. Two distinct styles of group interaction are found among grassroots dream groups. These are not mutually exclusive, and most groups combine them in some way, though one or the other tends to predominate. The first style can be termed the *study-group* approach. In it, the group serves as a forum for sharing and discussing dreams in a manner that is largely unstructured and conversational. Attention may be given to skills like remembering dreams and keeping a dream journal, as well as to building a repertoire of techniques for both shared and private dreamwork. But while various hands-on methods are usually sampled in the study-group format, it lacks the consistent experiential tone of the second approach.

There, the group members act primarily as catalysts for the dreamer, using techniques to help the latter become more intimate with the shared dream. Groups that have this *experiential* style tend to be more structured, whether they stay with a single, preferred dreamwork method or opt to practice several approaches.

Ullman's *experiential dream group* process epitomizes the second approach. Avoiding specific interpretive theories, it views dream images as metaphors for feelings and assists the dreamer in connecting the imagery with the life situations that gave rise to it. Ullman maintains that dream appreciation "requires work and takes energy." His group process has been carefully designed to enable the necessary work, while preserving the emotional safety of the dreamer.

At the heart of this method is a projective exercise in which the dreamer listens, while the rest of the group imaginatively try to make the dream "their own." By exploring, in this way, the various feelings and metaphors suggested by the dream, they generate a pool of possible meanings to which the dreamer can inwardly respond. Afterwards, the dreamer has a chance to actively reply to the group's projections and then to engage in a kind of focusing dialogue with the group.

A principle underlying Ullman's method, and shared by most dream groups, upholds the exclusive authority of the dreamer when it comes to the meaning of a dream. Accordingly, the various methods are meant to stimulate the dreamer's inner knowledge, rather than to impose understandings from without. Since a hallmark of grassroots dreamwork as a whole is its sheer diversity of method, the full range of techniques cannot be encompassed in a chapter of this size. Unitarian-Universalist minister and dreamworker Jeremy Taylor has a delightfully inclusive attitude in the face of such abundance. He believes that "virtually all of the theories, styles of work, religious beliefs, community dream sharing practices, etc. of various cultures and periods of history have been born out of and are focused on some aspect of the multiple, whole truth about dreams." In his book *Dream Work*, Taylor offers numerous practical hints for working with dreams alone and in groups, encouraging dreamers to unravel the many threads of meaning contained in the tapestry of a dream.

CULTURAL IMPLICATIONS OF DREAM GROUPS

In mainstream American culture, to the extent that it values dreams, the current perspective is a therapy-centered one. It looks to one or another technical theory of dream interpretation and calls on an expert (the therapist) to make interpretive statements about the dream. It views the dream as a form of communication productive of therapeutic insight but does not concern itself with the dream as a resource outside the consulting room. Grassroots dream-appreciation groups share the assumption that dreams have meaning, but they act on the belief that the value of dreams transcends the clinical context. They hold that dreamers themselves can appreciate the significance of their dreams without having to rely on the interpretive guidance of experts. By thus widening the social framework within which we make dreams important, dream groups play a vital role in helping to raise our cultural appraisal of the dream.

Yet the cultural function of dream groups goes beyond their promotion of the value of dreaming and to the kind of social interaction they encourage. This is suggested by the work of Alexander Randall on the effects of dream sharing on group cohesion. Randall studied a group of fifteen people engaged in a month-long residential conference on themes relating to dreams, shamanism, and the work of the American psychic Edgar Cayce. Dream-sharing activities were part of the group's daily routine during the conference, and dreams were the primary focus of discussion. Randall discovered that "not only did the reflective nature of the dreams help to iron out interpersonal differences, but the very act of sharing dreams put the members on a personal level of intimacy.

Dream groups can also help us in the scientific task of learning more about the phenomenology of consciousness. Regular work
with dreams has a tendency to increase one's sophistication as a
dreamer, bringing about a wider experience of the full range of consciousness possible during sleep. Dreaming is not a "unitary phenomenon," as conventional wisdom would have us assume, and
lucid dreaming, out-of-body experiences, and other qualitatively distinct states must be included on our cognitive map. Furthermore,
by learning to value our dreams, and by expanding our knowledge
of dream states, we challenge the narrow cultural focus on the ordinary phenomena of waking.

In addition, dream groups offer an excellent opportunity to
begin exploring the social and cultural dimension of the dream itself.
In one of his more recent contributions to this theme, Ullman says:

> Cultural anthropologists have long viewed dreams as
> useful instruments for studying the mores and value sys-
> tems of exotic cultures. Logically, they should be as use-
> ful in the examination of our own society. Social in origin,
> our dream imagery has an intrinsic bidirectionality that
> points inwardly to the innermost and often hidden aspects
> of our personal being and outwardly to the source of their
> origin and to their possible connection to prevailing social
> realities that otherwise tend to be obscured from view.

An eloquent example of how and why we should attend to this
"social intelligence" of dreams is provided by political scientist John
Wikse. He points out that in a social environment in which dreams
are customarily suppressed, we tend not to be aware of our inner
knowledge of how that environment impinges on our feelings. But
by sharing dreams "in a context in which it is possible to become
reflective about the conditions and circumstances of social life," we
gain access to that liberating intelligence.

Part of the process of tapping the social and cultural dimension
of dreams is using the information to reshape the outmoded myths
and images we find there. Some feminist dreamworkers, for example, in exploring their identities through dreams, have sought to transform Jungian archetypal imagery along less gender-stereotyped lines.

As psychologists David Feinstein and Stanley Krippner point out in their book *Personal Mythology*, "gaining a measure of autonomy from the limiting mythic images of your culture and from other early influences increases your psychological freedom and strengthens your ability to cope with a rapidly changing world."

In the broadest sense, dreamwork has the capacity to help heal the collective wounds resulting from our social dividedness. Jeremy Taylor writes passionately about this transformative potential:

> As a community organizer I realized that dream work could bring people together across all the barriers of race, age, sex, class, et al. to join in the work of changing society. I came to understand that dream work has the potential to be deeply "radical," not only in the original sense of *radix*, getting to the "root" of things, but also in the political and social sense of dramatic transformation of collective fears, opinions, attitudes, and behaviors.

Finally, just as the therapy process is a common dream theme for those who are engaged in it, so is the dream-group experience often depicted in the dream lives of its participants. As with other aspects of the social world, we can learn more about the role of dream groups if we begin examining our collective imagery about them. I can offer a small start by reporting one of my own dreams, which occurred when I was regularly involved in experiential dream-group work.

Our group met weekly in the living room of a Manhattan apartment, where there was a nice, but very undistinguished, carpet. Yet one night I dreamed that marking the area where we assembled was an Oriental rug of extraordinary subtlety and richness. While the transformative nature of this image speaks to my personal experience of dreamwork, it points to a larger meaning, as well. For as Taylor suggests, dream groups have a role in helping to enrich and repair the complex social fabric weaving us together.

PART 3

Understanding
Dreams

Caesar:

Calpurnia here, my wife, stays me at home:
She dreamt to-night she saw my statue,
Which, like a fountain with an hundred spouts,
Did run pure blood: and many lusty Romans
Came smiling, and did bathe their hands in it:
And these does she apply for warnings, and portents,
And evils imminent; and on her knee
Hath begg'd that I will stay at home to-day.

Decius Brutus:

This dream is all amiss interpreted;
It was a vision fair and fortunate:
Your statue spouting blood in many pipes,
In which so many smiling Romans bathed,
Signifies that from you great Rome shall suck
Reviving blood, and that great men shall press
For tinctures, stains, relics and cognizance.
This by Calpurnia's dream is signified.

William Shakespeare,
Julius Caesar

20

Dreams, the Dreamer, and Society

MONTAGUE ULLMAN

MANY, IF NOT most, people have a natural curiosity about their dreams. However, there are very few resources at hand to help them pursue this interest in a serious way. Dreams have a low priority in our society (in all civilized societies) and, as a consequence, little or no attempt is made to encourage their pursuit or to provide the necessary means to do so. The only socially sanctioned arrangement available is to seek a professional who, for a fee, will offer the help necessary to interpret the dream. In this respect, we have not advanced much from the way dreams were handled in ancient times. The skills and prerogatives around dreamwork continue to be vested in a small group of people who are acknowledged as experts by virtue of their specialized knowledge. The question I wish to explore is whether the skills necessary for dreamwork can and should be shared with the public at large. Can we transform dreamwork from a therapeutically valuable operation in the hands of specialists to a universally accessible experience that is available to anyone who wishes to take the time and trouble to learn how to go about it?

In recent years, many books have appeared for the general public which address this issue. They speak of the benefits to be gained by working with dreams and offer several approaches to them. My own work emphasizes the skills necessary for dreamwork and the importance of a small group as the optimal supportive and helping agency. I will present what I consider the basic information that is needed if serious dreamwork is contemplated and a description of how I structure a small group setting to meet the needs of the dreamer. Finally, I will explore dream images in a larger social frame of reference, seeing them as pointers not only to personal issues but to related social issues as well.

In our society we grow up rather ignorant about the nature of our dream life. This is unfortunate because it leaves us without any understanding of a language we have been speaking all our lives and, therefore, without the means to connect to our dream life. We fail to introduce dreamwork into the family system, the educational system, or any natural system. For the most part, we come together only as adults to find a way to work with dreams. Much learning has to take place before we are ready to proceed.

The new recruit to dreamwork needs several different kinds of information, namely, clarity about the distinction between dreaming and what we call the dream, a grasp of those qualities of dreaming that make the dream a significant event in our lives, an understanding of the dreamer's predicament, the kind of help the dreamer needs, and the way that help can be provided.

DREAMING AND THE DREAM

Dreaming and the dream refer to two different, though closely related, events. Dreaming is an intrinsic part of the sleep cycle that recurs every ninety minutes during sleep and is associated with distinct psychological changes that signify a state of arousal. The dream is a remembrance in the waking state of whatever we can bring back from the previous night's dreaming episodes. The two are not the same. The dream originates in the dreaming experience, but it is that experience transformed into the waking mode of expression. These two modes of consciousness resort to different languages to say different things about the same organism. In order to understand the dream, we must begin with an understanding of the way in which the two languages differ and what it is we are saying when we use dream language.

Our Two Languages

Waking language appears to have evolved as a way of speaking to each other about the world and the way we experience ourselves in that world. The world is broken down into manageable and agreed-upon categories which can then be communicated through a structured grammar that conveys the way our experiences are organized in space and time in a logical manner. Language is a way of categorizing reality to be able to talk about our experiences.

But our needs go beyond what can be transmitted in this fashion through language. We seem to need a more direct way of encountering and expressing the impact upon us of the world in which we live. We need a more effective language for the expression of feelings. In waking life we resort to the arts, music and poetry. While asleep and dreaming, a pictorial, figurative language takes over and reflects our feelings. This dream language has much in common with poetry in that both rely on metaphor for their expressive effect. There are, however, at least three significant differences in the way the poet and the dreamer use metaphor. The poet rearranges words to create the metaphorical quality he or she needs to best convey the feelings he or she wishes to communicate to others. The dreamer shapes images into metaphorical statements. The poet addresses an audience outside himself or herself. The dream is a private message to oneself. Finally, writing poetry is a task of greater or lesser difficulty. Dreaming and the creation of visual metaphors is something that *happens* to us through no deliberate or volitional effort on our part.

The neophyte in dreamwork has to learn to look at these images not as photographic reproductions of reality but as metaphorical ways of conveying the nature of the predicament felt by the dreamer. We have adapted what, in all likelihood, is a primitive imaging capacity that we probably share with animals lower on the evolutionary scale, and we use this as an instrument for symbolic rather than literal expression. Our sleeping self is concerned with managing certain residual feelings. Metaphorical imagery is a most suitable symbolic vehicle for containing and conveying feelings. A person who pictures himself or herself in a dream driving down a steep hill and having the brakes suddenly fail will experience the sensation of being in an uncontrollably dangerous situation far more powerfully than ordinary language could convey. In the dream we are part of the metaphor we ourselves are creating, a fact that places us in an immediate relationship to the feelings being generated. We are the actors, not the reporters, of the scene taking place. There is no way out except through terminating the dream either by generating feelings strong enough to awaken us or by somehow resolving the issue so there is a natural passage back into dreamless sleep. The concept of the visual metaphor is basic to dreamwork, and its importance cannot be overly stressed. We are more like poets than scientists when we sleep. We express our personal poetry in a language we have been using since childhood, yet this language continues to feel strange and unfamiliar to us as adults. To understand this fully we must also take into account the content of our dreams, what is being expressed through this language.

Dream Content

When we use this pictorial language what are we saying that makes the remembered dream so potentially illuminating when awake? Our imaging capacity provides the form that our consciousness takes, but where does the content come from?

As we fall asleep we close off our input channels. No new information is coming in, so whatever we become conscious of during this period of dreaming has its origin some time before falling asleep. Freud spoke of the "day residue" as the starting point of the dream.

Some recent event sets up a lingering tension that surfaces at the onset of a dreaming period and acts as a shaping influence on the content to be developed. What gives this recent residual feeling its extraordinary power lies in the fact that, regardless of how trivial or insignificant it may seem at the time, it connects with unresolved issues from the past. It touches on vulnerable areas still being worked over. We are unaware of this connection when awake, but when we are asleep, it comes clearly into view. The first important point, then, is that the dream starts in the present. The issue it addresses derives from our past but continues to be of some importance for us in the present.

What we do with this residue while dreaming is quite extraordinary when judged by waking standards. We seem able to do many things at once. We scan our entire life history for events and experiences that are emotionally related to it; we explore our past ways of coping with whatever vulnerable areas may have been exposed; we mobilize the resources at our disposal and try to come to some resolution. In short, while dreaming we are reassessing the significance of recent events in the context of our past. In a rather clever way we express it all through pictorial metaphors that highlight the feelings evoked in the course of this self-exploratory adventure. And it is all done effortlessly and seemingly instantaneously. We have brought a current residue into a relationship with past residues. In so doing we bring together important information relevant to what we are struggling with now. The range and extent of that information is not easily available to us in the waking state. If aspects of it are available, they are not readily seen in relation to the current issue. This is the second significant feature of our dream life that contributes to its value as a potentially healing instrument.

This brings us to the most important quality of our dream life, particularly in its relation to the question of healing. We are alone when we sleep and dream, perhaps more alone than at any other time in our life. We have temporarily disconnected from the world around us. We have temporarily suspended our social roles and our social façades. We no longer are in need of our social defenses, those various ways of protecting ourselves from truths we cannot or do not

wish to see. In the act of going to sleep we undress not only physically but psychically as well. When our brain gets the signal to start
dreaming we are emotionally nude.

What happens next is best described by analogy. There is a
magical mirror in this place where we find ourselves. It is a mirror
capable of reflecting a profoundly honest picture of who we are
rather than who we would like to think we are or who we would like
others to think we are. Another bit of magic in this mirror is that
only the dreamer can use it. No one else can look into it. Being alone
and confronted with a mirror that provides a private view, the
dreamer risks looking into it himself. The view reflected back is the
view rendered by the imagery of the dream. It is a view without pre-
tense. It is the truth. In a sense it is a privileged portrait of intrinsic
value to the dreamer in search of a more honest self-concept. For
the most part, our dreams are not understood or appreciated in their
individual and social significance, and we are largely unaware of the
personal and social choices and opportunities offered through our
dream life. Once we are awake, there is an overwhelming tendency
to slip back into a familiar character structure and behavioral pattern. At a social level the dream is also of dubious value to the
dreamer who is concerned more with fitting *in* than with whatever
he or she is fitting *into*.

It is much easier to adapt to the social blinders we have grown
up with and are accustomed to than to challenge and reevaluate
them in terms of the social truths they may be hiding from us. Both
the individual and society are the losers.

21

A Brief History of Dreams

PHYLLIS R. KOCH-SHERAS AND AMY LEMLEY

THROUGHOUT THE world, dreams have been seen as an integral part of life, and their contents were akin to the sacred. Whether sent from a god, a demon, or an ancestor, or merely an expression of a wish or a fear, dreams were believed to contain a mystery worth deciphering.

What were these nocturnal adventures, and what might early humans have thought about them? We can only imagine. But one thing is clear: At least from the dawn of recorded history, people were compelled to interpret the meaning of the stories and images in their dreams. In fact, in centuries past, societies invested dreams with even more power and importance than the experiences of their waking lives. In ancient Greece and Rome, for example, dream interpreters actually accompanied military leaders into battle, so essential was the understanding of dream content. Over time, the Christian belief that dreams were the work of the devil influenced Western culture to such an extent that dream interpretation was discouraged, perhaps out of a fear that the content of dreams could undermine the moral teachings of the Church. But dream interpretation continues today, and while the focus has largely shifted from decoding a divine message sent by a deity to uncovering a meaning anchored in the dreamer's own psyche, the tendency to look for meaning remains, as it has for thousands and thousands of years, possibly from the beginning of time. Delving into the past to learn the history of dreamwork allows us to derive a cultural context for our own dream lives today. Just as tracing our family history builds stronger bonds with our relatives, tracing the history of dreamwork can enrich our lives as dreamers, making a connection with the past and forging a bond with our world community.

ANCIENT CULTURES

From the earliest days of written language, dreams and dream theories have been documented extensively. Sumerian texts, inscribed with sticks on clay tablets in 3000 to 4000 B.C., describe this Mesopotamian people's practice of dream interpretation, and indicate that dreams were believed to be messages from the gods. Dream reports in these now-fragmented texts seem to follow a particular format, experts report, that is not unlike the common guidelines for a dream journal today. Not only is the dream recounted, but background details about the dreamer are included as well, including where and when the dream took place, how the dreamer felt about the dream, and what message he or she derived from it.

The field of dream study originated in a religious context. In ancient Egypt, the dream interpreters were priests known as "masters of the secret things," who documented their findings in hieroglyphics, their picture alphabet. One such volume exists as part of an archeological discovery known as the Chester Beatty papyrus, an early dream interpretation book that is more than two thousand years old.

In many ancient cultures, priests and seers who had a talent for interpreting dreams were considered to be divinely gifted. A person who had a particularly significant dream was also believed to be blessed, and only certain people were considered worthy of such dreams. Artemidorus, author of the *Oneirocritica*, a five-volume book on the dream interpretation practiced by his Greco-Roman contemporaries, wrote in the second century A.D. that "Dreams are proportioned according to the party dreaming. Thus those of eminent persons will be great . . . if poor, their dreams will be very inconsiderable." (The *Oneirocritica* takes its name from Oneiros, a Greek dream messenger sent by the gods.)

In the *Oneirocritica*, Artemidorus refers to an already extensive body of literature on the subject of dreams. In the days of the Greek epic poet Homer (eighth century A.D.), "The dream was not conceived of as an internal experience, a state of mind, or a message from the irrational unconscious to the conscious ego," Susan Parman writes in *Dreams and Culture*. "Rather, it was an objectified messenger, a supernatural agent sent by a deity (Zeus in *The Iliad*, Athena in *The Odyssey*), or in some cases by the dead." Later, she explains, ancient Greek authors such as Plato, Horace, Virgil, Statius, and Lucian embraced the concept of "true and false dreams," some prophetic, and some red herrings.

In ancient times, dreams were often — but not always — believed to be prophetic, and people of all cultures shared what they had dreamed in hopes of catching a glimpse of the future or receiving a message of advice or warning. The Egyptians, for instance, relied on an elaborately constructed list of interpretations, a kind of early dream dictionary. Author Raymond de Becker cites a few of these in his book *The Understanding of Dreams*: "If a woman kisses her husband, she will have trouble; if she gives birth to a cat, she will have many children; if she gives birth to an ass, she will have an idiot child." The ancient Carthaginian philosopher Tertullian said, "Nearly everyone knows that God reveals himself to people most often in dreams." For this reason, dreams figured prominently in ancient cultures' religious rituals intended to evoke the dream spirits or gods who would send these vivid messages. Even the ancient Greek philosopher Socrates considered dreams to be prophetic, emanating from the gods.

In Buddhist culture, as in Taoism, Hinduism, and Sufism, the specifics of dreamwork were kept secret, considered to be sacred. In fact, there is a particular type of dream called *Milam Ter,* or "dream treasure," which, according to Michael Katz, editor of *Dream Yoga,* are "teachings that are considered to be the creations of enlightened beings. The training for dream awareness or lucidity, apparently thousands of years old, was purposefully hidden or stored in order to benefit future generations." Again, there was a decidedly prophetic overtone to this class of dreams. For instance, the mother of Buddha, Queen Maya, supposedly dreamed that a white elephant with six tusks entered her womb and foretold that she would give birth to a child who would become a universal monarch. Buddha's father is also reported to have had a dream about his son and the sadness of their future separation. In the sixth century, the mother of Prince Shotokutaishi, who established Buddhism in Japan, dreamed just before she became pregnant that a god came to her asking to take shelter in her womb.

The Old Testament, written between about 750 and 100 B.C. according to the *Dictionary of the Bible,* contains about fifteen references to dreams, which the Hebrew people considered to be gifts from God, just like waking visions that occur frequently in Scripture. The folk art toy called Jacob's Ladder is, in fact, named for an element in a dream recounted in the Bible: Jacob dreamed that a ladder connected earth to heaven, and that God stood at the top, instructing him and his family to spread God's word. This dream illustrates the phenomenon of *theophany,* the direct and powerful experience of God through a dream, vision, or other spiritual event. Ancient Jews turned frequently to their dreams for such messages. In fact, Joseph, Jacob's son, achieved notoriety by interpreting the dreams of the Egyptian pharaoh. Apart from a belief in dreams as gifts from God, there was also an element of belief in soul travel. The idea of recent waking experience and even the sleeping environment having an influence on dream content was another part of the framework. Remarkably, even these ancient people made a practice of expunging or changing dreams that were upsetting to them.

The Talmud, the collected commentary on biblical text that, along with the Old Testament, is part of the foundation of the Jewish religion, also mentions the use of dreams to predict the future, citing the potential of dreams to influence the decisions of kings and governments. Compiled between 200 B.C. and 300 A.D., the Talmud discusses the purpose of dreams extensively, containing 217 references to dreams. The Talmud purports that dreams have meaning subject to interpretation and serving as a notable precursor to some contemporary theories. Its two thousand authors were primarily Phoenician (Hebrew) and Babylonian, and it assumed they were influenced greatly by the nearby cultures of Greece and Rome, which in turn would be influenced by the Talmud. There were two different schools of thought expressed in this document: that dreams come from higher powers, and that dreams are generated by the psyche, perhaps as opposing forces of the mind. Interestingly, the Talmud also contains references to dreams as wish fulfillment, which is how Sigmund Freud would later characterize all dream content.

The New Testament, written between 75 and 400 A.D., also includes countless references to dreams. Well known to many Christians is the biblical account of St. Joseph's dream revealing Mary's immaculate conception to him. Another dream from the New Testament instructs the Eastern Magi not to reveal the whereabouts of Jesus to King Herod. The interpretations have evolved over time. In Christianity's early days, for example, dreams were thought to be the work of God, designed to offer messages for both the dreamer and those to whom he reported the dream. Synesius of Cyrene, an early Christian bishop who wrote a book entitled *On Dreams*, found dreams to be of immeasurable inspiration and significance. Synesius saw dreams as a state in which the mind could work unfettered by the conventions dreamers adhered to in their waking lives, and therefore considered dreams to hold the power of transforming the dreamer by offering new insights and talents. This belief, dating to the writings of this fifth-century religious leader, evidences itself today in the current dreamwork movement.

In the fifth century, St. Jerome substituted the phrase *observing dreams* for the term *witchcraft* in his translation of the Bible from Greek and Hebrew, leading to the dogmatic statement, "You will not practice soothsaying or observe dreams." (The word *witchcraft* is used correctly elsewhere in the translation, so this appears to be a deliberate use of the term.) For the next fifteen centuries, the Roman Catholic church had a negative attitude toward dreamwork of any kind.

Dreams were in large part discounted as fanciful nonsense, perhaps because the nightly wanderings of an unchecked mind allowed for visions and experiences that sometimes went against religious dogma. In time, while some Western Christians continued to see dreams as divine gifts, others came to believe they were the work of demons. Perhaps most prominent was the thirteenth-century priest St. Thomas Aquinas, whose writings remain influential today, particularly in the Catholic church. Aquinas attempted to discount the possibility that dreams had special meaning, and attributed them to three different causes: waking experiences, physical sensations, and the work of God or demons. While he did not believe it was sinful to interpret the first two types of dreams, as earlier Christians had held, he did consider it "unlawful and superstitious" to derive meaning from dreams sent by demons.

The prophet Muhammad (570–632 A.D.), the Arabian founder of Islam to whom Moslems believe the Koran was dictated by God, considered dreams to have vital significance, and to have some bearing on the matters of waking life. He would inquire of his disciples every morning what their dreams were, discuss their interpretations, offer his own, and then recount his own dreams. According to Nathaniel Bland, writing in *The New World of Dreams*, "By [one] dream attributed to him, the Sunnis justify the still-disputed rights of his three successors; and the origin of a strife, political and religious, which convulsed the whole Muhammaden empire and threatened its destruction, which still divides the followers of Islam by a schismatic and irreconcilable hatred, is founded on a revelation made to its founder Muhammad in his sleep." Some of the followers of Muhammad question whether his revelations occurred in dreams, arguing that such a highly evolved mind would not have a dividing line between the "conscious" and "unconscious."

Whatever the case, the attitude of the prophet Muhammad toward dreams had ramifications that reached beyond his own experiences to affect centuries of cultural and religious conduct. For example, a dream by one of his followers, Abdullah ben Zayd, led to the Islamic call to prayer for the faithful that is still used today. It was during Muhammad's lifetime that dream interpretation was elevated to a science, called *Ibn ul Tabir*. Dream books called *Tabir Namehs*, which commented on sleep and dreams, offered specific guidelines for their interpretation. Writes Bland: "*Tabir* is set forth as being a noble science, first taught by God himself to Adam, from Adam passing to Seth, and from Seth to Noah, by whom the Deluge was foretold in his explanation of dreams to Canaan's mother."

Ancient Arab dream practices proved to be a fascinating precursor to contemporary dreamwork. Their custom held that in order "to get a clear vision of what is happening or what will befall you in this life, you should do certain things before going to bed," writes Yehia Gouda, author of *Dreams and Their Meanings in the Old Arab Tradition*. Rituals such as this one for bedtime—which involves careful bodily cleansing, sleeping in a certain position, speaking a prayer of meditation, and fasting—are common in many cultures around the globe, and are quite similar to some modern dream practices described in chapter 6. Ancient Arabian dream interpreters, held in high esteem, followed certain rules in offering interpretations. According to Gouda, they believed the ideal time for recounting or interpreting a dream "is the early morning, when the dreamer's memory and the interpreter's mind are still fresh, before both of them get entangled in the worries and necessities of everyday life." Dream interpreters gave credit where they thought credit was due, to the dreamer him- or herself: "The best interpretation is that given by the dreamer himself, even if he knows nothing about the science or conventional symbols of dreams, for people have their own concepts and codes." And they acknowledged that dream symbolism could vary from one dreamer to the next: "The same dream experienced by two different persons could have two different meanings, depending on each person's nature and character," Gouda continues.

The ancient Arab ideas are strikingly similar to those expressed by contemporary Western dreamworkers and many psychotherapists. But they were in fact "the synthesis of at least four or five introductions I read in Arabic," Gouda explains. "The marvelous things about the Arabs of ancient times is that they understood very well that dreams belonged to the realm of absolute freedom. To them nothing was taboo."

Indeed, since history's earliest days, dreams have influenced not only religious belief and conduct but the decisions of leaders in politics and battle, the choices of individuals in personal crisis, and the actions of medical professionals in treating illness. It is common in our culture for people to experience healing dreams, which contain some kind of message that speaks to the health concern of the dreamer; a dream of loose teeth, for instance, might lead to a necessary trip to the dentist. In some ancient cultures, dreams were considered a vital clue to the health of the dreamer. In ancient Greece, for example, physicians used the information contained in dreams to make a diagnosis. Sometimes, a doctor would turn to his own dreams for help in treating a patient. For example, Galen, a well-know surgeon of second-century Greece, would seek instruction from his dreams, relying almost solely on this guidance to perform operations. People would visit temples and other holy places for the specific purpose of having a dream experience that could aid in healing them. Aesclepius, a skilled physician living in eleventh-century Greece, came to be regarded as a god for his power as a healer. He was often represented by a snake, so dreamers would sometimes seek out a place to sleep and dream where snakes were known to live. Aesclepius would listen to the words of his dreaming patients in order to devise a cure. And legend has it that even after his death there were hundreds of sleeping temples dedicated to him where the ill and infirm could go to dream their own cures.

In many ancient cultures, dream life and waking life were simply two different dimensions of a single existence, a viewpoint that shows itself in many modern cultures and that is shared by many contemporary dream theorists as well. For the ancient Egyptians, the world of dreams was indeed an actual place they visited when their souls left their bodies to travel freely during sleep. The Talmud, too, refers to these soul travels, but suggests that the world the soul visits is not a different world from the one the dreamer inhabits in waking life.

Another ancient topic of dreams is sexual content, which received notice in all cultures long before Sigmund Freud's theories of sexuality gained prominence. In numerous cultures, a sexual dream indicated visitation from a sexual demon, the *incubus* and *secubus* of Greek legend. Like the mythical Greek faun, the Talmud's erotic demon is hairy and goatlike. Lilith is another erotic demon of Talmudic origin; taking on either a masculine or feminine form, she attacks only people sleeping alone in a house. This character is essentially the same as *incubus/secubus*, perhaps not surprising given the influence of Greco-Roman belief on the writings of this ancient document.

In ancient China, writes psychologist Robert Van de Castle in *Our Dreaming Mind*, dreams were believed to be "nighttime excursions to the land of the dead," embarked upon by the soul, or *p'o*, which could separate from the body during sleep in order to make these visits. Almost a thousand years ago, a Chinese mathematician wrote a document entitled *Chou Kung's Book of Auspicious and Inauspicious Dreams*, which categorizes dreams and offers interpretations that today sound rather like fortune cookie pronouncements. If you dream that you witness the flight of a swallow, for instance, "a friend will come to visit you from far away." Dream rituals pervaded ancient Chinese culture. Like the people of ancient Greece, the Chinese would habitually visit temples, sleep on graves, or perform rituals so as to incubate their dreams, looking for answers that might lead them to a course of action. Indeed, dreams were held in such high esteem that political officials routinely sought guidance from their dreams, which they then shared with their colleagues. Interestingly, Van de Castle also points out, this culture's ancient beliefs about the dream state still resonate today: Because the ancient Chinese believed a soul could fail to return to the body if the dreamer were suddenly awakened, some Chinese people today are quite wary of alarm clocks.

In ancient India, as in so many other ancient cultures, dreams have received much attention in sacred writings over the centuries. Hindu tradition, in fact, holds that all phenomenal existence is the dream of God or Vishnu. Many sacred paintings show a sleeping Vishnu with a cord from his navel becoming a beautiful lotus flower. The belief is that everything emanates from the mind of God and that we are a part of that image, dreaming our own worlds into existence and eliminating them upon awakening into consciousness. As always, people were inclined to translate dreams, identifying certain dream symbols as omens of good or bad things to come. Curiously, the Vedas, the sacred books of ancient India that were written as long ago as 1500 B.C., contain references to different periods of sleep which Western researchers did not identify scientifically until the mid-twentieth century! Briefly, these periods of sleep were established as a measure of how soon after the dream its prophecy would come true. Indian dream texts also suggest that a dreamer who remembers several dreams upon waking should interpret the final dream. This belief is remarkably like that of modern dream interpreters, who refer to the dream remembered upon awakening as most likely the last dream dreamed and the one most closely connected with waking experience.

CONTEMPORARY NON-WESTERN CULTURES

Dreams continue to be held in high esteem in cultures outside Western culture. There are still dreamers throughout the world who accept their dreams' gifts, heed their dreams' warnings, and seek out their dreams' adventures as a regular part of their cultural life. In many cultures today, among them New Guinea's Arapesh, Mexico's Tarahumara, and several Native American tribes, dreams serve as an alternate dimension to waking life, with knowledge to be gained from the experiences that unfold each night. Like some ancient cultures, Australia's Aborigines, the continent's native hunters and gatherers, today maintain their belief that the dreamworld is an actual place, a spiritual dimension they call "Dreamtime"; it is here that they look to connect with their ancestors, whom they call "Dreamings." These ancestral beings are considered to be more powerful than living people and to have nonhuman manifestations such as rocks or trees. Rather than creating the dreams, like a god or demon would, these ancestors merely live in dreams, and it is to dreams that the living must travel in order to make contact. One way in which contact is useful is in the creation of art: Songs, stories, and artwork inspired by dreams are considered to be the gifts of the ancestors, channeled through the dreamer, who is merely the vehicle of reproduction for the ancestor's original creation. These traditions continue among the Aborigines today, echoing the ancient practice in many cultures of creating song, dance, painting, sculpture, and household objects based on dream content.

Other twentieth-century cultures, too, have chosen to incorporate dreams into daily life as a matter of course, often with remarkable results. In the 1930s, archeologist Kilton Stewart traveled deep into the mountains of what is now Malaysia to study the Senoi, a minority tribe of 12,000 people who he said appeared at that time to live in extraordinary harmony, with very little fighting, stealing, anger, upset, or mental illness. In search of an explanation, Stewart came to regard their intense dreamwork activity as the reason for their peaceful existence. Although it is unclear how many of the Senoi people participate in these dream practices, his reports are still fascinating and useful for dreamers today.

According to Stewart, the Senoi believed the dreamworld to be just as real as the waking world, however different. They believed the conflicts they experienced in waking life found expression in their dreams. By talking about these dreams, Stewart suggested, the conflicts were put to rest, rather than causing the dreamer to take some physical action that could result in strife. Unlike most Westerners, who are at times embarrassed by their dream content, the Senoi saw nothing wrong with dreams, instead viewing even incestuous dreams as merely "facets of one's own spiritual or psychic makeup." Interestingly, the beliefs of these isolated Malaysian forest dwellers are strikingly similar to some contemporary dream theories put forward by Western dreamworkers, especially the idea that every person, place, and thing in a dream is in fact representative of a part of the dreamer.

From childhood, Stewart reported, Senoi children learned to participate actively in their dreams, confronting danger, interacting with even the most sinister dream characters, and gathering "gifts" of insight and information that they can bring back with them to their waking world. Being aware of a dream while in the dream (an experience called lucid dreaming) enables the dreamer to make decisions and take actions that influence the dream's outcome and,

therefore, its usefulness in waking life. It is a rare skill among Western dreamers, but Stewart reported that Senoi children were encouraged to perfect it from the time they could first recount their dreams.
Each morning, the Senoi gathered for dream sharing, looking to the
content of the tribe's dreams for all kinds of information, from where
to hunt that day to what songs and dances to add to their rituals.

Interestingly, Stewart's findings were later disputed. Although
Senoi dreamwork was found to occur, Stewart apparently exagger-
ated the extent of it, as well as the Senoi's resulting peacefulness.
There were in fact occasional incidences of discord, violence, and
mental illness in Senoi life. (One anthropologist, who went to live
among the Senoi in the 1930s, learned this the hard way: When H.
D. "Pat" Noone forbade his Senoi wife to sleep with Noone's adopted
Senoi brother, the brother shot him to death with a blowpipe.) Soci-
ologist G. William Domhoff sought to determine the truth about
Stewart's much-disputed claims in his 1985 book *The Mystique of
Dreams: A Search for Utopia Through Senoi Dream Theory*.
Domhoff concludes that Kilton Stewart's "preoccupation [with] the
major social problems that faced the civilized world" led him to
ascribe to Senoi dream traditions a kind of healing power that could
solve the problems of violence and mental illness. "His desire to be
a great healer and prophet led him to imbue his dream principles
with the mystique of the nonviolent and easygoing Senoi," writes
Domhoff. "It was Kilton Stewart who developed the novel idea that
societies can benefit from sharing their dreams and that they can
shape them through . . . mind control."

Exposure to dominant peoples and the amenities of modern
life has irrevocably changed the Senoi way of life. Nonetheless, Kilton Stewart's theories are worth noting, if only because Senoi dream
theory has enjoyed popularity among Western dreamworkers and
dream researchers for several generations. Times have changed,
even for the Senoi, and their once idyllic life has lost its innocence
as the twentieth century has invaded their culture. Yet while some
of Stewart's claims have been questioned, it is still interesting to consider the effect regular dreamwork can have on individuals and an
entire culture.

On the African continent, there are many variations in the way different tribal peoples view dreams and dreamwork. Some look to dreams for their healing power, others might look for divine messages, and still others rely on dreams to guide their artistic creation. Among Zezuru healers in Zimbabwe, for example, dreams are said to be the source of all training on the medicinal use of plants, and also serve as a diagnostic tool, according to the University of Zimbabwe's Pamela Reynolds, who worked with sixty traditional healers of the region. And for all Zezuru people, dreams hold special interpretive possibilities that can shape waking experiences. She writes, "Zulu believe that without dreams, true and uninterrupted living is not possible. Zezuru believe the same: dreamless nights are said to be unhealthy."

The Temne of Sierra Leone, too, look to dreams for divine training. "Among the Temne, the vision and knowledge of diviners are largely attributed to accomplishment in dreaming, through which they become experts on the dreams of their clients. Not only, then, do their dreams have power; they have power over other people's dreams," writes Rosalind Shaw, coeditor of *Dreaming, Religion, and Society in Africa*. This same volume includes an essay by Roy M. Dilley of the University of St. Andrews about the Tukolor, who believe dreams are associated with spiritual agents, and that in dreams the soul is allowed to roam free. To the Tukolor, some dreams are utter nonsense, others are meaningless entertainment, and still others are incubated to reveal new techniques they can use in their traditional weavings. Africa is a massive continent, and it is not surprising that dream beliefs vary from culture to culture. And, contrary to the stereotypes that are associated with native peoples, not all African tribes invest dreams with special significance. The Berti, for instance, "are not encouraged to dream and to remember their dreams," according to Ladislav Holy, also of the University of St. Andrews. In fact, they rarely tell their dreams to others, and claim not to dream very often at all, despite the biological evidence Western researchers have gathered showing that all people (and mammals) dream every night.

Like many societies on the African continent, the Native American tribes of North America have traditionally looked to dreams for healing, which they believe is often symbolized by the appearance of an animal or bird. Despite vastly diverse cultures among the few thousand Native American tribes who populated this continent when the Europeans first landed, every tribe placed a great deal of importance on dream life. Contacting supernatural spirits and borrowing from their power was common in all of these cultures. A dream interpreter, like a medicine man, had special status in the tribe, and was consulted regularly. Rituals designed to filter bad dreams and attract good ones incorporated the use of a dream catcher, a small, hand-crafted net that is decorated with symbolic objects such as feathers and beads.

The seventeenth- and eighteenth-century Iroquois tribe held that dreams shed light on human nature and could also provide insight and guidance, according to Susan Parman, author of *Dream and Culture*. Parman writes: "The Iroquois took their dreams very seriously, and interpreted them as the wishes of supernatural beings, or as enactments of personal fate they were destined to fulfill." The dream as destiny is a theme that surfaces in other Native American cultures as well. . . .

Whereas some cultures embraced dream life as an important dimension, worthy of interpretation and exploration, Western Christian culture emphasized only the most literal or transparently symbolic interpretations, so threatened was that culture by the possibility that dream content might undermine the morality being handed down by the Church. Despite numerous biblical references to dream interpretation, the practice was discouraged as frivolous, if not dangerous, perhaps partly influenced by the early Christian belief that dreams were sent by the devil. Philosopher Jeremy Taylor, writing in 1650, warned readers to pay dreams no mind: "If you suffer impressions to be made upon you by dreams, the devil hath the reins in his own hands, and can tempt you by that, which will abuse you, when you can make no resistance."

22

Dreams for Personal and Spiritual Growth

LOUIS M. SAVARY

FROM EARLIEST recorded history, people have observed their dreams and found in them a source of meaning, wisdom, and guidance. Through the centuries, the dream was presumed to be a spiritual event, a gift of God or a gift from some source beyond the ordinary. And, in all major religions and most minor ones, of both East and West, dreamwork was an accepted spiritual practice. In many religious and spiritual traditions—from the most primitive to the most civilized cultures—the dream was viewed as a holistic event, an experience reflecting the wholeness of the individual. Sometimes, as in biblical and shamanic traditions, the dream was viewed as benefitting not only the individual dreamer, but also the entire community to which the dream belonged.

In contrast, among Christians the practice of dreamwork has been discouraged for the past centuries by the official Church, probably because, in the Church's eyes, dream interpretation has turned from a spiritual activity into a superstitious one. By the fifth century, it seemed many Christians were no longer using dreamwork to develop their moral and spiritual growth, but rather to predict their fortunes and further their material goals. As one person put it, "Many Christians were no longer interested in the God-life, but only in the 'good' life." Even so, dreamwork continued to be practiced throughout those centuries by holy Christian men and women, many of whom were canonized as saints by the Roman Catholic Church. Now, in the present generation, the practice of dreamwork is again finding a place in Christian spirituality as it had throughout the first five centuries of the nascent Christian Church.

SPIRITUALITY AND CONSCIOUSNESS

I define spirituality as "a way of being, acting in light of ultimate values." According to this definition, all persons, by virtue of their nature as spiritual, value-seeking beings, have a potential spirituality. Their ultimate values may be conscious or outside of awareness, healthy or destructive. In turn, the spirituality that is built upon those values may be clear or confused, simple or complex. Part of my work as a "technician" of the spiritual path is helping people bring their spirituality to light.

I have learned through my experience that dreams can help you clarify and live up to your ultimate values. Clarifying and living up to those values is a major part of the process of becoming conscious.

Consciousness is a very important term in spirituality, but not one whose definition is universally agreed upon. For some, consciousness refers to awareness, perceptions, thoughts, and feelings; for others, it implies intention and will. Strephon Kaplan Williams, with whom I wrote *Dreams and Spiritual Growth*, gave a simple and clear definition of the term: "Consciousness is awareness PLUS appropriate action." According to this definition, an insight never becomes truly conscious until you somehow put it into action in your daily life.

Spiritual practices, such as meditation or dreamwork, serve as ways of tapping into your inner resources, so that insights from these resources may be brought back and integrated into your ordinary life choices. I believe that spiritual practice is primarily a matter of consciousness, as defined above, and that a spiritual practice is complete only when the insights and gifts it releases are being incarnated in your life. Spirituality almost always involves values and choices being made in everyday activity.

For example, a forty-year-old woman named Marie dreamed that she had given birth to twins. Though one of the infants was well-loved and healthy, the other had been forgotten. Not only was the forgotten child hungry and angry but its head had also, somehow, become completely encased in a seamless golden metal mask.

This dream did not make any decisions or choices for Marie. Rather, based on the data revealed by the dream and her dreamwork, she made choices about nurturing parts of her life that had been forgotten and masked over. On one level, most dreams metaphorically reveal what is going on in your life and portray a current situation in a fresh light, from which you can grow spiritually. In spiritual practice, the waking ego becomes conscious by raising insight to the level of action. When using dreams and dreamwork as an authentic spiritual practice, there is no substitute for ego-reflection and choicemaking.

In almost all traditions, the purpose of bringing the discipline of spiritual practice into your life is to live more in line with your goals and higher life-purposes. The call to a full and whole life is often experienced during the moments of spiritual practice with striking clarity. During dreamwork, Marie realized that the angry cry of the forgotten and hungry child in her dream was a clear call to live her life more fully and wholly, as well as an indication that she had the inner strength to do what was required. From the standpoint of spiritual growth, the purpose of dreamwork, as with other spiritual practices, is to tap into the deepest resources of your self in order to bring up hidden potentials and integrate them into your waking life, that is, bring them into consciousness.

SOME PREMISES OF DREAMS AND SPIRITUALITY

Here are a few of the premises, or assumptions, about dreams and spirituality that I hold. Many of you also may study dreams from other perspectives. As a psychologist, a physician, a neurologist, or other practitioner, you may not hold some of these premises; it is not unusual in science even to hold some contradictory positions. For example, two psychotherapists may hold contradictory premises about the function of emotions, yet both may be successful in helping people. Or two physicists may hold contradictory assumptions about the physical universe, yet both may create valid mathematical equations to describe physical reality. As long as people listen to each other, I believe they can undoubtedly learn from one another. As a technician of the spiritual realm, I focus on the spiritual aspects of dreams and dreamwork.

The dream is usually presented symbolically and/or in the language of metaphor. In some ways, your dreams may speak a universal language, and therefore they belong not only to you but to the larger community. Others may find wisdom for themselves in your dream. Many people who have heard Marie tell her dream of the golden mask have been able to acknowledge that they, too, have gone through life wearing masks. Metaphor is the dominant language of spirituality. Dreams provide holistic data in metaphoric form for the choices and decisions that the waking ego—the choice-making part of the personality—will be called upon to make.

The dream is, among other things, a spiritual event. Many have called the dream "the voice of the soul." Your dream presents symbolically the options available to you—and others—at the level of the human spirit. During her dream, Marie discovered her resourcefulness by telephoning a goldsmith, who agreed to come and remove the mask. As a result of dreamwork, she decided to work with a therapist to help her remove the emotional masks she wore in daily life.

The dream can provide healing and wholeness. It is, in part, the dream's purpose to put you in touch with your ultimate values. It can get you involved in your own development and growth. Marie realized that the golden mask would need to be removed before she could become a whole person. Others, too, have found wisdom and healing insights for themselves from her dream.

The dream releases energy or insight. It is possible for you to bring the dream's insights into waking life and integrate them into the choices you make at the conscious level. Sometimes, the waking ego's ranking of ultimate values is dysfunctional or conflictual. When this happens, the deepest self, in dreams, is likely to reveal the problem. For example, upon reflection, Marie began to recognize her own anger at being forced by her family to live behind a mask for most of her adult life, and she realized she wanted to begin living in an emotionally honest way.

The dream allows your waking ego to establish a relationship with your deepest self. From the spiritual technician's perspective, dreamwork offers a way for building and using a line of communication between the waking ego and the deepest inner self. For Carl Jung, this self is the center and integrator of all life experiences, conscious and unconscious. Establishing a relationship between the waking ego and the inner self is perhaps your most important spiritual task in bringing yourself to spiritual maturity.

In light of spiritual growth, the dream is more powerful when viewed as a question rather than as an answer. A question invites growth in any relationship much more effectively than a command, especially in the ego–self relationship. Questions evoke consciousness. Marie discovered that her golden mask posed many questions: "How did I forget this other child I had? How did the golden mask get put on the child? Do I sometimes find my mask valuable to me? What professionals would help me take it off?

The dream is incomplete without dreamwork. In spirituality, the dream is the gift; dreamwork is what we do with it. Like a gift, the dream is meant to be opened, used, and cherished. Since a dream often speaks a universal language and triggers insights in others beside the dreamer, I believe the richness of its gifts may sometimes be more fully recognized when dreamwork is done with a partner or in a small dreamwork group. Nevertheless, it remains the dreamer's task to realize the dream's healing insight.

In pursuit of spiritual growth, the purpose of dreams and dreamwork is to bring you to higher levels of consciousness—that is, to awareness plus appropriate action. Marie found that her mask dream was of such profound depth and meaning that for the next ten years she continued to profit from dreamwork on it. She discovered she had been wearing layers of masks, and as one layer was taken off, another was discovered beneath it.

Dreamwork provides a way to channel the energy and insights of the dream into daily life. For Sigmund Freud, dreams were the royal road to the unconscious. The unconscious realm was a boiling cauldron of energy, and dreams led to this energy source. For Freud's disciple Carl Jung, dreams used symbols to reveal different kinds of energies in the unconscious realm that were available to us in waking life. Jung called these energy sources archetypes. For Jung, archetypes were bundles of energy, like the myriad strands of electrical wire bundled together in a power cable carrying energy from one place to another. Dreams and dreamwork can be used to release these spiritual energies. Whenever Marie worked on her golden-mask dream, she found energy to make everyday choices that helped her put aside the mask.

In the Western tradition, spiritual energies are called virtues. (*Virtus* is the Latin word for energy.) In the Eastern traditions, these energies are associated with spiritual energy centers called *chakras*. Major spiritual energies include creativity, the transmitting of life, self-awareness, courage, forgiveness, empathy, willpower, wisdom, meaning, discernment, unity, vision, and cosmic perspectives.

DREAM TASKS

Many approaches to dreams simply help you find meaning in them; so that once you have discovered what your dream is all about, the problem is considered solved and the process is over. Perhaps in certain approaches to the dream, it is enough to stop there. But in spiritual practice, which involves the way you live and act in light of your ultimate values, the purpose of the dream and dreamwork is consciousness: awareness plus appropriate action.

For this reason, the final step in dreamwork is to turn the energy and insight of the dream into choices and actions. At this stage, it is up to the waking ego, after reflecting on the energy and insight of the dream, to make choices for living and acting in the world. The easiest and most effective way of doing this is to create a list of possible dream tasks that could be accomplished to keep the energy of the dream alive, then to choose some of these tasks and actually carry them out.

Why actually carry them out? If you don't use the energy released in the dream, it will slip back into the unconscious and no longer be as readily available. How many of us have had insights about our lives that we recognized as important, intended to do something about them, but never turned those insights into concrete tasks? Consequently, our lives were never changed. The great insight soon became merely a vague memory, taking up a forgotten line or two in our personal journal. Marie kept her golden-mask dream alive by returning to it periodically over a period of years.

Furthermore, the accomplishment of such tasks keeps the energy of the dream alive and growing. The more Marie used her gift, the more that energy became available to her. This principle is true in all domains of life: the more you exercise your muscles, the stronger they become and the more energy they make available to you. The more you discipline yourself to keep the dream energy alive, the more access you have to it. If your dream reveals to you that you have the courage to face an important issue in your life, create a set of tasks to keep that energy alive and exercise that courage. In doing so, you will develop courage to face not only that particular issue but future issues as well.

There are three different kinds of dream tasks that you can use to keep the energy of the dream alive. The first are *Dreamwork Tasks*, techniques to clarify and nurture the energy revealed by the dream or by a symbol within it. Dreamwork tasks might include reflecting on dream symbols, having a dialogue with a dream figure, bringing an unfinished dream to resolution, and using artwork to concretize a dream image. For example, Marie conducted dialogues with her dream figures—the mask itself, the good baby, the forgotten baby, and the goldsmith—and all of them had wisdom for her. She also researched the meaning of "mask" and "persona" in the writings of Jung.

The second kind of dream tasks are *Personality Tasks*. These are *inner activities* that you, your dreamwork partner, or someone acting as a spiritual technician (such as a member of the clergy, a spiritual director, or a shaman) might suggest to keep the dream energy alive. Personality tasks might involve you in making a list of the ways you are like or unlike a certain dream figure, jotting down what positive things might happen if you were to incorporate dream energy into your daily life, or practicing some reflection or personal discipline that keeps you connected with the dream energy, such as marking down every time you affirm yourself. Marie made lists of the places in society where she still wore her golden mask and of the diminishments to her life the mask had caused. She even attended a mask-making workshop.

The third set of dream tasks are *Outer Life Tasks*. These are *outer activities* that you or your dreamwork partner might suggest to keep the dream energy alive. Outer Life Tasks might include taking actions that involve other people or the work you do. If your dream revealed that you had the energy to enhance your courage, you might choose to practice a simple act of assertiveness, or to stand up for yourself among your friends, or to write a letter of complaint to some company. Not only did Marie enter psychotherapy, but she also realized that without the mask she might appear angry and critical, so she chose to tolerate these unfamiliar feelings and consciously express them appropriately in public as validation that she was indeed removing her mask. Notice how each of these three kinds of dream tasks support and enrich each other.

The objective with dream tasks is to choose tasks to keep the energy alive, not to exhaust it. Therefore, you should choose tasks that you are able to accomplish in a finite amount of time and at which you are likely to succeed. Success breeds success, and a successful expression of dream energy is most likely to keep that energy alive. It is best to have a string of successes to keep you motivated and actively involved.

I believe dreamwork has made a revolutionary contribution to spirituality in recent years. Dreamwork is really a spiritual exercise that almost everyone can learn with some degree of proficiency and use effectively without having to depend upon someone else as a dream expert. Versatile and adaptable, it can be used individually, with partners, and in small dreamwork groups.

Since you dream every night, there is never a dearth of material for spiritual growth. On the other hand, there is no need to become compulsively attached to the dreamwork process. You may use it regularly without engaging in it compulsively. You don't need to do it every day. Whenever you choose to explore your dream resources, your deepest inner self will help you realize your true potential.

23

The Interpretation of Spiritual Dreams Throughout History

KELLY BULKELEY

DREAMS HAVE always been a fertile source of spiritual reflection, thought, and speculation. Throughout history dreams have challenged people to expand, deepen, and refine their understandings of the sacred. This [chapter] will provide an overview of the various ways that people have tried to make sense of their religious dream experiences—how people have tried to analyze, classify, categorize, explain, interpret, and understand dreams in their capacity as spiritual revelations. Such efforts are the province of hermeneutics, the discipline concerned with the rules and principles guiding our interpretations of religious, artistic, and historical texts. The term "hermeneutics" stems from the Greek deity Hermes, god of journeys, passages, and exchanges. One of Hermes' chief tasks was the delivery of messages (often in the form of dreams) from the gods of Mount Olympus to the humans residing below on earth. A hermeneutics of dreams, then, involves the attempt to interpret and understand dreams as possible messages from the gods, as possible revelations of the sacred.

The simplest, and perhaps safest, hermeneutic stance toward the realm of dreaming is this: dreams cannot be trusted as spiritual guides, so for all practical purposes they should be *ignored*.

. 1. The Old Testament is filled with passages warning that dreams are deceptive, unreliable, and frequently dangerous. One of the best known passages is from Ecclesiastes: "For a dream comes with much business, and a fool's voice with many words. . . . For when dreams increase, empty words grow many" (Eccl 5:3, 7). But the most vigorous denunciation of dreams comes in the apocryphal book of Sirach: "A man of no understanding has vain and false hopes, and dreams give wings to fools. As one who catches at a shadow and pursues the wind, so is he who gives heed to dreams. The vision of dreams is this against that, the likeness of a face confronting a face. From an unclean thing what will be made clean? And from something false what will be true? Divinations and omens and dreams are folly, and like a woman in travail the mind has fancies. Unless they are sent from the Most High as a visitation, do not give your mind to them. For dreams have deceived many, and those who have put their hope in them have failed. Without such deceptions the law will be fulfilled, and wisdom is made perfect in truthful lips." (Sir 34:1–8).

2. The Roman writer Lucretius (95–55 B.C.) is our best source for the philosophical teachings of the Epicureans, who offered a highly rationalist vision of the universe as consisting solely of atoms moving in a godless void. In his book *On Nature* Lucretius says this about the deceptiveness of dreams: "And when sleep has prostrated the body, for no other reason does the mind's intelligence wake, except because the very same images provoke our minds which provoke them when we are awake, and to such a degree that we seem without a doubt to perceive him whom life

has left and death and earth gotten hold of. This nature constrains to come to pass because all the senses of the body are then hampered and at rest throughout the limbs and cannot refute the unreal by real things. Moreover memory is prostrate and relaxed in sleep and protests not that he has long been in the grasp of death and destruction whom the mind believes it sees alive."

3. Wang Ch'ung, a Chinese philosopher from the first century A.D., takes a dim view of the supposed "realness" of dreams. Commenting on the well-known story of Shu-sun Mu-tzu's dream of heaven, Wang Ch'ung says, "Shu-sun Mu-tzu dreamed that heaven weighed down upon him. If this had been real, then heaven must have descended and reached the earth. Upon reaching the earth, it would have met the barrage of mansions and terraces. Hence it could not have touched him. For if it had, then the mansions and terraces would have been crushed. That they remained intact indicates that heaven did not reach earth. If it did not reach the earth, then it did not weigh down upon the man. If it did not weigh down upon him, then what did weigh down upon him was not heaven itself but rather the image of heaven."

4. In the sixth century A.D. leaders of the Eastern Orthodox church began denouncing the heretical threats posed by dreams. As historian Steven Oberhelman notes, church leaders begin to view dreams as satanic torments and seductions. "Resorting to ancient views on physiology and to Christian demonology, Eastern fathers like Evagrius and John Climacus reduced the vast majority of dreams to demon-inspired torments; the few dreams not so reduced were considered nonimportant images of mental illusion or warnings sent by God to sinners to beware of judgement and punishment. Dreams, in other words, fall into complete mistrust. Not even images of Jesus, angels, or saints can be trusted, since Satan and demons can and will disguise themselves as the Lord and heavenly beings, in order to destroy the dreamer's peace of mind. Any dream, therefore, should be considered the devil's deceit."

5. Antiochus Monachus, a seventh-century A.D. Christian monk living in a monastery near Jerusalem, gave a homily on dreams in which he condemned virtually all dream experiences: dreams, Antiochus argues, "are nothing other than things of the imagination and hallucinations of a mind led astray. They are the illusions of evil demons to deceive us and result from their enticements with the attendant purpose of carrying off a man to pleasure . . . Now then, if a light or some shape in the form of fire appears to one of those who strive (for a spiritual life), let him in no way whatsoever admit this vision. It is a patent delusion of an inimical and wicked scheme. It is this that the apostle teaches us, saying that he (Satan) is transformed 'into an angel of light.' . . . Even though, as is likely, a vision may have been sent down to us by divine revelation, let us not pay attention to it lest we accept smoke in lieu of light. In this way we do not stir up the Lord's anger, but rather He may also approve our guarding, with the help of fear, the treasure (i.e., the divine revelation) entrusted by Him to us."

6. The sixteenth-century Protestant reformer Martin Luther also refused to have anything to do with the seeming revelations of dreams: "I care nothing about visions and dreams. Although they seem to have meaning, yet I despise them and am content with the sure meaning and trustworthiness of Holy Scripture."

7. Thomas Nashe, a sixteenth-century English playwright and novelist, provides one of the most florid denunciations of dreams ever written: "A dream is nothing else but a bubbling scum or froth of the fancy, which the day hath left undigested; or an after-feast made of the fragments of idle imaginations. . . . No such figure of the first Chaos where the world was extraught, as our dreams in the night. In them all states, all sexes, all places, are confounded and meet together. Our cogitations run on heaps like men to part a fray, where everyone strikes his next fellow. From one place to another without consultation they leap, like rebels bent on a head. Soldiers just up and down they imitate at the sack of a city, which spare neither age nor beauty; the

young, the old, trees, steeples, and mountains they confound in one gallimaufry. . . . There were gates in Rome out of which nothing was carried but dust, and dung, and men to execution; so, many of the gates of our senses serve for nothing but to convey out excremental vapours and affrighting deadly dreams that are worse than executioners unto us. Ah, woe to the solitary man that hath his sins continually about him, that hath no withdrawing place from the devil and his temptations!"

8. In his classic work of political philosophy *Leviathan* (1651), Thomas Hobbes discusses the relationship of dreaming to waking perceptions. He says dreams are "caused by the distemper of some of the inward parts of the body"; however, people rarely recognize the absurdities of their dreams for what they are. Thus, Hobbes says, "from this ignorance of how to distinguish dreams, and other strong fancies, from vision and sense, did arise the greatest part of the religion of the gentiles in time past, that worshipped satyres, fawnes, nymphs, and the like; and now arises the opinion that rude people have of fayries, ghosts, and goblins; and of the power of witches. . . ." Hobbes believes such ignorance poses a threat to a well-ordered society: "In a common-wealth, a subject that has no certain and assured revelation particularly to himself concerning the will of God, is to obey for such, the command of the common-wealth: for if men were at liberty, to take for God's commandments, their own dreams, and fancies, or the dreams and fancies of private men; scarce two men would agree upon what is God's commandment; yet in respect of them, every man would despise the commandments of the common-wealth."

A thorough distrust of dreams is certainly the safest hermeneutic attitude one can take from a *political* perspective — rejecting all dreams keeps a person out of trouble with the authorities. The writer of the book of Sirach, the Eastern Orthodox fathers, the monk Antiochus, and Martin Luther all warn that dreams can lead people to stray from religious orthodoxy; and Hobbes is explicit in saying that supposed revelations through dreams pose a threat to a well-ordered society, an argument similar to the one made in Plato's *Republic* about the political dangers of dreams. Dreams frequently have the effect of challenging the official doctrines of churches, movements, and governments. It is understandable that people who prize social and religious stability would denounce dreams in general as dangerous, heretical, and subversive.

A total distrust of dreams is also the safest hermeneutic stance one can take from a purely *intellectual* perspective. For those who believe that rationality is our greatest faculty, the stubbornly irrational phenomenon of dreaming can only be regarded as a nuisance. Lucretius dismisses dreams as nonsensical fancies that are able to arise only because reason, memory, and the senses lie "prostrate" during sleep. Similarly, Wang Ch'ung ridicules those people who are gullible enough to believe that dreams are *real*, when their contents are so obviously contrary to fact and common sense. And Thomas Nashe rejects dreams for their absurd irrationality, their "fragmentary," "undigested," "chaotic" nature; how, Nashe asks, can we take seriously a phenomenon that "confounds" all the rational categories of waking life into one great muddled "gallimaufry"?

However, the severe distrust we find in these examples is relatively rare; from a cross-cultural and historical perspective, such absolute skepticism appears very infrequently. By far the most common and widespread hermeneutic attitude toward dreams involves making distinctions—classifying *some* dreams as true, meaningful, and/or spiritually valuable, and classifying *other* dreams as false, meaningless, and/or spiritually insignificant (even in the preceding examples, many of the writers grudgingly admit that some dreams may be significant). What follows are accounts of some of the classification systems people have developed to distinguish various types of dreams:

9. The native people of Hawaii have a number of different dream classes, according to anthropologist E. S. Craighill Handy. Hawaiians distinguish dreaming in deep sleep (*moe uhane*) from the swift vision in half sleep (*hihi'o*). They also differentiate

between unpremeditated dreams (*me ka noonoo mua ole*) and premeditated dreams (*i loaa mamuli o ka mana'o*). Handy quotes Kepelino, a native folklorist, as saying, "some dreams were true dreams and some not true. In olden days dreams were taught by dream interpreters and their teachings spread everywhere even to this day. . . . Their meanings were memorized like a catechism learned by memory in childhood. . . . There were two important kinds of dreams as regards the dreamer, unpremeditated dreams and those which were the result of premeditation on the part of the dreamer. Of all dreams the most significant ones were those which were the result of premeditation on the part of the dreamer. Of all dreams the most significant ones were those which came when one was startled in a very deep sleep or just as the eyelashes closed together when falling into a doze. These were true dreams."

10. We have already noted the Mohave distinction between "the traditional power-bestowing dream (*sumach ahot*, 'dream lucky') and the less significant, everyday sleep experiences (*sumach*, 'dream')." Anthropologist W. J. Wallace goes on to say that for the Mohave, "not all dreams are equally significant. The criterion used in determining what is important is often difficult to ascertain. The real test sometimes seems to be whether or not the dream comes true. A few dreams are regarded as having no meaning whatsoever. [An informant said] 'Some dreams, like if I dreamt I went to the store, don't mean anything and people forget about them right away.'"

11. A leader of the Jamaa movement, a charismatic movement that flourished in the Congo in the 1950s, described to anthropologist Johannes Fabian this theory of significant and insignificant dreams: "So, there are dreams that come from man alone, and dreams that come from God to teach man, to make him understand how God loves. . . . And then there are just dreams. . . . Therefore, the dream we receive from the *mawazo* [spiritual teaching] of God, the dream that comes from God, we may take as *mawazo*, yes. Because God has thought out and given the

dream. It's a *mafundisho* [instruction] by God himself. But the dream that comes only from us: this is the second case. We have a dream that comes from us, the dream we have at night. One dream we receive as a holy dream, the one we regard as *mawazo* coming from God; that's how we call it, yes, that sort of dream is *mawazo*. Another dream is just a dream, senseless things that come from man alone, yes."

12. The Mehinaku of central Brazil distinguish between dreams of greater and lesser significance, according to anthropologist Thomas Gregor: "A dream, for the Mehinaku, is an experience well worth remembering. It is, they say, like a shaman's prophecy in that the dreamer can learn much of what is to occur in the future. Upon entering periods of seclusion associated with ado- lescence, for example, boys have dreams that are regarded as sure indications of their longevity, health, and social status. Other dreams, admittedly rare, can herald the career of new shamans. These so-called true dreams *(jepuni yaja)* are given the closest attention by the initiates and their parents. Ordinary, everyday dreams *(jepuni he te*, literally 'mere dreams') are also important, however. Each morning the villagers recall such dreams and weigh them for their possible significance. The Mehinaku are aware, for example, that dreams are often constructed out of the residue of daily events. A man may explain a dream in which he went fishing or went hunting monkeys by recalling that he had done these things the previous day. Alternatively, the villagers may occasionally interpret their dreams as expressions of wish ful- fillment. One young man told me he dreamed he had received a certain gift because he had wanted it for a long time."

13. In book 19 of Homer's *Odyssey* Penelope describes a dream in which twenty fat geese are slaughtered by a mountain eagle. She tells the dream to a kind beggar, whom she does not recognize as her husband Odysseus; he has disguised himself, and is plotting revenge against the suitors who have plundered his home. Odysseus assures Penelope that the dream's meaning is clear: her husband will return and kill the suitors. Penelope, however, is not

so certain, and says, "Friend, many and many a dream is mere confusion, a cobweb of no consequence at all. Two gates for ghostly
dreams there are: one gateway of honest horn, and one of ivory.
Issuing by the ivory gate are dreams of glimmering illusion, fantasies, but those that come through solid polished horn may be
borne out, if mortals only know them. I doubt it came by horn,
my fearful dream—too good to be true, that, for my son and me."

14. John Brennan, a scholar of Chinese literature, tells of how dream
interpretation was an official function of the Chinese government
as far back as the middle of the second millennium B.C. A text
called the *Zhou li*, which describes the governmental structure
of the Zhou dynasty (eleventh century to 221 B.C.), includes dream
divination among the various bureaucratic positions of the ancient
Chinese state and provides a table of organization for officers
involved with divinatory practices. The text goes on to outline the
duties of the Examiner of Dreams *(zhan meng)*. Brennan says,
"The Examiner of Dreams is charged with divining the good or
ill fortune of the six types of dreams, taking into account the positions of the sun, moon, and stars, distinguishing between the yin
and the yang, observing the conjunction of heaven and earth
according to the seasons. The six types of dreams are given as:
1) Regular or restful dreams *(zheng meng)*; 2) Startling or disturbing dreams *(e meng)*; 3) Reflective dreams *(si meng)*; 4) Day-
dreams *(wu meng)*; 5) Happy dreams *(xi meng)*; 6) Frightening
dreams *(ju meng)*. This is the first typology of dreams encountered in Chinese literature. There is no correspondence between
the type of dream and whether it is divined as auspicious or
inauspicious. Startling or frightening dreams, though unsettling,
can be favorable omens and happy or restful dreams may be
unlucky. . . . The lack of linkage between the typology of dreams
in the *Zhou li* and the divinatory significance of dreams strongly
suggests that the basic meaning and cause of dreams is not to be
found in the mental state of the dreamer, but in a broader, impersonal system of signification and causality such as that which
underlies the *Book of Changes* [*I Ching*].

15. An ancient Indian medical text attributed to Caraka presents this classification of dreams, as described by Wendy Doniger O'Flaherty in *Dreams, Illusion, and Other Realities*: Caraka's text "divides dreams into several categories: dreams that reflect what has been seen in waking life *(drsta)*, dreams that reflect what has been heard in waking life *(sruta)*, dreams that reflect what has been experienced *(anubhuta)*, dreams that foretell the future *(bhavika)* . . . dreams that reflect the disturbance of a particular bodily humor *(dosaja)* . . . dreams that dramatize individual fantasies (i.e. things unseen), though perhaps based on memory data *(kalpita)*; and dreams that are wish-fulfillments, gratifying desires that could not be gratified in the waking state *(prarthita)*. These seven categories of Caraka thus cover waking experiences, somatic impulses, imagination, and the influence of the supernatural."

16. The Jewish philosopher Philo (born c. 20 B.C.) wrote a three-part work, *On Dreams, That They Are God-Sent*, of which only the last two parts have survived. Philo introduces the final section by saying, "the first kind of dreams we saw to be those in which God originates the movement and invisibly suggests things obscure to us but patent to Himself: while the second kind consisted of dreams in which the [human] understanding moves in concert with the soul of the Universe and becomes filled with a divinely induced madness, which is permitted to foretell many coming events. . . . [The] third kind of dreams arises whenever the soul in sleep, setting itself in motion and agitation of its own accord, becomes frenzied, and with the prescient power due to such inspiration foretells the future." Philo says that the first kind of dreams are perfectly clear, "of the nature of plain oracles"; the second kind are enigmatic, but "not in very high degree concealed from the quick-sighted," as in the case of Jacob's dream at Bethel of the heavenly ladder; and the third kind are more "obscure . . . owing to the deep and impenetrable nature of the riddle involved in them"; these require interpretation by men skilled in this science (e.g. Joseph, Daniel, etc.).

17. In his *Oneirocritica*, Artemidorus begins by making some distinctions among the different types of dream experiences. He says there is a major distinction between *enhypnion* and *oneiros*. *Oneiros* indicates a future state of affairs, while *enhypnion* relates to a present state of affairs. Examples of the latter type, Artemidorus says, would be a lover dreaming of his beloved, a frightened man dreaming of what he fears, a hungry man dreaming of eating. Another major distinction is between allegorical dreams and theorematic dreams. Allegorical dreams signify one thing by means of something else; theorematic dreams are those that present themselves plainly and directly. Artemidorus says he does not speculate about whether dreams are sent by the gods or not; he uses the term "godsent dreams" in the customary sense by which we speak of anything that is unforeseen.

18. In his *Treatise on the Soul*, the Christian theologian Tertullian categorizes dreams in this way: "We declare, then, that dreams are inflicted on us mainly by demons, although they sometimes turn out true and favorable to us. When, however, with the deliberate aim after evil, of which we have just spoken, they assume a flattering and captivating style, they show themselves proportionately vain, and deceitful, and obscure, and wanton, and impure. And no wonder that the images partake of the character of the realities. But from God . . . must all those visions be regarded as emanating, which may be compared to the actual grace of God, as being honest, holy, prophetic, inspired, instructive, inviting to virtue, the bountiful nature of which causes them to overflow even to the profane. . . . The third class of dreams will consist of those which the soul apparently creates for itself from an intense application to special circumstances. . . . Those [dreams], moreover, which evidently proceed neither from God, nor from diabolical inspiration, nor from the soul, being beyond the reach as well of ordinary expectation, usual interpretation, or the possibility of being intelligibly related, will have to be ascribed in a separate category to what is purely and simply the ecstatic state and its peculiar conditions."

19. *The Commentary on the Dream of Scipio*, by the fourth-century A.D. Roman writer Macrobius, presents a classification of dreams that has had a huge influence on western thinking about dreams. "Scipio's Dream" was originally the concluding section of Cicero's *Republic*, a work of political philosophy arguing that the Roman Republic represents the ideal state. The "dream" involves Scipio being led by his long-dead grandfather on a tour of the cosmos; by discovering the rewards and punishments given to departed souls, Scipio gains new motivation to lead an upright, law-abiding life. In his commentary on the dream, Macrobius begins by describing the various types of dreams recorded in classic literature. He says that dreams may be classified into five different categories: enigmatic dreams, prophetic visions, oracular dreams, nightmares, and apparitions. Macrobius says, "the last two, the nightmare and the apparition, are not worth interpreting since they have no prophetic significance. Nightmares may be caused by mental or physical distress, or anxiety about the future: the patient experiences in dreams vexations similar to those that disturb him during the day. . . . The apparition comes upon one in the moment between wakefulness and slumber, in the so-called 'first clouds of sleep.' . . . To this class belongs the incubus, which, according to popular belief, rushes upon people in sleep and presses them with a weight which they can feel. . . . We call a dream oracular in which a parent, or a pious or revered man, or a priest, or even a god clearly reveals what will or will not transpire, and what action to take or avoid. We call a dream a prophetic vision if it actually comes true. . . . By an enigmatic dream we mean one that conceals with strange shapes and veils with ambiguity the true meaning of the information being offered, and requires an interpretation for its understanding. . . . The dream which Scipio reports that he saw embraces the three reliable types mentioned above. . . . [T]he purpose of the dream is to teach us that the souls of those who serve the state well are returned to the heavens after death and there enjoy everlasting blessedness."

20. Alex Wayman's "Significance of Dreams in India and Tibet" describes several dream classification systems found in these cultures: "In the sixty-eighth *parisista* of the *Athara-Veda* [a sixth-century A.D. Hindu religious text] men are said to have the temperaments bilious (fiery), phlegmatic (watery), and sanguine (windy). Different dreams are attributed to such persons respectively: for the bilious, dreams, for example, of arid land and of burning objects; for the phlegmatic, dreams, for example, of nature in splendor and burgeoning life; for the sanguine, dreams, for example, of racing clouds and of forest creatures running in terror. In the *Questions of King Milinda* [a famous Buddhist text from the second century A.D.], there are said to be six men who dream: the foregoing three, 4) those under influence of a deity, 5) those who dream under influence of their experiences, and 6) those with prophetic dreams. . . . The Buddhist Mahayana text '*Meeting of the Father and Son*' (*Pitrputrasamagama*) gives dreams based on all six senses, the usual five plus the mind as the sixth sense; but here again the basic classification is three-fold by the three 'poisons,' lust (=attraction), hatred (=repulsion), and delusion (=incapacity), because the text gives a sample dream for each of the three in terms of each of the senses [making 18 different categories in all]."

21. The Muslim philosopher Ibn Arabi (1164–1240 A.D.), who created a grand metaphysical system merging Islamic theology with Greek philosophy, argued that there are three basic type of dreams. As described by historian Rom Landau, "Ibn Arabi regards dreams as *khayal*, or metal images (imaginings) which represent something between the real and the phenomenal worlds. . . . It is during dreams that imagination is at its most active, producing ordinary dreams. According to Ibn Arabi, it is then that imagination gets hold of experiences of daily life, and presents them to the 'inward eye' (of the heart). In the inward eye, they are magnified as though in a mirror, and it is the subsequently distorted image of those experiences that fill our dreams. Usually these images become the foci or symbols of our

desires. There also exists a second type of dream, which Ibn Arabi regards as of far greater significance, the material for which comes not from our ordinary daytime experiences, but direct from the Universal Soul or, as Ibn Arabi sometimes calls it, the 'Guarded Table.' In such a dream man's (rational) soul perceives the archetypal ideas contained in the Universal Soul. But even in such dreams imagination gains possession of the received ideas, and distorts them. As a result, man's 'inward eye,' while in direct contact with the Universal Soul, nevertheless does not act as a perfect mirror but as a 'running, yet undefiled, stream wherein are reflected illuminated objects of all descriptions.' . . . In consequence, these dreams, being symbolical, have to be interpreted. . . . There is, however, one type of dream that is not symbolical but a direct revelation of Reality. Imagination does not enter into it, and the 'inward eye' reproduces the exact reflection of the impression received. . . . They are the direct vision of Reality, of Universal Truth."

22. *The Sefer Hasidim*, the work of thirteenth-century German Jewish pietists, distinguishes between different types of dreams: "In the prophetic dream the prophets' personal thoughts were not intermingled, nor were the words of the demon. In the dreams of ordinary people, however, the words of the demon are intermingled." The text goes on to say that if a man goes to sleep thinking about a woman, he will dream of "intimacies with a woman," and that if a man needs to "evacuate" he will dream of being weary. "All such dreams are not dreams told by the angel but come from one's thoughts, and in these one sees their symbol. . . . But a dream that comes through an angel, even though one did not imagine things or speak, before rising the angel comes to tell him; for his thoughts and sinful fancies had already ceased. . . . The angel turns the thoughts into thinking about those things that God decrees. It is certainly so when one sleeps and reason does not direct the mind: For it is said 'I will bless the Lord, who hath given me counsel; Yea, in the night seasons my reins instruct me [Ps. 16:7].'"

23. In his fourteenth-century A.D. work *Muqaddimah* ("An Intro-
    duction to History") the Muslim scholar Ibn Khaldun explained
    the different types of dreams in this way: "Real dream vision is
    an awareness on the part of the rational soul in its spiritual
    essence, of glimpses of the forms of events. . . . This happens to
    the soul [in the form of] glimpses through the agency of sleep,
    whereby it gains the knowledge of future events that it desires
    and regains the perceptions that belong to it. When this process
    is weak and indistinct, the soul applies to it allegory and imagi-
    nary pictures, in order to gain [the desired knowledge]. Such alle-
    gory, then, necessitates interpretation. When, on the other hand,
    this process is strong, it can dispense with allegory. Then, no
    interpretation is necessary, because the process is free from imag-
    inary pictures. . . . One of the greatest hindrances [to this
    process] is the external senses. God, therefore, created man in
    such a way that the veil of the senses could be lifted through
    sleep, which is a natural function of man. When that veil is lifted,
    the soul is ready to learn the things it desires to know in the world
    of Truth. At times, it catches a glimpse of what it seeks. . . . Clear
    dream visions are from God. Allegorical dream visions, which
    call for interpretation, are from the angels. And 'confused
    dreams' are from Satan, because they are altogether futile, as
    Satan is the source of futility."

24. In his book *Pitron Chalomot*, the sixteenth-century Jewish
    scholar Solomon Almoli reminds his readers that most dreams
    involve representations of the ordinary dreamer's thoughts and
    daily concerns. The interpreter of dreams has the responsibility
    of recognizing that "this type of dream is insignificant, as its
    source is not the Master of Dreams [the archangel Gabriel]; it
    is simply the product of one's imagination." Almoli says that the
    best way of distinguishing true from untrue dreams is "by the
    degree of excitement experienced by the dreamer. If one dreams
    of powerful fantasy images that cause him to be excited or to
    feel anger during the dream itself, this is a true dream; but if the
    images are insipid and arouse no strong feelings, the dream is

not true. The reliability of any dream is thus in proportion to its level of excitement."

25. The Islamic theologian Abdalghani an-Nabulusi (1641–1731) wrote an encyclopedic work on dream interpretation in which he provides an elaborate classification system. Dreams can be divided into three basic categories: glad tidings from God (e.g. dreams cited in religious texts); dreams of warning from the devil; and dreams that originate from the dreamer's own self. Nabulusi says that dreams from the devil are false and require no interpretation. Examples of dreams that originate in the self are the person dreaming of being with a loved one, seeing something he is afraid of, or eating when he is hungry. Nabulusi goes on to divide false dreams into seven types: 1) dreams originating in desire and ambition; 2) sexual dreams, which require the dreamer to purify himself upon awakening; 3) warnings from the devil; 4) dreams shown by sorcerers; 5) dreams shown by Satan; 6) dreams that result from disturbances in the humors; and 7) "reversion" dreams, in which the dreamer sees himself as he was many years in the past. True dreams, Nabulusi says, are of five different types: 1) the trustworthy dream, which is a form of prophecy; 2) glad tidings from God; 3) dreams shown by the angel of dreams; 4) symbolic dreams, from spirits; and 5) the dream "that is valid for the viewer and exerts an overpowering influence upon him."

If nothing else, this group of dream classification systems should put to rest forever the notion that people in non-western, premodern cultures are fundamentally *ignorant* about dreams—i.e., they cannot distinguish between "dreams" and "reality," they gullibly believe that all dreams come from the gods, and they do not understand how dreams are rooted in the mundane experiences of a person's daily life. The historical and cross-cultural fact is that people have *always* distinguished between dreams that are more spiritually significant and dreams that are less spiritually significant. People from many, many different cultures have found a clear-eyed skepticism toward some dreams to be entirely compatible with a reverential appreciation of the deep religious value of other dreams.

Looking more carefully at the examples above, we find in a number of them a clear recognition of the rootedness of dreams in the dreamer's personal life. For instance, the Mohave acknowledge that some dreams "don't mean anything". Macrobius says that in most nightmares "the patient experiences in dreams vexations similar to those that disturb him during the day". Caraka's Indian medical text speaks of dreams stemming from what has been seen, heard, and experienced in waking life. Nabulusi describes dreams that "originate in the aspirations of the self," as when a hungry man dreams of eating. These examples, with their matter-of-fact awareness of the connection between dreams and recent waking life experiences, give us a new perspective on the twentieth-century dream theories of Sigmund Freud and Calvin Hall. Freud claims that every dream can be related to some incident or experience from the dreamer's recent past, and Hall's "continuity hypothesis" proposes that there is a close correspondence between people's dreams and their acts and thoughts in waking life. In this regard, then, Freud's and Hall's theories simply reformulate a point that has been made countless times through history. The difference is that the non-western, pre-modern classification systems assert that while some dreams seem to be rooted in the experiences of our ordinary waking lives, other dreams seem to be rooted in powers and realities that *transcend* our personal existence. This is a notion that Freud, Hall, and many other modern dream researchers have difficulty accepting (although Freud does say, in one of the most cryptic footnotes in *The Interpretation of Dreams*, that "There is at least one spot in every dream at which it is unplumbable—a navel, as it were, that is its point of contact with the unknown").

We also find in many of these examples an awareness that dreams differ in terms of their clarity: some dreams are relatively straightforward in their images and meanings, while other dreams are more enigmatic. Artemidorus distinguishes between "theorematic" (or direct) and "allegorical" dreams, although he does not explain why a dream takes one form or the other. Both Ibn Arabi and Philo account for the difference between clear and symbolic dreams by referring to the distorting effects of the human imagination: symbolic dreams occur because our limited human faculties can only imperfectly perceive the sacred, while clear dreams are revelations received directly and immediately from God. Ibn Khaldun claims that "confused dreams" are caused by the deceptive influences of Satan, and the *Sefer Hasidim* likewise accounts for murky, unintelligible dreams by referring to the malevolent activities of demons.

    Occasionally a false, deceptive dream is attributed not to evil spirits, but to the gods. The Islamic prophet Muhammed was sent a false dream by Allah so that he would lead his troops into a difficult but ultimately successful battle. Muhammed writes in the *Koran*, speaking of himself:

26. You were encamped on this side of the valley and the unbelievers on the farther side, with the caravan below. Had they offered battle, you would have surely declined; but Allah sought to accomplish what He had ordained, so that, by a miracle, he that was destined to perish might die, and he that was destined to live might survive. Allah hears all and knows all. Allah made them appear to you in a dream as a small band. Had He showed them to you as a great army, your courage would have failed you and discord would have triumphed in your ranks. But this Allah spared you. He knows your inmost thoughts.

    But not everyone is as fortunate as Muhammed, whose deceptive dream actually helped him. The second book of Homer's *Iliad* presents a dream sent by the almighty Zeus to Agamemnon specifically in order to trick the Greek warrior into a deadly trap on the battlefield:

27. Zeus "cried out to the dream and addressed him in winged words: 'Go forth, evil Dream, beside the swift ships of the Achaians [Greeks]. Make your way to the shelter of Atreus' son Agamemnon; speak to him in words exactly as I command you. Bid him arm the flowing-haired Achaians for battle in all haste;

since now he might take the wide-wayed city of the Trojans. . . .'
So he spoke, and Dream listened to his word and descended. . . ."
After finding Agamemnon, who was sleeping in his tent with the
other Greek troops, "Dream stood then beside his head in the
likeness of Nestor, Neleus' son, whom Agamemnon honoured
beyond all elders beside. In Nestor's likeness the divine Dream
spoke to him: 'Son of wise Atreus breaker of horses, are you sleeping? . . . Listen quickly to what I say, since I am a messenger of
Zeus, who far away cares much for you and is pitiful. Zeus bids
you arm the flowing-haired Achaians for battle in all haste; since
now you might take the wide-wayed city of the Trojans. . . .' So
he spoke and went away, and left Agamemnon there, believing
things in his heart that were not to be accomplished." When
Agamemnon awakened, he reported the god-sent dream to his
comrades; they believed it to be a favorable omen, and roused
themselves to arms. But the ensuing battle brought not the vic-
tory Agamemnon thought his dream promised, but the bloody
death of countless Greek warriors.

   Agamemnon's "evil dream" illustrates the dangers posed by all
dreams: how to tell what exactly they mean. Throughout history, people have feared the consequences of misinterpreting their dreams.
These fears have been widely expressed in myths, stories, and legends from around the world. For example, when Gilgamesh has three
horrible nightmares at Cedar Mountain, his friend Enkidu misin-
terprets them as omens of success in battle. King Nebuchadnezzar,
as we have already seen, completely misses the warning in his dream
of the great human statue, misinterpreting it as a sign that he should
build such a statue. Euripides' tragedy *Iphigenia in Tauris* opens with
the heroine recounting a nightmare, which she mistakenly believes
is an announcement of her brother Orestes' death. An especially
moving account of the anxiety people have felt over misinterpreting
dreams comes in the Indian epic *The Ramayana*. The princess Sita
is a captive in the castle of demon king Ravana; but when the monkey Hanuman, ally of her husband prince Rama, sneaks into the

castle and tells Sita that help is on the way, she is afraid to believe it. Sita says:

28. Today I have seen a grotesque dream, the dream of a monkey. . . . But this cannot be a dream, for I am so tortured by sorrow and misery I cannot sleep. . . . I have been thinking constantly about nothing but Rama all day today, obsessed by the mental image of him alone, and that is why I have seen and heard these things. This is just wishful thinking—but nevertheless, I wonder about it, for this monkey speaks to me and has a clearly visible form. . . . What if you are a form of Ravana himself, the master of illusion, once more engaging in magic illusion to make me suffer? . . . I have been held a captive for so long that I find great happiness in a dream. If I saw Rama and Laksmana [Rama's brother] even in a dream, I would not despair; even a dream can be exhilarating. But I don't think this can be a dream, for if you see a monkey in a dream it is an omen of nothing good, but something good has happened to me. This could be a delusion in my mind, or some disturbance caused by indigestion, or madness, or a mental distortion, or a mirage. But it is not madness or delusion, for I am in my right mind, and I see both myself and this monkey.

It would require [an] entire book to make an adequate survey of the various strategies people in different cultures have used to interpret the meanings of symbols in dreams. We can note, however, that many of these strategies correspond closely to the basic methods of dream interpretation used by contemporary psychotherapists—for example, relating the dream to the dreamer's personal life context; looking for evidence of puns and wordplay in the dream; trying "a contrario" interpretations (i.e. interpreting a dream of death as meaning "new life"); connecting the dream to religious, philosophical, and/or psychological beliefs in the dreamer's culture; viewing recurrent dreams as bearers of especially important meanings; and discussing dreams in group settings.

Looking at these different classification systems, we can draw some very general conclusions regarding what humans dream about. People dream about their daily experiences, their bodies, their relations with other people, their fears and wishes, their futures, and their relations with the sacred. We can also conclude, again in a very general sense, that people have historically distinguished between "ordinary" dreams and "extraordinary" dreams—the former referring to the dreamer's waking life experiences, and the latter bringing the dreamer into contact with sacred powers and realities.

But I would be hesitant to draw conclusions about human dreaming experience that are any more specific than this, at least given the present state of our historical and cross-cultural knowledge. In particular, I would caution against efforts to try to reconcile the various dream classification systems we have discussed, to try to devise a "system of dream systems." The primary obstacle to such a tempting goal is that the different dream classifications presented above answer to extremely different questions, concerns, and interests. For example, some of them distinguish dreams according to their meanings (e.g. true vs. false, happy vs. fearful, clear vs. confused), some of them distinguish dreams according to their causes (e.g. the gods, the soul, the body, demons, angels), and some of them distinguish dreams according to both meanings and causes. I find it hard to imagine how such different conceptual systems could be intelligibly, let alone usefully, reconciled.

Perhaps the best example of these difficulties regards one of the classification systems that seems clearest and most straightforward to us—the gate of horn vs. gate of ivory distinction that Penelope makes in book 19 of Homer's *Odyssey*. Most western readers have assumed that Penelope's distinction is merely a poetic way of saying that some dreams are true and others false. Horn is a relatively clear and transparent substance, while ivory is opaque; thus, true dreams can be said to pass through a "gate of horn" and false dreams through a "gate of ivory." But classicist Anne Amory argues that a closer reading of the passage reveals this common reading of the text to be mistaken. The distinction, Amory says, is not between true and false dreams, because the first lines of the passage ("Friend, many and many a dream is mere confusion, a cobweb of no consequence at all") indicate that virtually *all* dreams are confused and perplexing; Amory says: "Penelope means that dreams are bewildering things and hard to understand; confronted with them, the dreamer tends to feel helpless. . . . [A]t this point she is speaking of dreams in general, not just those which come through the gates of ivory." So there is not a sharp contrast here between qualitatively different types of dreams; rather, there is a contrast between the different *effects* that dreams can have in waking life. According to Amory,

> Penelope is saying that the dreams which come through the gate of horn have power, or are effective, in reality. The previous contrasted phrase for the dreams which come through the ivory gate . . . will then mean that these dreams bring mere words, without any consequences in actuality. . . . In sum, Penelope's speech does not seem, upon careful examination, to lend any support to a thesis . . . that there are two radically different kinds of dreams. The impression given is rather that she is expressing metaphorically the common belief that some dreams predict the future and come true, while others merely seem to predict, but do not come true in reality, although both kinds of dreams are hard to interpret.

If it is easy to misunderstand a dream classification system that appears so simple and familiar to us, we should be very cautious in trying to make broader generalizations about how people have distinguished different types of dreams through history.

Penelope (like Sita, another captive woman) knew that dreams often bear valuable and important revelations, but she also knew that they are terribly difficult to understand. I can be dangerous to ignore dreams, and yet dangerous to interpret them incorrectly. Penelope's fearful uncertainty illustrates what I believe is the deepest and most widespread feeling people have about dreams: *ambivalence*. A profound ambivalence lies at the heart of human experience with dreams. Some dreams bring us closer to the gods, to the divine, to the realm of the spirit; other dreams are trivial, insignificant, and/or false; still other dreams seem to mix potent revelations with vain

self-deceptions. And no matter what, it is extremely difficult to interpret the true meaning of any one particular dream. This ambivalence
cannot be relieved by sternly rejecting all dreams as worthless, nor
by gullibly embracing all dreams as divine inspirations.

In this regard, it is worth remembering that Hermes is not only
the messenger of the gods—he is also the great *trickster*; Hermes is
a wily thief, a cunning liar, a sly seducer. A true "hermeneutics of
dreams," then, recognizes that dreams *reveal* as well as *deceive*. Our
fate as mortals, it seems, is to struggle over the difference.

24

Context and Metaphor: The Message of the Dream

MONTAGUE ULLMAN

DREAMS START with the tensions and preoccupations we bring to bed with us at night. To what extent can we reconstruct the recent past to shed light on these emotional currents? What aspects of our recent past left us with emotional residues? What feelings or thoughts surfaced in our mind just prior to falling asleep? The dream is a continuation at night of feelings stirred up during the day. Any technique that professes to work with a dream without stressing the importance of identifying the recent emotional context will fall short of embedding the imagery in the concrete life situation of the dreamer and will run the risk of superimposing theoretical or speculative ideas on the dream to fill in the gap.

THE SEARCH FOR THE ASSOCIATIVE CONTEXT

The next step involves bringing to each image in the dream, and to each detail of each image, whatever associations occur to the dreamer. What contact, past or present, has the dreamer had with that image? What might that image mean?

The important thing about the work at this stage is that it be done systematically. The goal of the dreamer is to recover information first and, in so doing, lay the basis for linking the dream to his or her life. The most effective way to do this is to begin by breaking the dream down into its various scenes, consider each scene first as a unit, and then work with the individual elements in that scene.

Consider the first scene as a whole. Are there more things you can say about it? Are there more things you can say about the individual images or elements (such as numbers and colors) that appear in that scene? Play back your thoughts about the scene against what you have noted about the recent emotional context of your life. Do any further associations occur as to why you chose those particular images that night? Do this with each succeeding scene. The work you do on each scene enables you to bring a richer network of associations to the next one and often sheds light on why one scene follows another.

IN PURSUIT OF THE
METAPHORICAL MESSAGE

In most instances, as more and more associations are brought to light, the dreamer will begin to make the connections between image and reality and catch on to the way the image reflects metaphorically a certain feeling, trend, or life situation. For a dreamer working alone, this may not be an easy matter even after doing one's best to elaborate the associative matrix. There are many helpful hints in the literature to overcome this block. One is for the dreamer to take an objective point of view about a particular image that remains puzzling, without regard to this particular dream. Sometimes in doing this, the dreamer will come across a message that suddenly feels right in its application to the dream.

Having done this work, it can sometimes help to let some time elapse; then, on coming back to the dream, the dreamer may be surprised to find some meanings emerge that escaped him or her the first time around. This is mostly likely to happen if enough ground-work has been done at the time the dream occurred. It can't be over-stressed that dreams have a current meaning. Although they engage with our past, they start in the present.

There remains an intrinsic reason why a dreamer working alone may have difficulty in grasping fully all that the dream has to say. This can, perhaps, be best understood by viewing dreamwork as involving a series of steps designed to socialize the dream. In effect, dreamwork is the socialization of a part of the psyche that has not yet been socialized, a part that has had a kind of underground exis-tence. *Socializing* it is making it a felt and viable part of our waking social existence. We are introducing a relative stranger to our inner circle of friends (all that goes into perpetuating our self-concept). At the outset, we can never be quite sure how the stranger will fit in.

The preceding outlined the first two stages in the socialization process that any teaching technique has to address. The first has to do with the transformation of the dreaming experience into the dream. On awakening, we are once again active social creatures, and the remembered dream now becomes an item on our waking social agenda. Most books outline some of the many helpful techniques to aid recall.

The next step in the socialization of the dream is to use the instruments of waking consciousness, such as language, associations, feelings, and memories, to explore the basis for the dream's con-nection to our lives. As we do this, the dream becomes more deeply embedded in our ongoing social existence. The orientation of many current books is focused on the dreamer working alone and stops at that point.

It has been my experience, based on the work I have done on my own dreams as well as my work with patients for thirty years and with groups for fifteen years, that sharing and working on dreams in a supportive and stimulating group setting is the most natural and effective method. It is as if our dreams require this level of social-ization to bring out their full healing potential. Nor should that be surprising. Confronting the message of the dream alone, regardless of one's degree of sophistication, is to do so with all one's defensive apparatus ready to spring into operation should one get too close to an unpleasant truth. One is more apt to risk that confrontation in a supportive social context where trust has been established and where, through the sharing that has taken place, our human frailties have become known to each other. Our dreams cry out for this level of socialization.

Many books do encourage a group approach. There are certain minimum requirements for such an approach if it is to be effective. The atmosphere has to be that of a learning experience in which dreamers have the freedom to learn at their own rate and to the extent they feel ready. A leader should be there to teach whatever process is being used, not to confront the dreamer as the expert on his or her dream. The basics of group dreamwork should stress the following factors:

The safety of the dreamer. The dreamer who shares a dream should be in control of the process. The dreamer has the responsibility to set his or her own limits and is never to be pushed beyond that. In its effort to provide assistance, the group should always follow the associative track offered by the dreamer and never lead him or her. Leading questions take the control away from the dreamer. They arise from a concern with issues in the mind of the questioner that have not been opened up by the dreamer.

To maintain the dreamer's control, certain constraints on the group are necessary. In addition to avoiding leading questions, the group must respect the privacy of the dreamer at all times. That means, in effect, that however one conducts the dialogue between dreamer and group member, the questioning is never intrusive—that it never goes beyond areas opened up by the dreamer.

Respect for the authority of dreamers over their dreams. This entails never superimposing an interpretation on the dreamer. All interpretive ideas, be they right or wrong, should be considered as projections on the part of the person offering them unless they are accepted as meaningful by the dreamer. In my opinion, group work with dreams is best carried out in the absence of a single ideological metapsychological system. Working within the framework of any one system will constrain the imagination of both dreamer and group members to what is consistent with that system.

Both Freud and Jung endowed us with very powerful metaphors that are often, but not necessarily always, applicable to particular dream images. One should be free to draw upon them when indicated but, at the same time, remain aware that a dreamer may use any image in a highly idiosyncratic way. This accords true respect for the dreamer's individuality.

An atmosphere where all the participants, including the leader, share their dreams. This flattens the structure, lessens dependency on the leader, and diminishes his or her role as an authority. The only authority is that of someone teaching the particular process being used. In all other respects, the leader should be a fully participating member of the group.

The time factor. It takes a good deal of time to work through a dream in its entirety. It is not always possible to capture the meaning of every element of a dream, but there should be time to work on each element. If the dream is not treated with the thoroughness and care it deserves, it is best left alone.

All of the above can be summarized by saying that group work is best carried out in an atmosphere that generates safety and trust and that respects the dreamer's privacy, authority over the dream, and control over the work being done with it. The dreamer is left to manage his or her own defensive structure. The safer one feels, the more open one will be to explore the message of the dream.

25

Personal Myths and Dreamwork

STANLEY KRIPPNER AND JOSEPH DILLARD

SOLUTIONS TO problems do not spring full-blown from one's dreams like children from the head of Zeus. Preparation and incubation often are necessary stages if illumination and inspiration are to occur, either in dreamworking or during some similar activity. Indeed, dreams have been known to respond to a request by the dreamer for help by delineating the fears and doubts that block a resolution. One way this is done is by identifying "personal myths" that may be helping or hindering a creative insight.

Personal mythologies consist of people's ever-changing systems of complementary and conflicting personal myths—those patterns of thinking and feeling that give meaning to the past, definition to the present, and direction for the future. A personal myth serves the functions of explaining, guiding, and sacralizing experience for the individual in a manner analogous to the way cultural myths once served those functions for society.[1]

Frequently, when one's underlying mythic structure is incongruous with a personal experience, it is the task of the dream to resolve the difference. A dream can emphasize weaknesses in one's mythic structure, giving that structure an opportunity to adjust to the new experience. A dream can point out that a dysfunctional personal myth is not adequately accounting for the dreamer's experiences by revealing an emotional blind spot.

Personal myths serve the individual in the same way that cultural myths used to function in primitive and ancient societies. One's personal mythology includes all the interacting and sometimes conflicting thoughts and feelings a person harbors about the world, both in and out of awareness. These myths shape the actions that people take and the interpretations they give to their experiences. A myth functions well if it provides an emotionally satisfying reflection of reality; it does the individual (and the society) a disservice if it obscures gaps that exist between one's feelings and reality.

An individual is most likely to become aware of a myth when a change is occurring within that myth. Maggie was a commercial artist who had terrifying dreams in which she was fleeing from a huge and ugly monster. She was so troubled by these dreams that she tried to draw pictures of the monster but couldn't quite capture the image. The next time she had the dream, Maggie was so determined to remember what the creature looked like that she actually turned to face it, but the monster disappeared. The dream took place again, but this time when the monster faded into the distance, Maggie ran after it, finally catching up with it and actually touching it. As she touched the monster, she screamed in terror and at that moment it turned into a beautiful, horselike creature. Maggie rode it, whirling in a sky of clouds, until she found herself in the embrace of a man.

Maggie awoke, realizing that she had once had the same feeling of terror in an early dating experience. As a result, she had held herself distant and aloof from men, acknowledging that the sexual response was difficult for her. Taking clues from the dream, Maggie allowed herself to permit more sexual fantasy into her awareness and, later, into her life. She finally was able to draw the sequence of events in her dreams. Maggie began to open up to intimate contact on both the emotional and sexual levels. Her old personal myth's insistence that intimate contact was monstrous gave way to a new myth stating that interpersonal closeness could transport her to new realms of understanding, just as the flying horse did in her dream.

Personal Myths and Dreamwork

The mass media continually remind people that they are surrounded by extremely talented individuals who have skills in areas about which most others know very little. Upon comparing oneself with these celebrities, a person may ignore or minimize one's personal creative potentials. A person may know an area of expertise thoroughly but it may have ceased to be new, unusual, or inspirational. Abilities are taken for granted and unique capabilities are ignored. Personal myths become constricted, limited, and mundane. The hero's or heroine's journey, a common theme of cultural mythology, is bypassed in favor of myths that emphasize a habitual, passive existence. Yet, effective dreamwork is based on the reality that creative potential is a nearly universal human trait.

Dreams can be a source for constant inspiration, giving the dreamer permission to make mistakes, discard old habits, and indulge in spontaneous and nonrational behavior. The dreamer can become less concerned about other people's opinions and about traditional ways of understanding projects. If a business deal is successfully consummated in a dream, the dreamer may become more confident in waking life. The approach used in the dream may even reveal some hitherto overlooked strategy that might yield success.

Old Myths and Counter-Myths

Dreams play an active role in the ongoing revision of an individual's personal mythology. Though dreams probably serve many physiological and psychological functions, one function that receives the greatest attention in working with personal myths is the dream's role in synthesizing the dreamer's existing mythic structure with the data of his or her life experiences. As Montague Ullman notes, "Our dreams serve as corrective lenses that, if we learn to use them properly, enable us to see ourselves and the world about us with less distortion and with greater accuracy."[2]

Frequently, a conflict in one's personal mythology affects his or her behavior, feelings, or thoughts, and a mythic crisis becomes apparent in that person's development. This crisis typically occurs when a prevailing myth becomes so outdated or otherwise dysfunctional that the psyche generates a counter-myth to organize perceptions and responses along different lines. This process has been observed by developmental psychologists over the years, although they have described it in different terms (Feinstein & Krippner, 1994).

When this occurs, the psyche is in conflict; each myth becomes a psychological entity that starts to dominate the same situation with its own particular mode of perceiving and responding. Typically, the conflict between the old myth and the counter-myth proceeds outside of awareness. The counter-myth may become crystallized, developing within one's cognitive system and emerging in response to the old myth's limitations. It challenges the old myth, and the two engage in a dialectical process. The old myth becomes the *thesis*, and the counter-myth becomes the *antithesis*. The way that internal conflict develops is similar to the way that the Aztec religion was opposed by the newly arrived Roman Catholic religion; or the way that Eastern thought was confronted with Western thought when Alexander the Great invaded India.

There are nine ways in which dreams appear to handle old myths and counter-myths. First, a dream could emphasize past experiences that validated the old myth. For example, a man is told in a dream, "You really are a failure and always have been, your promotion at work notwithstanding." Second, a dream could force a fit between the old myth and daily experience: A woman who stays out later than she had planned dreams about being berated by her husband, a punishment her old myth felt she deserved, even though her spouse never would have taken such an action in real life. Third, a dream could preview the future according to the script of the old myth, often with a sense of irreversible fate: A young woman on the verge of moving away from her dominating parents dreams about herself ten years in the future, still living at home. Some people misinterpret these dreams as confirming the validity of the old myth rather than as reflecting and often caricaturing it.

On the other hand, there are three ways a dream may strengthen a counter-myth that has grown out of the old myth's deficiencies. First, the dream may rework old experiences and interpret them in a less self-limiting, more affirming manner providing an alternative to the old myth's template of reality. For example, a young man who had worked many years for an unstable, vindictive employer dreams about making the best of the situation, learning what he can before moving on to another job. Second, the dream may accommodate the old myth to fit new experiences so that the old myth corresponds more closely to the counter-myth: An aspiring vocalist, somewhat disappointed that her first engagement turns out to be a small nightclub, dreams about how much she can learn by trying out new material with her audience. Third, the dream may organize possibilities into a future with wish-fulfillment qualities: A newly arrived immigrant dreams about the possibilities she envisions for her life in the new country.

Finally, there are three ways that the dream may facilitate an integration between the two myths. As ongoing experiences bring the two together, making them more compatible, the essential elements of each become integrated. The forces that work against dissonance begin to unite the two. This is evident in dreams that highlight experiences from the past in which the mythic conflict was evident, showing ways it could have been integrated at that time. For example, a man works on resolving a new conflict by dreaming of a past psychotherapy session in which he had resolved a related problem. Second, a dream may highlight the conflict as it has emerged in current experiences and show ways of resolving it: A woman dreams about a conflict with a neighbor, considers ways of resolving the problem in the dream, and is instructed to attempt one of these by an inner voice. Third, a dream may portend that the conflict is resolved: A woman, anxious because her children are about to leave home, dreams about how she will enjoy her free time once they go to college.

The integration of the thesis and antithesis is called the *synthesis*. Although the Roman Catholic Church became the official religion of Mexico, syncretic underground rites developed in some parts of the country, combining Aztec deities with Catholic saints. After Alexander the Great left India, Greek themes continued to influence Indian sculpture. Western ideas had a major impact on Japan after the historic "opening" of Commodore Perry; the success of Japanese technology and industry is a more recent example of synthesis. Sometimes the counter-myth predominates, as in Mexico; sometimes the old myth retains most of its power, as in India; and sometimes a true synthesis is accomplished, as in Japan.

Once one learns how to interpret dreams on this basis, one can quickly identify which of these nine possibilities is present. Sometimes none of them will appear. Sometimes more than one will be present in a dream. This system also demonstrates the value of working with a *series* of dreams because the struggle between the old myth and the counter-myth often is played out in one's dreams over time.

This system interfaces with portions of several other dream theories. The counter-myth would be seen by Adlerians as the psyche's attempt to solve problems around dilemmas caused by the prevailing myth. Freud's wish-fulfillment notion involves the counter-myth, as do Jung's compensatory dreams, which allegedly express an underdeveloped part of the psyche. Gestalt psychologists' view of dream elements as conflicting parts of the psyche focuses on the conflictual aspect of this system. The information theory approach to dreams is congruent with the adaptive function that this system perceives dreams as serving.

Emotional tone and bodily feelings often give the dreamer clues about the function of the dream. Old myth dreams typically feel pessimistic and hopeless, and seem to drain the dreamer of energy and vitality. Counter-myth dreams usually feel hopeful, optimistic, and exhilarating. Integration or synthesis dreams tend to produce a calm, positive, assured feeling. Of course, emotion and mood in a dream are dependent on the dreamer's thinking and feeling style.

However, one cannot claim that all dreams revolve around personal myths any more than one can claim that a Freudian client's sexual dreams prove Freudian theory, or that a Jungian client's compensatory dreams prove Jungian theory. Ullman suggests that dream theories are basically waking metaphors for expressing, in highly condensed language, the therapist's preferred way of perceiving and understanding the client's predicament. When the therapist's metaphorical construct fits well with the metaphors of the client's dream imagery, a sense of contact between the dreamer and the therapist develops.

Indeed, Ullman suggests that professional help is needed when the dreamer's self-deceptive myths are so intrusive that he or she is not open to what is coming through in the dream. But for the dreamer who is in touch with internal processes, personal myths can be seen in dreams as accommodating developmental needs and unknown parts of the psyche. Personal myths capitalize on opportunities and strengths, and deal with a person's deficiencies realistically. Personal myths can resolve polarities and enable a healthy dialectic to occur that leads the dreamer to higher levels of synthesis.

Creative behavior can reflect one's ongoing struggle or the mythic synthesis that marks the temporary end of the conflict. Abraham Maslow pointed out that a hallmark of creative people he studied was their ability to resolve dichotomies: "The great artist is able to bring together clashing colors, forms that fight with each other, dissonances of all kinds, into a unity. And this is also what the great theorist does when he puts puzzling and inconsistent facts together so that we can see that they really belong together. And so also for the great statesman, the great therapist, the great philosopher, the great parent, the great inventor. They are all integrators, able to bring separates and even opposites together into unity."[3] It is this same process that marks the creative synthesis of two opposing personal myths.

However, today's synthesis often becomes tomorrow's old myth, a belief, theme, or script that may outgrow its usefulness as an individual continues to develop his or her latent capacities. Dreams can provide continual access to one's ongoing development, allowing a creative use of each step in self-discovery. Dreams appear to synthesize the dreamer's existing mythic structures with the information gleaned by his or her life experiences. Personal myths seem to develop in a manner that is parallel to the way dreams develop because they are related to the brain's propensity for language, imagery, and storytelling. These are the raw materials for myth, and we believe that dreams play an active role in the ongoing revision of the dreamer's personal mythology.

In Summary

- Personal myths can block one's creativity if they are not understood and taken into account.

- Some dreams attempt to eliminate discrepancies between one's personal myths and one's daily life events. Other dreams point out these discrepancies.

- Whether a person is aware of them or not, personal myths structure one's actions as well as one's explanations for what occurs.

- The old myth states the accepted worldview of the dreamer while the counter-myth provides alternatives to this view.

- Integrative dreams may state the procedure for synthesizing the old myth and the counter-myth.

Exercises

1. *Emerging Myths.* Emerging myths often require people to take risks in order to test their potential value. These risks may be previewed in dreams, as they give dreamers an opportunity to behave and experience in new and unusual ways. Review your dream notebook. Have you engaged in unusual activities in your dreams

that might suggest a novel opportunity for developing your personal or professional life? Dreams typically reflect one's daily concerns and customary lifestyle. A departure from conventional behavior in your dreams may anticipate the possibility of a new direction in your waking life.

2. *Alternative Answers.* Dreams can present not one but several "right answers" by expressing a number of different points of departure in a single dream or a series of dreams. Tonight you may be presented with alternative answers to a life dilemma. Examine which of these is the most feasible, and try to determine the basic personal myth that each "right answer" reflects.

3. *Alternative Values.* Unquestioned attitudes and assumptions often reflect prevailing myths that have a paralyzing effect on your creativity. But waking ethical and moral standards can be violated with impunity in dreams. Priests may find themselves sleeping with nuns; judges may find themselves committing perjury; business executives may find themselves squandering the company's profits. The dreamer may feel futility and be horrified by such behavior, but these alternative value standards may reflect emerging myths that are attempting to gain the dreamer's attention. Examine your dreams; identify an instance in which your dream behavior was immoral by your waking standards. What was your dream attempting to tell you? Consider the possibility that what Jungians call your shadow might reflect an emerging myth.

4. *Alternative Role Models.* People's desire to actualize themselves often is the mainspring in both creativity and psychotherapy. This tendency also can be found in many dreams. However, one personal myth that blocks self-actualization is the presence of inappropriate role models. Have you identified with role models that are inhibiting your development? Do these represent old myths in any of your dreams? Do your dreams contain images of emerging myths that challenge these role models? Do any of your dreams challenge the messages given you in the past by people or institutions that supported your adherence to these role models?

5. *Alternative Myths.* The hero's quest is only one myth that appears in dreams, legends, and works of art. Some alternatives are myths of creation, destruction, nurturance, finding a community, overcoming obstacles, completing a task, attaining wisdom, reconciling opposites, and empowerment, initiation, and/or transformation. Find one or more of these myths in your dreams and construct a fairy tale that reflects your life situation.

NOTES

1. Feinstein, D. & Krippner, S. (1997). *Your Mythic Path.* New York: Tarcher/Putnam.
2. Ullman, M. (1979). The experiential dream group. In B. B. Wolman (Ed.), *Handbook of Dreams* (pp. 406–423). New York: Van Nostrand Reinhold.
3. Maslow, A. H. (1976). Creativity in self-actualizing people. In A. Rothenberg & R. Hausman (Eds.), *The creativity question* (pp. 86–92). Durham, NC: Duke University Press.

26

Nightmares: Terrors of the Dreaming World

FRANKLIN GALVIN AND ERNEST HARTMANN

ALMOST EVERYONE has had a nightmare on occasion, most likely in childhood. Although people tend to forget their childhood nightmares, some have had particularly frequent or especially vivid ones that are remembered clearly throughout their lives.

Nightmares are definitely more frequent in children than in adults and are particularly common at ages three through six. Evidence suggests that they probably occur as early as age one. While they become less frequent after age six, their incidence may increase again in adolescence between ages thirteen and eighteen. The incidence of nightmares generally decreases with age and in healthy adults is relatively low.

Based on many survey studies, sleep researchers estimate that approximately 50 percent of the adult population have no nightmares at all, though they may have had them as children. Most others remember an occasional nightmare, and the average is perhaps one or two per year. Between 5 and 10 percent of the population report nightmares once a month or more. Only a small percentage have nightmares that are frequent enough or severe enough to be significantly disturbing to their lives. Men are probably as likely to have nightmares as often as women, but they tend to be much more reluctant to mention them.

What Produces Nightmares?

For centuries the word *nightmare* has been used loosely to mean anything that wakes one up in fright, a creature that produces such terror, the frightening dream itself, or the actual awakening. Most scholars now agree that the root *mare* derives from the Old English and Old German root *mara*, meaning "an incubus or succubus," and not from *myre*, meaning "a female horse." The folklore of peoples' experiences during the night inspired the eighteenth-century Swiss artist Henry Fuseli to depict both images in his well-known painting *The Nightmare*.

We no longer believe that demons or evil spirits produce nightmares, nor is there any solid evidence that eating something disagreeable will cause them. Recent evidence also contradicts another widely held view that a lack of oxygen gives rise to nightmares. Obstructive sleep apnea is a disorder in which air does not get through the throat to the lungs of the sleeper because of some obstruction at the back of the throat. This may happen 100 or more times in one night. The chest and abdomen of the sleeper heave but no air gets through, and after ten to twenty seconds there is a brief awakening, allowing normal breathing to resume. Sleep-apnea sufferers very rarely report nightmares, indicating that a lack of oxygen is not causally related to nightmares.

One factor that does appear to precipitate nightmares is physical illness, although it is unclear whether illness itself or the stress that accompanies it is more important. Children who do not otherwise have nightmares report them during times of illness, particularly febrile illness. Adults, too, seem to have more nightmares during high fever or around the time of an operation. In addition, certain neurological disorders sometimes have been associated with nightmares—notably epilepsy and postencephalitic parkinsonism.

Mental illness is often associated with nightmares. In certain individuals nightmares occur at the onset of psychosis, especially schizophrenic episodes. Depression can also be associated with an increase of nightmares.

Stressful events seem to be causally related to frequent and severe nightmares in susceptible persons. Stressful periods in adulthood, such as times of examinations, job changes, moves, or the loss of significant persons, may produce or increase nightmares.

The one generalization that seems to hold true for nightmare sufferers is that their nightmares almost always involve feelings of helplessness, most often helplessness dating from childhood. The most frequent situations in their nightmares involve being chased, attacked, thrown off a cliff, or generally feeling at the mercy of others. Almost invariably it is the dreamer who is in danger and utterly powerless—not someone else. A decrease or sometimes a cessation of adult nightmares usually occurs as the dreamer feels more confident, more mature, and thus less close to the helpless feelings of childhood.

PROFILE OF THE NIGHTMARE SUFFERER

Recent in-depth studies carried out at Ernest Hartmann's sleep laboratory at Shattuck Hospital in Boston have provided information about the personalities of people clearly reporting nightmares rather than night terrors. Using newspaper ads, subjects were recruited who had frequent nightmares as a long-term condition. One study examined thirty-eight adults reporting nightmares at least once per week for at least one year and beginning in childhood. A second study compared another twelve frequent nightmare sufferers with twelve people who reported vivid dreams but no nightmares and twelve others who reported neither nightmares nor vivid dreams. All the subjects were interviewed and given a battery of psychological tests including the Rorschach Inkblot Technique and several personality inventories; some were also monitored in the sleep laboratory.

Individuals in the nightmare groups from both of these studies were no different in intelligence from those in the comparison
groups, and likewise there were no clearcut physical differences in
appearance distinguishing the groups. The nightmare subjects were
different in having jobs or lifestyles related to the arts or other creative pursuits; they ranged from painters, poets, and musicians to
craftspersons, teachers, and nontraditional therapists. No blue-collar
workers or white-collar executives or office personnel were found
who had frequent nightmares, but there were many such workers in
the comparison groups.

The artistic and creative interest of the nightmare subjects was
a lifelong characteristic. These subjects felt themselves to be in some
way unusual for as long as they could remember and often described
themselves as sensitive in various ways. Some were sensitive to bright
light or loud sound, most could be easily hurt emotionally, and some
were quite empathic or sensitive to others' feelings. However, no
extreme trauma could be discerned in their histories.

More commonly than in the comparison groups, those with
nightmares described their adolescence as stormy and difficult, often
with bouts of depression and thoughts of suicide. They tended to
rebel by using drugs and alcohol, fighting with parents, or running
away. From adolescence on, the nightmare sufferers appeared to be
extremely open and trusting people—perhaps too trusting, making
them defenseless and vulnerable. They often became quickly
involved in difficult, entangling friendships and love relationships
from which they could not easily escape.

However, these nightmare sufferers were *not* especially anxious,
angry, or depressed people. Some were vulnerable to mental illness:
70 percent of them had been in psychotherapy, and 15 percent had
previously been admitted to mental hospitals; but at the time of the
interviews, as a group they were functioning quite well in life.

Hartmann and his associates described the creative, sensitive,
and vulnerable nightmare subjects as having "thin boundaries" in
many different senses. They had thin interpersonal boundaries—that
is, they became involved with others very quickly; thin ego boundaries, being extremely aware of their inner wishes and fears; and thin

sexual boundaries—they easily imagined being of the opposite sex, and many fantasized or engaged in bisexual activity. They also had thin group boundaries, for they did not strongly identify themselves with a single community or ethnic group. Their sleep-wakefulness boundaries were thin, for they often experienced in-between states of consciousness, unsure whether they were awake, asleep, or dreaming. Some would awaken from one dream only to find themselves in another.

TREATMENT OF NIGHTMARES

Treatment is not usually required for nightmares. Parents of children ages three through six, when nightmares are most common, should be aware that the occurrence of nightmares is not abnormal. Talking with these children and allowing them to express any fearful feelings may be helpful, as is checking the children's environment at home and school for any potential sources of fear or anxiety.

Most of the adult subjects with frequent nightmares in the above-mentioned studies had never sought treatment specifically for their nightmares, though many had sought it for other conditions, such as stress or depression. The majority had accepted their terrifying dreams as part of themselves and sometimes made use of them in their creative endeavors. However, some sufferers wanted treatment specifically for their nightmares. Judging from published accounts of case reports and a few controlled studies, a variety of therapeutic techniques have been used with success.

In a recent review of psychological therapies for nightmares, psychologist Gordon Halliday suggested four distress-producing features of the nightmare and proposed that treatment may reduce the distress by altering any of these features: the nightmare's uncontrollability, its perceived sense of reality, the dreadful and anxiety-producing story line, and the nightmare's believed importance. He categorized treatment techniques into these classes: desensitization and related behavioral procedures, psychoanalytic and cathartic techniques, story-line alteration procedures, and "face [the danger] and conquer [it]" approaches.

Desensitization and related behavioral procedures first identify the fear-generating components of the nightmares and then desensitize the dreamer to those elements through relaxation procedures, invoking pleasant imagery, or repeated exposure of those elements to the dreamer in a therapeutic setting. Psychoanalytic and cathartic techniques attempt to convey to dreamers an understanding of their nightmares in the context of their life situations and developmental histories, to allow suppressed or repressed emotion to be appropriately released, and to strengthen their adaptive mechanisms. Story-line alteration procedures try to change the nightmares through imagination or hypnotic suggestion by rehearsing different endings, confronting the nightmare figures, or modifying some detail. The "face and conquer" approaches consist of instructions to the dreamer to face and confront the nightmare figures when the dreamer is next experiencing an actual nightmare dream state. Several other methods that have been used clinically but not yet reported in the case literature include teaching dreamers, especially children, to call upon a "dream friend" for help and restaging nightmares in collages or drawings.

We are currently investigating a "face and conquer" treatment procedure that attempts to teach frequent nightmare subjects to attain a lucid dream state in order to reduce the frequency and severity of their terrifying dreams. A lucid dream is one in which the sleeper is aware *during the dream* that he or she is dreaming and feels to be in full possession of mental functions as if awake. This awareness permits the dreamer to make choices as the dream occurs. For example, the dreamer may be walking through an unusual landscape, realize that the experience is a dream, and decide to fly into the air to see the dream landscape from a new perspective.

In nonlucid dreams, which are more common, there is generally a sense of the dream experience happening *to* the dreamer with little feeling of choice about what occurs. Thus, when confronted by a threatening figure in a nightmare, the dreamer usually tries to run away from it. By becoming lucid in the nightmare, the dreamer could then choose to turn and face the threatening figure and possibly master what is feared.

In nearly all of the published reports, clinical accounts, and first-person descriptions of utilizing the lucid dream state to deal with nightmares, the actual dreamers perceived and felt their encounters to be positive, enriching, and empowering experiences both during and after their dreams. However, given that most of these persons are from a normal population, it is possible that these observations may not generalize to a population of frequent nightmare sufferers. Also, though such a treatment has therapeutic potential, it does involve some risk, because there are isolated accounts of negative lucid dream experience.

The lucid-dream treatment approach has the potential to alter three of the four distress-producing aspects of the nightmare suggested by Halliday. Once one achieves lucidity within a nightmare, the nightmare's uncontrollability can be altered, because the dreamer can choose and act to change his or her response to the threatening images; the nightmare's perceived sense of reality can be altered, because the dreamer understands that the experience is a dream rather than part of everyday physical external reality; and the nightmare's dreadful and anxiety-producing story line can be altered as a result of the changed response of the dreamer. Other dreamworkers, such as Stephen LaBerge, may contend that the fourth distress-producing aspect, the believed importance of the nightmare, also may be altered, because lucid dreamers "realize that they themselves contain, and thus transcend, the entire dream world and all of its contents, because they know that their imaginations have created the dream."

The major limitation cited by Halliday in utilizing the lucid dream state as a treatment modality for nightmares is that it is not yet known how to reliably induce this experience. Psychologist Joseph Dane has developed a posthypnotic suggestion technique for inducing the lucid dream state in hypnotically susceptible women. Using this technique, seven of the eight women in one group of his study succeeded in having verified lucid dreams. This is a promising approach for frequent nightmare sufferers, because there is evidence that they have higher hypnotizability scores than others.

Two recent studies indicate that learning lucid dreaming could be a viable treatment method for frequent nightmare sufferers. The first is a study of boundary characteristics by Franklin Galvin, which matched forty spontaneous lucid dreamers with forty frequent nightmare dreamers and forty nonlucid and relatively nightmare-free dreamers (ordinary dreamers). In comparison to the ordinary dreamers, both the lucid dreamers and the nightmare dreamers were shown to have "thin boundaries." In addition, a number of the spontaneous lucid dreamers stated that they had first developed lucidity during frightening dreams.

The second is a case study by Andrew Brylowski, which related the treatment of a thirty-five-year-old woman, Ms. D., with a history of major depression and a diagnosis of borderline personality disorder. She reported one to four nightmares per week and had a history of recurrent nightmares of variable frequency and intensity since age ten. The treatment focused on alleviating her nightmares using lucid dreaming. Within the first four weekly sessions, the introduction of lucidity into the patient's dream life coincided with a decrease in the frequency and intensity of her nightmares.

The report of a dream by Ms. D. seven weeks into the treatment illustrates her ability to avert a potential nightmare by using lucidity to convert a threat into a learning experience.

> *Ms. D. was walking up huge grey stone stairs leading to a fortress or castle. Looking down she saw a colleague and felt thrilled. The stairs then extended over a moat. She stopped to look at the water and a vicious grey shark with big white teeth surfaced. It propelled itself along the stairs toward her. Ms. D. was frozen with fear and couldn't move. She then realized that she had been having a good dream until the shark appeared; then she thought: "It is a dream!" She was unable to do anything but stare at the shark. The shark changed into a huge whale that smiled and was no longer terrorizing. She awakened in peace.*

Though she had previously thought of things she might do when she became lucid in a frightening dream, at the moment of fear she could only stare and not run. When she stood her ground and faced the terror rather than attempting to flee, the threatening image was transformed into an acceptable figure positively acknowledging her. Facing the fear in her dream enabled her to wake in peace. Altering her nightmares also facilitated Ms. D. in making positive changes to deal with her waking emotions.

The skills Ms. D. learned in lucid dreaming extended into areas of her waking life. After another nine weeks of treatment, she reported a dream in which she was working on a painting with two colors, each scintillating. Upon realizing it was a dream, she created a third color by blending the first two. With this new color she added depth and dimension to the painting. This accomplishment in her dream prompted Ms. D. to complete other art projects in her waking life that she had left unfinished.

As Sigmund Freud's nightmare was able to retain "its imperishable value . . . by becoming a driving force in the making of a genius," and as Carl Jung was initiated into the secrets of the earth by a nightmare and later brought light into this realm of darkness, so too have the nightmares of others heralded some meaningful change in their lives. For those with frequent nightmares, the use of the lucid dream state could offer a unique opportunity to begin such a change.

27

Dream Sharing in Cyberspace

RICHARD CATLETT WILKERSON

DEBORAH J. HILLMAN[1] has characterized the dream movement as a massive sharing of information between fields of study and a leap from clinical to nonclinical settings. Dream sharing is no longer limited to psychological healing, and includes dream-inspired art, dream-inspired literature, dream journals as novels, dream education, and a host of new multimedia processes.

The Internet has served to open up a fabulous garden of dreamy delights for people who have never had the chance to experience dreamwork and dream play. A single dream-sharing group might include members from downtown New York, the Left Bank of Paris, and the back roads of Australia. Further, new forms of dream sharing are emerging that could not have been imagined before the Internet, such as low-cost, dream-inspired art galleries, virtual conferencing, and multi-identity attendance in dreamwork sessions. One site may embody art, text, theory, spirituality, and capitalism in a complex global network of events, organizations, and publishing.

THE DANGERS OF PUBLIC SPACE

Joseph Campbell often remarked that the gates of heaven are guarded by monsters. Sharing dreams online has its own share of monsters, and they don't always stay at the gate. Dream sharing in cyberspace challenges several notions, including what is inner and outer, private and public, appropriate and inappropriate, safe and unsafe, clinical and nonclinical, professional and fake.

In 1995, the executive board of the Association for the Study of Dreams (ASD) took a foresighted step and allowed me to develop a dream and computer tract at the 1996 Berkeley conference. The only proviso was that no dreamwork could be done via the Internet at the conference computer room area. This restriction developed out of the fear that unmoderated dreamwork online was dangerous and inappropriate as an ASD-approved event. This probably was a prudent decision, yet those of us who had been experimenting for years knew such fears were wildly exaggerated. The dream-sharing community I was working with, the Electric Dreams community, hadn't found a single case where a person complained of being harmed or abused.

Of course, the potential for abuse does exist, as it is still possible for people seeking and needing therapy to confuse clinical and nonclinical dreamwork. It also is difficult to determine the age and emotional maturity of participants online. Many topics discussed in adult dream sharing may not be considered appropriate for children.

A panel was formed at the Berkeley conference to discuss these issues. Besides myself, panel members included Sara Richards, a psychotherapist; Jayne Gackenbach, an Internet psychology pioneer and anthropologist; Jeremy Taylor, a longtime dreamworker who was running the America Online DreamShow at the time; and John Herbert, a pioneering researcher in computer-mediated dreamwork. The conclusion was unanimous that dream sharing online was a valuable activity and worth the risks involved. However, these conclusions were for nonclinical dreaming.

PERSONAL DREAM JOURNALS

One of the most powerful skills in dreamwork is journal keeping. However, one of the biggest blocks to keeping a dream journal has always been personal motivation. With the advent of dream sharing on the Internet, a boost in the motivation system may be supplied by a social network. An online journal now can be constructed or published at little or no cost to the dreamer. These journals can be fully public, or open to just a few people with an access password. They can be published anonymously, or with all the details and background of the dreamer's life. Many of the dream journals online include places to make public comments that become part of the overall journal. Others request that private messages be sent via E-mail to the dreamer [http://www.dreamgate.com/dream/resources/ (select "Online" and then "Personal Journals")].

Many people feel horror in hearing that such personal material is being made public. What happens when I dream about a friend engaging in an illegal activity and publish her name online? Will there be lawsuits? Will people lose their jobs? These fears reflect the current issues about online publishing and seem to be eternal problems.[2] They can never be fully resolved, but neither can we stop trying to solve them. They bring up our most cherished notions of what a dream is, where it comes from, what its purpose may be, and who gets to be the final authority in determining its meaning and value.

The potentials of public, online dream journals are quite fantastic. Soon we will be able to type in our dream text and receive a movie in return. The program simply will locate pictures on the Net and build a moving graphic. True, the show would be a collective representation of our dream, but who could resist not having one's dreams illustrated automatically?

A project by John Gallagher called the National Dream Registry is being developed to create a geographic weather map of dreams. Participants will send dreams into the registry in the morning, and the mapping program will give data on what different parts of the country are dreaming about. Although this may be seen as more of an oddity than as something useful, the eventual collections in the data banks will serve as resources for content analysis experts and special topic researchers. The Numinous Archives Dream Interactive System is a smaller project of the same kind and clearly demonstrates the potentials mentioned [http://www.nadis.netNADIS].

One of the earliest projects in group dream journaling, Dream-Mosaic [http://www.itp.tsoa.nyu.edu:80/~windeatr/dreamMosaic.html], was developed by Dan Cummings.[3] DreamMosaic allowed dreamers to post dreams and then link the words and phrases together to associated themes around the Net. A dream of an alligator could be linked to a whole site on alligators, or the worship of alligators among the Yanamamo.

Individuals who have been providing their own collections of personal journals are beginning to link together in Web rings. These rings of associated themes may allow researchers to quickly locate massive amounts of dream material and expand long-term dream journal projects. They also create a community among the dream journal keepers.

For the individual, online journals offer a way to express parts of the self often locked away from public view, helping the person to gain the insights from others. Comments and dialogues can occur anonymously, and the threat of exposing inappropriate psychological or personal material is minimal. The creative variations on the dream journal are limitless and include the additions of multimedia, interactivity, hyperlinking, and text modulation.

Dream Groups and Dreamwork in the Electronic Omnisphere

Jill Gregory, director of the Dream Library and Archive [http://members.aol.com/dreammzzz/index.htm], has said that the heart and soul of the dream movement continues to be the local dream groups. The Internet has extended this to the far corners of the earth and made dream groups available to people who might never have had the chance to share their dreams with others.

In 1994, while I was searching online for bibliographic information on dreaming, I noticed a post on the Usenet newsgroup alt.dreams. It was an invitation to join a dream group named Electric Dreams [http://www.dreamgate.com/electric-dreams]. This dream bulletin board (alt.dreams) allows individuals to post dreams and dream-related issues. Some people want advice on how to recall dreams, some want their dreams interpreted, some want to discuss books and topics on dreaming. The level of discussion is uneven and is predominantly used by people new to dreaming online. But there is the possibility that it may one day be a major discussion area for dreams and dreaming. Two more dream-related newsgroups have appeared, alt.dreams.lucid and alt.dreams.castaneda. For those interested in these boards, a simple news reader program is needed, which is usually provided by your Internet Service Provider.

Electric Dreams decided to run a group by passing around a set of dreams and having everyone ask questions and comment on them [http://www.dreamgate.com/dream/ed-backissues]. The comments and dreams were collected and sent out to the group about every two weeks. But there often was a gap of a week or two between sharing a dream and getting feedback. In the fall of 1994, I re-formed the Electric Dreams group, making it more like a discussion-based magazine, publishing dreams, comments, news, and articles and using it as a jumping-off point for connecting with outer groups. The E-zine, or electronic magazine, flourished as a free dream-sharing forum run by volunteers. Some saw the dreams and comments as a form of literary criticism, while others were aghast that personal dreams and comments on these dreams were made public.

The experimental dream groups were significantly enhanced in 1995 by John Herbert with his America Online (AOL) SeniorNet Dream Bulletin Board. Herbert's groups used a variation of the Ullman technique, which he had worked out on two popular Internet Services, the WELL and AOL.[4]

Herbert had a wonderful dream-sharing process for electronically mediated communications which he had developed earlier on local BBS and the WELL. One could call up a service via a com-

puter modem and join in a variety of activities and discussions. Like
Usenet newsgroups, there were topic areas and discussion boards.
John's degree work at the Saybrook Institute in California led him
to see that while electronic groups were not as efficient with han-
dling emotions, they did offer more satisfying insights to the participants. He had adapted his methods to the AOL SeniorNet bulletin
boards with great success [http://users.aol.com/johno417/HuSci/
Greet.html].

The process is very simple. Participants send in dreams to a
moderator, who picks one for the group to explore. The dream and
instructions are posted at an agreed-upon time. The participants can
log on to the message board and ask clarifying questions of the
dreamer, who may or may not respond within a day or two. A typical question might be about the color of a jacket or if the dreamer
recalled anything more about the contents of a box. Interpretations
on the part of the dreamer or participants are avoided. Once the flow
of questions and answers drops off, the moderator asks each person
to take the dream as if it were his or her own and to post their comments. Herbert modifies the Ullman Stage II dream process accen-
tuating the re-owning of projections, requesting that an implicit or
implied "In my dream..." attitude be applied before every statement.
Again, the dreamer may or may not post replies to the bulletin
board, but it seems to make for a more complete group when this
happens. The moderator then steps in again and creates closure for
the group and sets a date for the next dream to be discussed [sam-
ple session: http://users.aol.com/johno417/dmgp/dg16.html].

I took this process back to the Electric Dreams community and
modified the process for E-mail. After some experimentation we
found a process that worked very well.[5] In these groups, all participants would send in dreams to the moderator, who would then E-
mail the first dream and instructions to the group participants. This
may sound confusing, but the E-mail created a sense of group cohesion. The Electric Dreams groups use a mail list called dream-
on@lists.best.com. Subscribers join the list and any mail sent to that
address is distributed to everyone else on the list, allowing for group
discussions and cohesion. Participants can easily take themselves off

the list. The lists can easily be protected from unwanted subscribers and intruders [http://www.dreamgate.com/dream/temple].

E-mail lists can further protect the members by allowing for anonymous participation. For most participants, one's E-mail address and first name are all the anonymity required. But for clinical and other support situations, more protection may be needed and participants can either sign up with an E-mail address where the personal information is withheld or use what is called a re-mailer, in which all E-mail is forwarded and the final E-mail address is kept secret.

The Electric Dreams Dreamwheel groups have been continually offered since 1995 and have spawned variations and offshoots in other countries, most notably the groups run by Roger Ripert in France.[6] Usually the dream group is disbanded after a series of dreams is finished. But some groups decide to stay together for years.

REAL-TIME CHAT

Herbert found that the Internet bulletin-board groups lacked the emotional involvement of face-to-face groups. This gap has been somewhat lessened by dream groups that are hosted in electronic conferencing that approximates real time. Due to the constraints at present in bandwidth, real teleconferencing via the Internet is rare and slow. But text-based real-time chat has been popular since the early 1990s. The most popular is IRC, Internet Relay Chat,[7] which provides a group with a real-time screen that allows for several conversations via text to take place at once. As soon as one finishes typing, the message is displayed on the screen of everyone else who is participating in the chat room. Thousands of rooms are open at any specific time, and anyone who connects can create a topic room in a few seconds. One can use real names or pseudonyms. People from around the world can connect at the same time and give a sense to the participants that they are all in the same space. When everyone leaves, the room disappears.

The advantage to IRC dream sharing is that there is immediate processing of imagery which leads to more emotionally toned sessions and the sense of the person being there. Roger Ripert and his

Oniros colleagues in France regularly use IRC to meet and discuss dreams. However, IRC does require that additional software be installed and is more involved than E-mail or preset chat rooms on the Web, AOL, MSN, or Compuserve.

Jeremy Taylor, who has been conducting groups offline for decades, expressed some initial concern about how his techniques would be translated in cyberspace:

> *Initially, I had some reservations about working dreams through this distinctly "cool" and physically isolating on-line medium. When I imagined as carefully as I could what it might be like, I was particularly concerned that the "flat" and highly compressed computer communication format might inhibit the flow of imagination, intimacy, and mutual respect so necessary for good dream work.*[8]

However, after just one experimental session online, Taylor's enthusiasm grew: "I have found that the emotionally and physically flat format of computer chat between people in widely separated locations appears to enhance many important elements that make group exploration of dreams so productive." Favored techniques by these real-time groups include nondirective questioning, such as variations of Gayle Delaney's Interview Method, dream re-entry approaches such as those of Fred Olsen, and exploration techniques like those used by Jeremy Taylor.

ONLINE DREAM-INSPIRED ART GALLERIES

Cyber-dream-inspired artists have taken advantage of the Internet to create everything from traditional galleries with pictures on the wall, to interactive pictures that talk about themselves and allow you to chat with the artist. Even the most self-inspired of dream artists like feedback and communication about their work and dreams. The primary communication tool of the Internet, E-mail, can be imbedded directly into the gallery, so that viewers who wish to write to the artists can do so immediately. Others have set up message boards that allow the viewer to post a public message or join an ongoing written discussion of the art right at the site.

The Granny Gallery, a project by Nancy Richter Brzeski, includes several works that focus on the evolving relationship among dream, artist, and family members. The evolution of Brzeski's work can be seen in a brief glance on her index page, or in more depth in larger graphic reproductions. Thus, the viewing public enters into something between a catalog and a gallery. Brzeski includes a dream about her Hungarian grandmother, Dora Graubart, who inspired the many "Granny" pieces. Also included are biographies and notes about the artwork and the creation process. A feeling of ancient root-edness occurs, offering a sense of deep insight into how the creative process emerges and grows from our dreams [http://www.dream gate.com/dream/granny/].

Alissa Goldring's Dream, Life, Art Gallery uses a revelation-across-time approach. With each new month a new gallery room focusing on a specific piece is opened. Each art piece is connected to a specific dream or dream series, as well as a life lesson. Each month a new article and graphic appear. Does Goldring feel the dream art illustrates the text, or is the text part of the graphicness of the presentation? Like a meditation on life itself, one can sit at this site, gain decades of perspective, and at the same time achieve a quiet mind [http://www.dreamgate.com/dream/goldring]. Some other notable dream inspired galleries include Epic Dewfall's Man Against Eternity lucid dream gallery, Jesse Reklaw's Slow Wave/Con-cave Up Dream Comics Galleries, the Electric Dreams Cover Gallery, and the Fly-by-Night Communal Dream Magic Show.

Epic Dewfall travels at night in his lucid dreams and searches for pictures on the dream walls. With some concentration he will remember a few of these upon awakening and then reproduces them on paper. The pictures then get scanned (digitally copied) and put in his online gallery. The background gallery itself is clearly an art piece as well. The World Wide Web gives Dewfall the ability to work more closely with the staging environment and to change the set more often with less expense than a traditional gallery. Dewfall also happens to be a poet as well as a graphic artist, and the text is mixed in as hypertext, meaning that a viewer may jump to a page with an entire poem. Dewfall's pictures and poems bring about an intuition that what is material shimmers in the foreground of a larger story, one that can be accessed best during a dream [http://www.storm.ca/~lucid/].

The Dream Wave Theatre mixes text and graphics in a unique way to explore mythological, archetypal mysteries of dreams. There is no attempt to categorically exhaust the possibilities, but rather to generate a deep respect for those dreamy things that neither text nor graphics can circumscribe, only celebrate in wonder. In a traditional gallery this is usually done by having a labyrinth of rooms. On the Web this is accomplished by turning graphics into buttons that, once selected, reveal a whole new area. On Dream Wave these new areas are meant to lead one more deeply into a particular theme [http://www.dreamwv.com/uworld/theatre/index.html].

A creative approach taken by Jesse Reklaw has been to illustrate contributors' dreams in comic form and then add them to one of the galleries. The Slow Wave Gallery includes weekly additions, a short dream strip each week plus from weeks past. The Concave Up Gallery is more involved and connected with the offline publication of the dream comic *Concave Up*. With this approach Reklaw has developed an interactive cybersite that both feeds the Net and draws sustenance as well [http://www.nonDairy.com/slow/wave.cgi].

Linton and Becky Hutchinson's DreamLynx is one of the original feedback dream sites. They also accept dreams and distribute them to various artists for illustration. Those illustrations are then put on the Web with the dreams. The dreamer remains anonymous when he or she wishes to, and the dream also may be put on a message board/bulletin board for others to comment. Joint projects between DreamLynx and Electric Dreams have expanded the simple post-and-comment into dream groups much like the ones researched by John Herbert. The dreamer may, during the course of the group, produce more art, which can then be returned to start the process over [http://licensure.com/.dream/].

Dream galleries will be expanding and becoming more popular as people realize the low development and maintenance cost, the
potential audience, and the exciting new possibilities in multimedia
presentations. And of course, these galleries are on Web sites that
host a wide variety of dream-sharing information, education, contacts, and links to other sites [http://www.dreamgate.com/dream/
resources (select "Online" and "Dream Art")].

DREAM SHARING AND PUBLISHING

Dream Tree, Dream Time, Dream Network Journal, the French
Oniros, and the MENSA *Somnial Times* all offer information about
their publications and have begun to publish articles online. *Dream
Tree* offers an international dream network news service, *The Global
Dreaming News,* as well as regional resource and event forums
[http://www.dreamtree.com]. *Dream Network Journal* offers articles
and an extensive searchable list of issue titles [http://www.dreamnet
work.net/]. *Oniros* supports a project called Planetary Dreaming, in
which seasonal topics are incubated by dreamers and published
online [http://perso.club-internet.fr/oniros/index.htm]. The journal
Dreaming has promoted online discussions where particular articles
are discussed within an academic community [http://www.as
dreams.org/subidxjournaldiscussion.htm]. The ASD *Dream Time*
publication has sponsored an ongoing dream and Internet educational column, the Cyberphile, which is also available online [http://
www.dreamgate.com/dream/cyberphile/]. Julia Koberlein's Nocturnal
Postings accepts dreams as literature [http://www.servtech.com/
~juliak/NocturnalPostings/], and Linda Magallon's NightFlyer deals
with the notion that dreaming can be fun.

What I feel will eventually emerge are newsletters and groups
that will target a particular interest group or individual. Dream publishing, I predict, will focus on small, concentrated areas, such as
dream interpretation and the Enneagram, children and nightmares,
or research in sleep studies in dreaming.

DREAM-SHARING EDUCATION

Three of the most formally structured programs on the Internet include Jayne Gackenback's Dream Discovery program with Grant MacEwan Community College [http://www.outreach.org/dreams/], Linda Magallon's program on Psychic Creative Dreaming [http://members.aol.com/caseyflyer/fbnc/fbnc04.htm], and my own program on the History of Dream Sharing, which is taught through Dream-Gate and Canadian Access TV [http://www.dreamgate.com/class]. These pioneering dream classes use a variety of Internet venues to offer course material that can be posted online, sent via E-mail, and then later discussed on bulletin-board posting areas and real-time chat rooms. Dream groups such as the type developed by John Herbert are used to instruct students in basic techniques such as the use of metaphor, association, and imaging. Unique group projects can include dream incubation, mutual dreaming projects, and sharing of art inspired by dreams. As soon as Internet teleconferencing becomes more accessible, dream-sharing techniques that need face-to-face contact will be added.

The ASD maintains a Web bulletin board for members to mingle with folks who are just curious about dreams. They keep several months of posts in order to promote a sense of community and to develop conversations and relationships that continue over time [http://www.asdreams.org/subidxdiscussionsbboard.htm].

The Intuition Network and DreamGate maintain an E-mail list, Cyberdreams, that also develops a sense of community. People can meet, share ideas, and participate in projects suggested by subscribers [http://www.dreamgate.com/dream/cyberdreams/]. A more personal approach is offered on the Daily Analyst, run by Dutch psychiatrist Willem Linschoten, which teaches techniques related to Freud and psychoanalysis [http://callisto.worldonline.nl/~cb008448/].

Don Kuiken has mixed the bulletin board with an E-mail discussion list. He invited international researchers to discuss Raija-Leena Punamäki's paper on dreams and trauma. . . . The discussion was posted weekly on the public ASD bulletin board [http://www.asdreams.org/subidxjournaldiscussion.htm].

The Electric Dreams community also combines Web sites, E-mail lists, and Web bulletin boards to allow question-and-answer sessions among a wide variety of individuals [http://www.dream gate.com/electric-dreams]. The Lucidity Institute offers a more focused approach to online education, posting articles on lucid dreaming, answering questions directly via E-mail, and offering compilations of the most frequently asked questions and answers [http://www.lucidity.com/].

Of course, there also are online sites where individuals answer questions in the more traditional style of newspaper columns. Jeremy Taylor maintains a topics board on AOL and has now added a board to his Web site [http://www.jeremytaylor.com]. Charles McPhee combines educational material from his book on sleep and dreams with question-and-answer posting [http://www.dreamdr.com/]. DreamGate has set up several response areas, including the Dream Q&A on the popular Self Help and Psychology site [http://www.shpm.com/articles/dreams/drintro.html], the DreamWork forum on AOL's Alternative Medicine [AOL keyword: AltMed (select "Therapies" and then "Dreamwork")], and the Cyber-Dream Library [http://www.dreamgate.com/dream/library].

THE FARTHER REACHES OF ONLINE DREAM SHARING

Dream sharing on the Net participates in the emerging concern about the meaning, significance, and potential value of the electronic omnisphere. How can such a network be used to communicate real wisdom? What unforeseen possibilities will arise? Preliminary speculations range from dire warnings to beatific visions. Some see the Net as falsely promising world peace while enslaving us to mere simulations of reality. Lonny Brown, on the other hand, sees the Net as a multidimensional link-up that amounts to nothing less than the next step in the evolution of human consciousness. Either way, people will be using the Internet to share dreams, create connections, and expand the notion of dreamwork beyond the recognized categories of today.

NOTES

1. Hillman, D. J. (1990). The emergence of the grassroots dreamwork movement. In Stanley Krippner (Ed.), *Dreamtime and dreamwork*, and Hillman, D. J. (1987). Dream work and field work: Linking cultural anthropology and the current dream work movement. In M. Ullman and C. Limmer (Eds.), *The variety of dream experience*. New York: Continuum.

2. Wilkerson, R. C. (1996). Dangerous dreams—the risks of online dream sharing. *Electric Dreams* 3(6). [Online]. Available: http://www.dreamgate.com/dream/ed-backissues/.

3. Cummings, D. (1995). The dream of cyberspace: Mosaic based dream interface to the Internet. *ASD Newsletter*, 12:7.

4. Herbert, J. W. (1991). *Human science research methods in studying dreamwork: Qualitative and quantitative analysis of face-to-face and computer dream work groups*. Unpublished manuscript, Saybrook Institute, San Francisco.[Online]. Available: http://users.aol.com/johno417/HuSci/Greet.html.

5. The content of some of these dream groups has been published on *Electric Dreams*, volume 5, issue 9, and *Electric Dreams*, volume 3, issue 4. [Online]. Available: http://www.asdreams.org/asd-13/2lb12.html.

6. EASD, the European Association for the Study of Dreams and Oniros, hosts dream groups via IRC. [Online]. Available: http://perso.club-internet.fr/oniros/.

7. Wilkerson, R. (1997). Dream sharing in cyberspace continues. *Dream Cyberphile Column*, Association for the Study of Dreams, *Dream Time 14*, volumes 3 and 4.

8. Taylor, J. (1996 June). Dreamwork in cyberspace. *Electric Dreams* 4(6). [Online]. Available: http://www.dreamgate.com/dream/ed-articles/ed4-6jt.htm. Originally posted on the DreamShow: The Hub on America Online. Also available in the *Dream Network Journal* (1996), 15(1), 35, 45.

28

How Dreams Reflect Neurological Disorders

OLIVER SACKS

HOWEVER DREAMS are to be interpreted—the Egyptians saw them as prophecies and portents; Freud as hallucinatory wish fulfillments; Crick and Mitchison as "reverse learning" designed to remove overloads of "neural garbage" from the brain; Jouvet as rehearsals for complex motor programs and behaviors—it is clear that they may also contain, directly or distortedly, reflections of current states of body and mind.

Thus it is scarcely surprising that neurological disorders—in the brain itself, or in its sensory or autonomic input—can alter dreaming either quantitatively or in striking and specific ways. Every practicing neurologist must be aware of this, and yet how rarely do we question patients about their dreams. Though there is virtually nothing on the subject in the literature, I think such questioning can be an important part of the neurological examination, can assist in diagnosis, and can show how sensitive a barometer dreaming may be of neurological health and disease.

I first encountered this many years ago while working in a migraine clinic. It became clear that there was not only a general correlation between the incidence of very intense dreams or nightmares and migraine auras (a correlation now well established by EEG studies) but also, not infrequently, an entering of aura phenomena into the dreams. Patients may dream of phosphenes, or zigzags, of expanding scotomas, or of colors or contours that wax and then fade. Their dreams may contain visual field defects, or hemianopias, or more rarely the phenomena of "mosaic" or "cinematic" vision. One patient of mine with an occipital angioma knew that if his normally black-and-white dreams were suddenly suffused with a red color, if they "turned red," he was in for a seizure.

The neurological phenomena may, in such cases, appear direct and "raw," intruding into an otherwise normal unfolding of a dream. But they may also, given a chance, combine with the dream, fuse with, and be modified by, its images and symbols. Thus the phosphenes of migraine are commonly dreamed of as firework displays, and one patient of mine often "embedded" his nocturnal migraine auras in dreams of a nuclear explosion. He would first see a dazzling fireball with a typical, iridescent, zigzag margin, coruscating as it grew, until it was replaced by a blind area with the dream round its edge. At this point he would usually wake, with a fading scotoma, intense nausea, and an incipient headache.

Another patient, who had focal sensory and motor seizures, once dreamt that he was in court, being prosecuted by Freud, who kept banging on his head with a gavel as the charges were being read. But the blows, strangely, were felt in his left arm, and he awoke to find it numb and convulsing, in a typical focal fit. But the most common neurological or "physical" dreams are of pain, or discomfort, or hunger, or thirst, at once manifest and yet camouflaged in the "scenery" of the dream. Thus one patient, newly casted after a leg operation, dreamt that a heavy man had stepped, with agonizing effect, on his left foot. Politely at first, then with increasing urgency, he asked the man to move, and when his appeals were unheeded, he tried to shift the man bodily. His efforts were completely useless, and now in his dreams, in his agony, he realized why: the man was made of compacted neurons—neutronium—and weighed six trillion tons, as much as the earth. He made one last, frenzied effort to move the immovable, then woke up with an intense viselike pain in his foot, which had become ischemic from the pressure of the new cast.

If there are lesions in the visual cortex, patients may observe specific visual deficits in their dreams. One patient with a central achromatopsia remarked that he no longer dreamt in color (Sacks and Wasserman, 1987). When dreaming, patients with prestriate lesions may be unable to recognize faces, a condition called prosopagnosia. If there is diffuse damage to the occipital cortex, visual imagery may vanish completely from dreams. I have encountered this, on occasion, as a presenting symptom of Alzheimer's disease.

The central effects of blindness can manifest themselves in dreams: there are few or no changes in dream imagery for a year or two after becoming blind; there then tends to be a loss of color in dreams, then a loss of recognizable faces and places; and finally, as the patient enters "deep blindness," a complete loss of all visual elements. This probably corresponds with a slowly progressive secondary (Wallerian) degeneration of the visual cortex.

Patients may sometimes dream of the onset of a disease. One patient, stricken with an acute encephalitis lethargica in 1926, had a night of grotesque and terrifying dreams about one central theme: she had dreamed she was imprisoned in an inaccessible castle, but the castle had the form and shape of herself; she dreamed of enchantments, bewitchments, entrancements; she dreamed that she had become a living sentient statue of stone; she dreamed that the world had come to a stop; she dreamed that she had fallen into a sleep so deep that nothing could wake her; she dreamed of a death which was different from death. Her family had difficulty waking her the next morning, and when she awoke there was intense consternation: she was parkinsonian and catatonic.

Another patient was admitted to the hospital three days before surgery to remove her gall bladder due to gall stones. She was placed on antibiotics for microbial prophylaxis; being an otherwise healthy young woman, no complications were expected. The day before surgery this patient had a disturbing dream of peculiar intensity. She was swaying wildly, in the dream, very unsteady on her feet, could hardly feel the ground beneath her, could hardly feel anything to her hands, found them flailing to and fro, kept dropping whatever she picked up.

She was distressed by this dream ("I never had one like it," she said. "I can't get it out of my mind")—so distressed that we requested an opinion from the psychiatrist. "Preoperative anxiety," he said. "Quite natural, we see it all the time." But within a few hours the dream had become a reality, as the patient became incapacitated by an acute sensory neuronopathy. One must assume in such cases that the disease was already affecting neural function, and that the unconscious mind, the dreaming mind, was more sensitive to this than the waking mind. Such "premonitory" or, rather, precursory dreams may be happy in content, and in outcome, too. Patients with multiple sclerosis may dream of remissions a few hours before they occur, and patients recovering from strokes or neurological injuries may have striking dreams of improvement before such improvement is "objectively" manifest. Here again, the dreaming mind may be a more sensitive indicator of neural function than examination with a reflex hammer and a pin.

Some dreams seem to be more than precursory. One striking personal example stays in my mind. While recovering from a leg injury, I had been told it was time to take the next step, to advance from using two crutches to just one. I tried this twice, and both times fell flat on my face. I could not consciously think how to do it. Then I fell asleep, and had a dream in which I reached out my right hand, grabbed the crutch that hung over my head, tucked it under my right arm, and set off with perfect confidence and ease down the corridor. Waking from the dream, I reached out my right hand, grabbed the crutch that hung over the bed, and set off with perfect confidence and ease down the corridor.

This, it seemed to me, was not merely premonitory, but a dream that actually did something, a dream that solved the very motor-neural problem the brain was confronted with, achieving this in the form of a psychic enactment or rehearsal or trial: a dream, in short, that was an act of learning.

Disturbances in body-image from limb or spinal injury almost always enter dreams, at least when they are acute, and before any "accommodation" has been made. With my own deafferenting leg injury, I had reiterative dreams of a dead or absent limb. Within a few weeks, however, such dreams tend to cease, as there occurs a revision or "healing" of body-image in the cortex (such changes in cortical mapping have been found in Michael Merzenich's experiments with monkeys). Phantom limbs, by contrast, perhaps because of continuing neural excitation in the stump, intrude themselves into dreams (as into waking consciousness) very persistently, though gradually telescoping, and growing fainter with the passage of years.

The phenomena of parkinsonism may enter dreams. One patient of mine, a man of acute introspective ability, felt that the first expression of parkinsonism in him was a change in the "style" of his dreams. He would dream that he could move only in slow motion, or that he was "frozen," or that he was rushing and could not stop. He would dream that space and time themselves had changed, kept "switching scales," and had become chaotic and problematic. Gradually, over the ensuing months, these Looking-Glass dreams came true, and the patient's bradykinesia and festination became obvious to others. But the symptoms had first presented themselves to him in his dreams. Perhaps parkinsonism itself is potentiated in dreams.

Another patient of mine, who has Tourette's syndrome, felt that he frequently had "Touretty" dreams—dreams of a particularly wild and exuberant kind, full of unexpectedness, accelerations, and sudden tangents. This changed when he was put on haloperidol, and he reported that his dreams had been reduced to ". . . straight wish fulfillment, with none of the elaborations, the extravagances of Tourette's."

Alterations in dreaming are often the first sign of response to L-dopa in patients with ordinary Parkinson's disease, as well as those with post-encephalitic syndromes. Dreaming typically becomes more vivid (many patients remark on their dreaming, suddenly, in brilliant color), more emotionally charged, and more prone to go on all night. Sometimes the "realness" of these dreams is so extraordinary that they cannot be forgotten or thrown off after waking.

Excessive dreaming of this sort, excessive both in sensory vivid-
ness and in activation of unconscious psychic content—dreaming
akin, in some ways, to hallucinosis—is common in fever, after many
drugs (opiates, cocaine, amphetamines, etc.), and in states of drug
withdrawal and REM rebound. A similar unbridled oneirism may
occur in other organic excitements, and at the start of some psy-
choses, where an initial mad or manic dream, like the rumbling of
a volcano, may be the first intimation of the eruption to come.
Dreaming, for Freud, was the "royal road" to the unconscious.
Dreaming, for the physician, may not be a royal road, but it is a
byway to unexpected diagnoses and discoveries, and to unexpected
insights about how one's patients are doing. It is a byway full of fascination, and should not be neglected.

29

From Chaos to Telepathy: New Models for Understanding Dreams

STANLEY KRIPPNER

FOR YEARS, dreaming has been equated with periods of rapid eye movement sleep. However, psychologist Allan Combs and I have found that episodes of dreaming often occur during other phases of the sleep cycle as well, and we have proposed a model that incorporates this evidence. Thoughts, emotions, memories, and other components of conscious experience change from moment to moment during wakefulness as well as during sleep to produce various mindbody states.

Combs and I use the term *mindbody state* to describe such experiences as ecstasy, sadness, joy, and confusion.[1] These mindbody states are embedded in "states of consciousness," one of which is sleep. During sleep, your awareness is turned inward and sensations from the external world are prevented from reaching your higher brain centers. Your muscular action and motor output is blocked so that you do not act out the scenarios of the dream. However, your fingers, toes, and eyes can move. Hence, rapid eye movements are a sign that a dream is very likely in progress.

The night's first period of rapid eye movement sleep generally begins ninety minutes after you fall asleep. The neurons at the base of your skull start to fire a random barrage of high-voltage impulses that unleash a cascade of potent neurochemicals that pour into your brain's visual and motor centers. This, in turn, triggers memories and images that are combined and presented in original, vivid, and often baffling ways. Immediately, your brain creates a story that will make sense of these fragments, either providing a script that has waited patiently for the material that would allow it to surface, or producing a narrative that matches—as best it can—the images and memories that have been evoked.

Sometimes these stories reflect basic problems in living with which you have wrestled for years. At other times they reflect the events of the past few days or hours, some of them trivial, some of them consequential. In other instances, as far as we know, the brain's search for meaning produces little more than a jumble of disparate pictures and events. This process of tale telling and story making is remarkably similar to what transpires when you use language while awake.

Combs and I have found that there are great individual differences in the way that mindbody states fluctuate from day to day, hour to hour, or even minute to minute. Patterns are produced that can be called chaotic, lending themselves to analysis by chaos theorists who look for the underlying tendencies of complex activities such as weather patterns, stock market fluctuations, and the rhythms of the brain itself.

Dreaming also can be matched with the neurological activity that originates in the lower brainstem. Allan Hobson and his associates have proposed that lower brain activity evokes unstructured stimuli that are then shaped by the higher brain into something meaningful.[2] This phenomenon is referred to as self-organization by chaos theorists. Indeed, Combs and I have worked with physicist David Kahn to describe how this self-organized activity often reflects the residues of daily life with its accompanying moods, concerns, and anxieties.

The part of the brain that is ordinarily involved during the day is less active at night, which allows other brain centers to organize dream content. As a result, many dreamscapes are bizarre, marked by abrupt transitions, quick changes of scene, and actions that would seem illogical in daily life. At the same time, as chaos theorist Christine Hardy points out, dreams can provide "networks of meaning" that reflect "emotional intelligence," helping dreamers understand emotional relationships and their own personal feelings.[3]

SUBTLE INFLUENCES ON THE BRAIN

Combs and I have proposed that there are two important qualities of the sleeping human brain that make it sensitive to subtle influences. The first of these qualities is the brain's susceptibility to what chaos theorists call the butterfly effect: that a shift in the sleeping brain's neurochemistry can introduce a new image into an ongoing dream narrative, which demonstrates, as Allan Hobson proposes, the brain's incredible creative potential.

The second remarkable quality of your sleeping brain is its capacity to respond to minute signals. This is known as stochastic resonance in chaos theory, which helps to explain how small, emotional residues of the day's experience (for example, a surprising scene from a movie, an intriguing face in the crowd, a sarcastic comment in a letter) may return during a nighttime dream.

In our opinion, the butterfly effect and stochastic resonance are qualities of the sleeping brain that make it susceptible to "telepathic reception" and other unusual interactions. We suspect that dreams often begin as chaotic attractors that pull together diverse images, memories, and even some events distant in space and time that are attracted to the dream's forming vortex.

Christine Hardy finds that dreams often depict conflicts between two chaotic attractors, for example, between dominance and cooperation, helplessness versus competence, activity versus passivity, or authenticity versus superficiality. For example, a person who tends to rely on authoritarian social interactions may have powerful dreams about cooperation and synergy. Such a dream—depicting the conflict between hierarchy and cooperation—might persuade the dreamer to adopt a new set of values that can lead to more effective ways of relating to people at work and in social settings.

Our colleague Ernest Hartmann has described how the brain's neural networks are more open to greater novelty and emotional impact when we are asleep, and that "telepathic" dreams often involve someone who is emotionally close to the dreamer.[4] In this manner, the self-organizing dream creates order from chaos, resulting in a unique story that may be a review of daily events, an attempt to resolve a life trauma, an inventive technological or artistic marvel, a metaphorical solution to a psychological problem, or a preview of an oncoming event in the dreamer's life.

Physicist David Bohm wrote about a subtle, underlying, interpenetrating component of the universe that he described as "order enfolded in chaos." Implicit within this order is a cooperative spirit and an inherent awareness that might explain how dreams can touch on distant and future events. Montague Ullman has suggested that the image-laden dream is closer to Bohm's concept of this subtle, underlying order than the mode of waking consciousness. When we work with our dreams, we can bring the implicit meaning of dream images and metaphors into explicit waking awareness.[5]

Some dreams appear to be profoundly mythological, containing images or activities that Carl Jung called archetypes. These powerful symbols and metaphors may qualify as chaotic attractors because they pull together personal experiences, cultural themes, and the emotional undergirding of both. I have observed archetypal images and activities in many "telepathic" dreams, some collected in the laboratory and others recorded in dream diaries.

When you record your dreams, you write a report that typically connects a series of visual and action-oriented images. Many scientists (including myself) believe that these reports can help you to understand your behavior, experiences, and intentions. Numerous psychotherapists also are convinced that dreams can help you to identify and work through waking problems and concerns.[6]

In summary, chaos theory may be an especially appropriate tool for understanding the highly complex dreaming process. But chaotic attractors do not occur only in dreams. During wakefulness, people's effective functioning is often hampered by inferiority complexes, self-defeating personal myths, and psychosomatic ailments that sap energy that could be better used for life-affirming purposes. "Bifurcation," change, and transition in a person's inner life can be stimulated by working intensively with his or her dreams. As a result, dreamwork may affect people's learning abilities, their personal relationships, their spiritual fulfillment, and even the ability of their immune system to maintain health and well-being.

The Greek historian Hesiod wrote that in the beginning there was Chaos, vast and dark. But from Chaos emerged the underworld and the night who, after their union, gave birth to the upperworld and the day. All dreamers have the opportunity to create order out of chaos, leading the night's treasure chest of dream symbols and metaphors from their underworld into the upperworld, where they can be appreciated, understood, and applied in the light of day.

NOTES

1. Combs, A., & Krippner, S. (1998). Dream sleep and waking reality: A dynamical view of two states of consciousness. In S. Hameroff, A. W. Kaszniak, & A. C. Scott (Eds.), *Toward a science of consciousness: The Second Tucson Discussions and Debates* (pp. 487–493). Cambridge, MA: MIT Press.
2. Hobson, A. J. (1988). *The dreaming brain*. New York: Basic Books.
3. Hardy, C. (1998). *Networks of meaning: A bridge between mind and matter*. Westport, CT: Praeger.
4. Hartmann, E. (1998). *Dreams and nightmares: The new theory on the origin and meaning of dreams*. New York: Plenum Trade.
5. Ullman, M. (1999). Dreaming consciousness: More than a bit player in the search for answers to the mind/body problem. *Journal of Scientific Exploration, 13*, 91–112.
6. Cartwright, R., & Lamberg, L. (1992). *Crisis dreaming: Using your dreams to solve your problems*. New York: HarperCollins.

30

Dying and Mourning: Transitional Dreams

IAIN R. EDGAR

IN MANY AREAS of applied welfare practice, such as in family therapy and groupwork, dreams are being used by practitioners. However it is, perhaps not surprisingly, the case that dreamwork has been most carefully considered in relation to work with the terminally ill and the bereaved. Welman and Faber used a Jungian approach to link the creativity of dream imagery to the 'unconscious processes intrinsic to terminal illness.' They aimed to show that dreams actually prepare people for death and dying. Dreams, they assert, do this by helping the individual to consciously orientate to the collective symbols produced by the unconscious in response to their actual situation. In their article they reported a sequence of seven dreams recorded by a terminally ill seventy year old man. This man had no particular interest in dreams or psychology and was resisting the prognosis that he was terminally ill. The dream imagery reported included the 'separation of the body into two parts,' being called, 'from the other side by friends,' 'driving towards a light at the end of a very long tunnel,' 'dancing with two very young and beautiful girls' and finally dreaming of a 'bright flower' that he had always wanted in his garden.

Whilst the Jungian analysis of these symbols in the article richly draws upon mythological sources to attempt to explain the universal meaning of the young girls dancing and the 'bright flower' of the dreams, the other symbols referred to here are more easily understood as possibly being related to dying. For instance the long dark tunnel leading to a bright light is now commonly referred to when discussing the near death experience. Similarly the evocative meaning of 'being called' from the 'other side' by friends is a very literal symbolization of the dreamer's state. The authors assert that merely by remembering and being exposed to these dreams, the images had a therapeutic effect on the dreamer. They suggest that 'an enlightenment of his conscious attitude followed' through his becoming orientated to the numinous power of the dreamt symbol. From this example the authors assert particular features to such dreaming. First they argue that dream imagery can be anticipatory; second, it is progressive; third, that there is a repeated reference to 'post-mortal psychical existence'; and finally, there is a 'concomitant transformation of the personality.' These important claims assert a value and a meaning to dream imagery that is beneficial to the dreamer even without an analysis of the imagery. The old adage of 'sleep on it' when faced with an insurmountable problem remains then still pertinent!

Even in other content analyses of the dreams of the dying which have not taken such a Jungian stance and which have not evidenced the dying as having archetypal dream imagery they concluded, with Weisman, that:

> dreams continued to function as metaphors in which problems and solutions are conveyed to consciousness.

If such progressive, anticipatory and therapeutic outcomes are possibly available from our dream imagery, it is important that such hypotheses are further researched and that professional therapists and welfare workers become acquainted and familiar with how to deal with such imagery. The theme of progression in dreams comes out in another recent article that studied dying, mourning and loss symbolism in the dreams of young adult students. 149 college students were asked to keep dream diaries and 1412 dreams were examined for imagery of any deceased person. Furthermore 96 college students, some of whom had experienced a recent bereavement, were asked specifically about any dreams of dead people that they had experienced. A fourfold categorization of dreams was developed by the author. Dreams of the deceased were typically about 'coming back to life' in which the dead wanted to 'discuss the situation surrounding their death,' 'advice dreams' in which the deceased proffered advice to the dreamer; 'leave-taking dreams' which were usually experienced as being very positive and beneficial for the dreamer; and finally 'state of death' dreams wherein the deceased, usually by telephone, described, often incompletely, the state of death.

Barrett develops this typology of dreams about the deceased as reflecting the stages of the bereavement process. For instance the 'back to life' dreams relate to the first 'denial' stage of grieving in which fantasies of the return of the loved one are common, whilst the 'leave-taking' category of dreams relates especially to the acceptance stage of mourning. 'Leave-taking' dreams often involved the completion of unfinished business between the deceased and the dreamer. Dreaming then is hypothesized as being a key feature of the grieving process in which the 'incorporation' of the deceased is a vital point in reaching a successful resolution of the mourning process. So far the material I have been presenting in this chapter about the dream aspect of the grieving process has been describing the dream as something 'given' to the dreamer and the client or patient appears passive in relation to the receipt of their night imagery.

Mogenson however advocates an imaginal approach to mourning. Jung's advocacy of active imagination is also central to this concept and practice. Mogenson, like Welman and Faber, advocates the activation and generation of the images of the unconscious into the conscious mind of the mourner. Particularly useful are the spontaneous images produced by our dreams, but the products of spontaneous or therapeutically assisted reverie are also potentially valuable to the reflective process. Mogenson advocates then an 'elegiac mourning' consisting of an active dialogue with our own bidden and unbidden images of the deceased. Gestalt and psychodramatic procedures are advocated to further generate and facilitate this process, and are described separately in the next chapter. Part of the resolution of the mourning process lies in the discovery of images by the mourner which 'immortalize the dead.' The imaginative work of the mourning and how it can be assisted by counselor, therapist or welfare worker is the crucial focus of an imaginal therapy. Mogenson, like Jung also, refers to the Tibetan Book of the Dead as being a unique example of a definitive crystallization of the imaginal journey of the deceased through the various Bardo planes leading to rebirth. Whilst the Tibetan Buddhist has such a collective resource through which to understand and even experience the impersonal journey of the loved one, such a resource is largely unavailable to the post-modern Western individual psyche. Hence the derivation of meaning from dreams and other products of imaginal thought have to be sifted in a much more eclectic way for possible transpersonal or archetypal meaning.

A further example of a more active and therapist assisted approach to the imagery of the deceased is described in Malon's case-study. In this example a social worker reflects on how they worked with a young woman's recurrent nightmare of seeing the skeleton of her dead mother. Despite extensive resistance the young woman was strongly advised to turn and face the frightening image of her mother in the dream. After some time the woman did report that she had spontaneously turned and faced the mother image in a dream and could describe what she had looked like and her famil-iar wedding rings. Following this breakthrough the nightmares appeared to stop. This therapist, like Mogenson, sees dreams as a process to be imaginally engaged rather than reductively interpreted as in a more Freudian approach.

Finally Golden and Hill report how they used dream imagery as a way to help patients creatively grieve the loss of the good par-ents that they had never in actuality experienced. The patient is offered the opportunity to 'reimagine' themselves within the safe space of therapy. The authors suggest that:

> . . . capacity for reverie, the ability to play, to imagine and
> to dream—using whatever signifiers are at hand—shifts
> the balance from the hopelessness of melancholia to the
> creative work of mourning.

The grieving process comes to completion with the creation of a definite image of the deceased in which the essence of the person is distilled. The authors refer to such an image as a 'psychic keepsake.' Jung's portrayal of the appearance of his dead wife in a dream is a fine example of such a psychic event:

> *After the death of my wife I saw her in a dream*
> *which was like a vision. She stood at some distance from*
> *me, looking at me squarely. She was in her prime,*
> *perhaps about thirty, wearing the dress which had been*
> *made for her many years before. It was perhaps the most*
> *beautiful thing she had ever worn. Her expression was*
> *neither joyful nor sad, but, rather objectively wise and*
> *understanding, without the slightest emotional reaction,*
> *as though she was beyond the mist of affects. I knew it*
> *was not she, but a portrait she had made or*
> *commissioned for me. It contained the beginning of our*
> *relationship, the events of thirty-five years of marriage,*
> *and the end of life also. Face to face with such a*
> *wholeness one remains speechless, for it can scarcely be*
> *comprehended.*

The mourning process and the imaginative contemplation of their future by the terminally ill has provided therapists interested in dreamwork and imaginal thought with a particularly well suited field in which to study the possible use and meaning of dream and imagework.

31

Dreams, Dying, and Beyond: A Conversation with Marie-Louise von Franz

INTERVIEWED BY FRASER BOA

Fraser Boa: *You have said that dreams in the first half of life aid ego development and in the second half focus on a search for meaning. What then do dreams say when death is on the horizon, when a person is terminally ill?*

Marie-Louise von Franz: Well, I have just started a study of the last dreams of people before they enter the coma. The dreams of dying people are not about death, but generally about a journey. They have to get ready for a journey, or they have to go through a dark tunnel and be reborn into another world, or they have to go through a disagreeable darkness or through a dark cloud to come out into another space, or they are going to finally meet their beloved partner. This meeting is the famous motif of death as a marriage, marriage with one's own other inner half. Or, when someone is so strongly identified with their body that they are inclined to think that when the body is finished, everything is finished, then they have dreams which try

to detach them from the body. I remember also the dream of an officer in the cavalry who dreamt, just before he died, that a soldier came
to him and said, "Officer, look at what I have to show you." And he
showed him the decaying corpse of his horse. Jung interpreted the
dream: "The warm-blooded animal which you are is going to die.
That's what's going to happen to it, but it's not you. It's only the warm-
blooded animal body which is going to decay, but not you yourself."
Jung made this interpretation because the dreamer's consciousness
still existed in the dream. He was able to look at the corpse.

The dreams of dying people show a tremendous variety. Generally they contain the same archetypal motifs which comparative
ethnology has discovered in its study of death rituals and the beliefs
about life after death among the different human populations: that
it is a rebirth, that it is a long, long journey into another country,
that it is a transformation, that it is a partial destruction out of which
something survives. There are many motifs.

At lunch today you told me the dream of a dying woman.

Yes, she was a very simple woman, and she told the nurse in the
morning after breakfast, "Last night I had a strange dream. I dreamt
that there was a candle on the windowsill. It was slowly burning
down and it began to flicker. I panicked and thought, 'My God, now
the great darkness is coming, the great darkness is coming.' And
then, suddenly, there was a change, and the candle was outside the
windowsill on the outer part of the window and was big and burning quietly again." Isn't that a strange dream? Four hours after that
dream she died.

The dream seems to tell her, "Yes, the candle of your life is
flickering. It's going out. But life will continue in another medium,
in another sphere. Beyond the isolating threshold of the window, that
very same life will be going on." She was very comforted by the
dream without understanding it. And that is a typical dream of a
dying person.

I remember another dream, which was published by a medical
doctor. A man dreamt that he saw an abyss, and at the bottom of the

abyss was a growing tree which was slowly losing its roots. Suddenly there was an earthquake, and the tree started falling, and the dreamer thought, "That's the end." Just at that moment, the tree began to hover in midair, and it continued to exist in midair without having roots in the earth. It just hung there in midair, as if the unconscious were saying, "Your tree of life is losing its contact with earthly reality, but it is not dying. The life process is going on in another medium."

That's the gist of most dreams of the dying, and that's why it is very worthwhile to continue analysis with dying people. Many psychological schools don't bother about old or dying people, because they think they have no further need of adaptation to life. After all, sex problems don't exist when you're on your deathbed. But you can see that the voice of nature or the voice of instinct, which is the dream, helps the people die in peace. It comforts them.

Many people to whom I told such dreams objected that it is wishful thinking, that dreams are wish fulfillments, but I don't believe it. As you see from the dream of the decaying horse, nature does say quite unsentimentally that the end is coming. In that woman's dream, the flickering candle does go out. But at the same time as the dream says that something is coming to an end, it also says that something is continuing in another medium. It's very difficult to imagine how it's going on, or what is going on. We can only take it as such.

Are there dreams that announce death, that say a person is actually going to die?

Well, I would say that until they are actually dead, you are never quite sure. A woman consulted me once who had cancer, metastases all over the body. She had shocking death dreams. She dreamt that her watch had stopped. She brought it to the watchmaker, and he said it couldn't be repaired. She dreamt her favorite tree was felled in the garden. I didn't even have to interpret the dreams for her. She said sadly, "That clearly tells me the outcome of my illness." The doctors told her in the usual way, "You will get better. You will be all right." But she was sure she was dying, and that terrible shock made her pull up her socks and face her problems. She had a problem she hadn't faced, and I can only say she's still alive after fifteen years. She had death dreams to give her a death shock. She could have died, and she could have not died. Out of shock, she chose to live.

After that experience I would say that even if people have death dreams, it might only mean that they should face death. It doesn't mean that death will actually happen but that they must come to a naked confrontation with the fact that their life might come to an end. That may give them either a salutary shock so that they continue to live, or it may mean, "Now it is finished." I would never dare to say what it means before the end has come.

But there is also sometimes a kind of uncanny smell around certain dreams where one has the feeling, "Umm . . . that forebodes death." But that's more of a parapsychological, mediumistic feeling one has about it. Scientifically, I couldn't give any reasons why one dream means actual death, while another means only the problem of death. Sometimes I get a gruesome shiver when people tell me a death dream, as if my sympathetic nervous system is saying, "Watch out, this really means death."

Does your work with dreams lead you to believe in life after death?

I wouldn't say I believe in it. That is a bit too strong. I would say that it seems to me from the dreams that there is life after death. I think that there is life after death. I think that dreams do not cheat, and because they are not wish fulfillments, there must be an aspect of life or the psyche going on. The question I would not dare to answer unequivocally is, "Does life go on impersonally, or does individual identity continue?" The dreams give contradictory evidence about that.

For instance, if you take the dream of that tree, you can say, "Yes, the life process of that man is going on, but not his ego. He himself is no longer around." On the other hand, there are other dreams which point to the fact that even the conscious identity continues. So it remains, for me, an open question.

Dr. von Franz, you've demonstrated how dreams reveal the fate of humanity, how they work at regulating the human psyche and are the key which unlocks the mystery of living one's own destiny. You've shown how they address even the most profound questions of life and death. But still one question puzzles me. If dreams are messages sent to inform our consciousness, why are they so obscure?

That has puzzled me too. I have often asked reproachfully, "Why does this damned unconscious talk such a Chinese difficult language? Why doesn't it tell us clearly what's the matter?" Now Jung's answer was that it obviously can't. It doesn't speak the language of the rational mind. Dreams are the voice of our instinctive animal nature or ultimately the voice of cosmic matter in us. This is a very daring hypothesis, but I'll venture to say that the collective unconscious and organic atomic matter are probably two aspects of the same thing. So the dreams are ultimately the voice of cosmic matter. Therefore, just as we cannot understand the behavior of atoms (look at the Chinese language modern physicists have to use to describe the behavior of an electron), so we have to use the same kind of language to describe the deeper layers of the dream world.

The dream takes us into the mysteries of nature strange to our rational mind. We can compare it to atomic physics, where the most complicated formulas are not sufficient to describe what is happening. I don't know why nature has constructed our rational mind in a way that prevents us from understanding the whole nature. We are born with a brain which seemingly can understand only certain aspects. Perhaps there will be later mutations on another planet where Nature will invent a brain which can understand these things.

Permissions

Chapter 20 has been excerpted from *New Directions in Dream Interpretation*, edited by Gayle Delaney. Copyright © 1993. Reprinted by permission of the State University of New York Press. All rights reserved.

Chapter 21 has been excerpted from *The Dream Sourcebook*, by Phyllis R. Koch-Sheras and Amy Lemley. Copyright ©1995, 1996, 1998. Reprinted by permission of Roxbury Park.

Chapter 22 has been reprinted by permission of Stanley Krippner. Copyright © 1990, 1999 by Stanley Krippner.

Chapter 23 has been excerpted from *Spiritual Dreaming*, by Kelly Bulkeley. Copyright © 1995. Reprinted by permission of Paulist Press, Inc.

Chapter 24 has been reprinted by permission of Stanley Krippner. Copyright © 1990, 1999 by Stanley Krippner.

Chapter 25 is an original essay by Stanley Krippner and Joseph Dillard. Copyright © 1999. Used by permission of the authors.

Chapter 26 has been reprinted by permission of Stanley Krippner. Copyright © 1990, 1999 by Stanley Krippner.

Chapter 27 is an original essay by Richard Catlett Wilkerson. Copyright © 1999. Used by permission of the author.

Chapter 28 has been excerpted from *Trauma and Dreams*, edited by Deirdre Barrett. Copyright ©1996 by the president and Fellows of Harvard College. Reprinted by permission of Harvard University Press.

Chapter 29 is an original essay by Stanley Krippner. Copyright © 1999. Used by permission of the author.

Chapter 30 has been excerpted from *Dreamwork, Anthropology, and the Caring Professions*, by Iain R. Edgar. Copyright © 1995 by Iain R. Edgar. Reprinted by permission of Ashgate Publishing Ltd., Avebury, England.

Chapter 31 has been excerpted from *The Way of the Dream*, by Fraser Boa. Copyright © 1988, 1992. Reprinted by arrangement with Shambhala Publications, Inc., Boston.

Contributors

FRASER BOA was a Canadian Jungian analyst, author of *The Way of the Dream* (and producer of the documentary series from which this book was made), and author of *The Way of Myth: Talking with Joseph Campbell*.

GREG BOGART, Ph.D., practices psychotherapy in Berkeley, California. His books include *Finding Your Life's Calling* and *The Nine Stages of Spiritual Apprenticeship*.

ROBERT BOSNAK, J.D., is a Jungian analyst on the faculty of the C. G. Jung Institute in Boston, Massachusetts. His books include *A Little Course in Dreams, Tracks in the Wilderness of Dreaming,* and *Christopher's Dreams: Dreaming and Living with AIDS*.

KELLY BULKELEY, Ph.D., a past president of the Association for the Study of Dreams, teaches at the Graduate Theological Union at the University of California at Berkeley. His books include *An Introduction to the Psychology of Dreaming, Spiritual Dreaming,* and *The Wilderness of Dreams*.

JENNY DAVIDOW, M.A., is a dream therapist, hypnotherapist, and creativity coach in Santa Cruz, California. She is the author of *Embracing Your Subconscious* (Tidal Wave Press, P.O. Box 2392, Aptos, CA 95001).

GAYLE DELANEY, Ph.D., is the founding president of the Association for the Study of Dreams. Her books include *All About Dreams, Living Your Dreams,* and *Sensual Dreaming.*

JOSEPH DILLARD, Ph.D., is a psychotherapist and health educator. He is the author of *Successful Meditation* and coauthor of *Dreamworking.*

IAIN R. EDGAR, Ph.D., is senior lecturer in social work at the University of Northumbria, Newcastle upon Tyne, England. He is the author of *Dreamwork, Anthropology, and the Caring Professions.*

BETTE EHLERT is an attorney in private practice in Albuquerque, New Mexico. She leads dream workshops in various New Mexico correctional facilities and has contributed a chapter on the topic to *Among All These Dreamers.*

FRANKLIN GALVIN, Ph.D., is a psychotherapist specializing in the treatment of post-traumatic stress disorder. He has written on the use of lucid dreaming in psychotherapy and has contributed chapters on the topic to *Dreamtime and Dreamwork* and to *The Variety of Dream Experiences.*

EUGENE GENDLIN, Ph.D., is Professor of Psychology at the University of Chicago and the founding editor of *Psychotherapy: Theory Research and Practice.* His books include *Let Your Body Interpret Your Dreams* and *Focusing.*

ERNEST HARTMANN, M.D., is Professor of Psychiatry, Tufts University School of Medicine, Medford, Massachusetts, and director of the Sleep Disorders Center at Newton-Wellesley Hospital in Massachusetts. His books include *Dreams and Nightmares, The Biology of Dreaming,* and *Boundaries of the Mind.*

CLARA E. HILL, Ph.D., is Professor of Counseling Psychology at the University of Maryland. She is a past president of the International Society for Psychotherapy Research and former editor of the *Journal of Counseling Psychology*. Her books include *Working with Dreams in Psychotherapy* and *Helping Skills: Facilitating Exploration, Insight, and Action*.

DEBORAH JAY HILLMAN, Ph.D., is a cultural anthropologist and psychotherapist with a special interest in community dreamwork. She has contributed chapters to *Dreamtime and Dreamwork* and to *The Variety of Dream Experience*.

PHYLLIS R. KOCH-SHERAS, Ph.D., is a clinical psychologist specializing in dreamwork. She is the coauthor of *The Dreamsharing Sourcebook*, *The Dream Sourcebook*, and *Dream On*.

AMY LEMLEY is the coauthor of several books, including *The Dream Sourcebook* and *Beyond Shyness*.

FRED OLSEN, a former researcher and NASA engineer, cofounded the Bay Area Dreamworkers Group in San Francisco and was a director of the San Francisco Dream House. He developed a dream imagery process known as Dream Reentry Healing.

AARON B. ROCHLEN, M.A., is a doctoral student in counseling psychology at the University of Maryland. He has published research studies on cross-cultural differences in dream content, physiological correlates of dream recall, depression and dream recall, and training procedures for dream interpretation.

RICHARD A. RUSSO is the editor of *Dreams Are Wiser Than Men*. His work has appeared in *Yellow Silk*, *Metier*, and *Heroic Visions II*.

OLIVER SACKS, M.D., is Professor of Clinical Neurology at Albert Einstein College of Medicine. His books include *An Anthropologist on Mars*, *The Man Who Mistook His Wife for a Hat*, and *Awakenings*.

LOUIS M. SAVARY, S.T.D., Ph.D., serves on the adjunct faculty of six universities, teaching courses on spirituality and religious studies. He is the coauthor of *The Sleep Book* and *Dreams and Spiritual Growth*.

PETER SHERAS, Ph.D., is Associate Professor of Psychology at the University of Virginia, Charlottesville, and the co-author of *The Dreamsharing Sourcebook*, *The Dream Sourcebook Journal*, and *Clinical Psychology: A Social Psychological Approach*.

GEORGE R. SLATER, Ph.D., is a psychotherapist, workshop leader, and author of *Bringing Dreams to Life*.

KATHLEEN SULLIVAN leads dream workshops in the United States and Europe. She is the author of *Recurring Dreams* and hosts the public radio show *Dreams, Another Way of Knowing*, on station KAZU, Pacific Grove, California.

GRAYWOLF SWINNEY, M.A., has degrees in chemical engineering and psychology. He practices as a dream mentor and psychotherapist in Grants Pass, Oregon, and the Puget Sound area. He is a contributing editor to the *Dream Network Journal* and other publications.

JEREMY TAYLOR, M.A., is a Unitarian-Universalist minister and former president of the Association for the Study of Dreams. His books include *Dreamwork*, *Where People Fly and Water Runs Uphill*, and *The Living Labyrinth*.

MONTAGUE ULLMAN, M.D., is Clinical Professor Emeritus, Department of Psychiatry, Albert Einstein College of Medicine. His books include *Appreciating Dreams*, *Dream Telepathy*, and the *Handbook of States of Consciousness*.

ROBERT L. VAN DE CASTLE, Ph.D., is Professor Emeritus at the University of Virginia Medical School and former director of its sleep and dream laboratory. He is a former president of the Association for the Study of Dreams, former senior editor for the *Dream Network Bulletin*, and the author of numerous articles and books, including *Our Dreaming Mind*.

MARIE-LOUISE VON FRANZ was a founder of the C. G. Jung Institute and an intimate colleague of Dr. Jung. She has lectured and published widely on dreams, analysis, and fairy tales, including such books as *The Cat: A Tale of Feminine Redemption*.

JANE WHITE-LEWIS is a Jungian analyst practicing in Guilford, Connecticut, and New York City. She is the author of numerous articles on nightmares and dreams and has contributed a chapter to *Among All These Dreamers*.

RICHARD CATLETT WILKERSON is the publisher for the online E-zine *Electric Dreams* and the Web manager for the Association for the Study of Dreams. He is the author of *Dream Guide to the Internet* and *The History of Dream Sharing* (available through www.dreamgate.com).

About the Editors

STANLEY KRIPPNER, Ph.D., is Professor of Psychology, Saybrook Graduate School and Research Center, San Francisco, and the former director of the Dream Laboratory, Maimonides Medical Center, Brooklyn, New York. A former president of the Association for the Study of Dreams, the Association for Humanistic Psychology, the Parapsychological Association, and two divisions of the American Psychological Association, he is the coauthor of *Dreamworking, Dream Telepathy,* and *The Mythic Path,* the editor of *Dreamtime and Dreamwork,* and the coeditor of *Broken Images, Broken Selves.* He serves on the editorial board for *Dreaming* and *The Dream Network Journal.*

Stanley is a Fellow in the American Psychological Association, the American Psychological Society, the Society for the Scientific Study of Religion, the Society for the Scientific Study of Sexuality, the American Society of Clinical Hypnosis, the Society of Clinical and Experimental Hypnoses, and the American Association of Applied and Preventive Psychotherapy.

MARK ROBERT WALDMAN practices counseling and therapy in Woodland Hills, California. He is the author of *Love Games* and the editor of *The Art of Staying Together*. He was the founding editor of the *Transpersonal Review* and is internationally published in the field of transpersonal psychology. He is a developmental editor for many publications and books on psychology, alternative medicine, and spiritual development.

Mark chairs the Los Angeles Transpersonal Interest Group and is a regional coordinator for the Spiritual Emergence Network, an international organization promoting psychospiritual development in counseling and education. He can be reached for telephone counseling through his Woodland Hills office, (818) 888-6690. Correspondence can be mailed to 21241 Ventura Blvd., Ste. 269, Woodland Hills, CA 91364. E-mail: markwaldman@cyberhotline.com.

Index